CREATED BY **JOSS WHEDON**

DAVID M. **BOOHER**   JEFF **JENSEN**   ANDRÉS **GENOLET**
JORDI **PÉREZ**   VINCENZO **FEDERICI**   FABIANA **MASCOLO**

firefly™

RIVER RUN

Published by

BOOM!
STUDIOS

Series Designer **Madison Goyette**
Collection Designer **Marie Krupina**

Assistant Editor
Gavin Gronenthal

Editor
Elizabeth Brei

Special Thanks to **Sierra Hahn**,
Becca J. Sadowsky, and **Nicole Spiegel**.

Ross Richie Chairman & Founder
Jen Harned CFO
Matt Gagnon Editor-in-Chief
Filip Sablik President, Publishing & Marketing
Stephen Christy President, Development
Lance Kreiter Vice President, Licensing & Merchandising
Bryce Carlson Vice President, Editorial & Creative Strategy
Hunter Gorinson Vice President, Business Development
Ryan Matsunaga Director, Marketing
Elyse Strandberg Manager, Finance
Michelle Ankley Manager, Production Design
Sierra Hahn Executive Editor
Dafna Pleban Senior Editor
Eric Harburn Senior Editor
Elizabeth Brei Editor
Kathleen Wisneski Editor
Sophie Philips-Roberts Editor
Jonathan Manning Associate Editor
Allyson Gronowitz Associate Editor
Gavin Gronenthal Assistant Editor
Gwen Waller Assistant Editor
Ramiro Portnoy Assistant Editor
Kenzie Rzonca Assistant Editor

Rey Netschke Editorial Assistant
Marie Krupina Design Lead
Grace Park Design Coordinator
Madison Goyette Production Designer
Crystal White Production Designer
Veronica Gutierrez Production Designer
Samantha Knapp Production Design Assistant
Esther Kim Marketing Lead
Breanna Sarpy Marketing Lead, Digital
Amanda Lawson Marketing Coordinator
Alex Lorenzen Marketing Coordinator, Copywriter
Grecia Martinez Marketing Assistant, Digital
José Meza Consumer Sales Lead
Ashley Troub Consumer Sales Coordinator
Morgan Perry Retail Sales Lead
Harley Salbacka Sales Coordinator
Megan Christopher Operations Coordinator
Rodrigo Hernandez Operations Coordinator
Zipporah Smith Operations Coordinator
Jason Lee Senior Accountant
Sabrina Lesin Accounting Assistant
Lauren Alexander Administrative Assistant

FIREFLY: RIVER RUN, May 2022. Published by BOOM! Studios, a
division of Boom Entertainment, Inc. © 2022 20th Television. Originally
published in single magazine form as FIREFLY: RIVER RUN No. 1,
THE FIREFLY HOLIDAY SPECIAL No. 1. © 2021 20th Television.
BOOM! Studios™ and the BOOM! Studios logo are trademarks of
Boom Entertainment, Inc., registered in various countries and categories.
All characters, events, and institutions depicted herein are fictional. Any
similarity between any of the names, characters, persons, events, and/or
institutions in this publication to actual names, characters, and persons,
whether living or dead, events, and/or institutions is unintended and
purely coincidental. BOOM! Studios does not read or accept unsolicited
submissions of ideas, stories, or artwork.

BOOM! Studios, 5670 Wilshire Boulevard, Suite 400, Los Angeles,
CA 90036-5679. Printed in China. First Printing.

ISBN: 978-1-68415-833-1,
eISBN: 978-1-64668-732-9

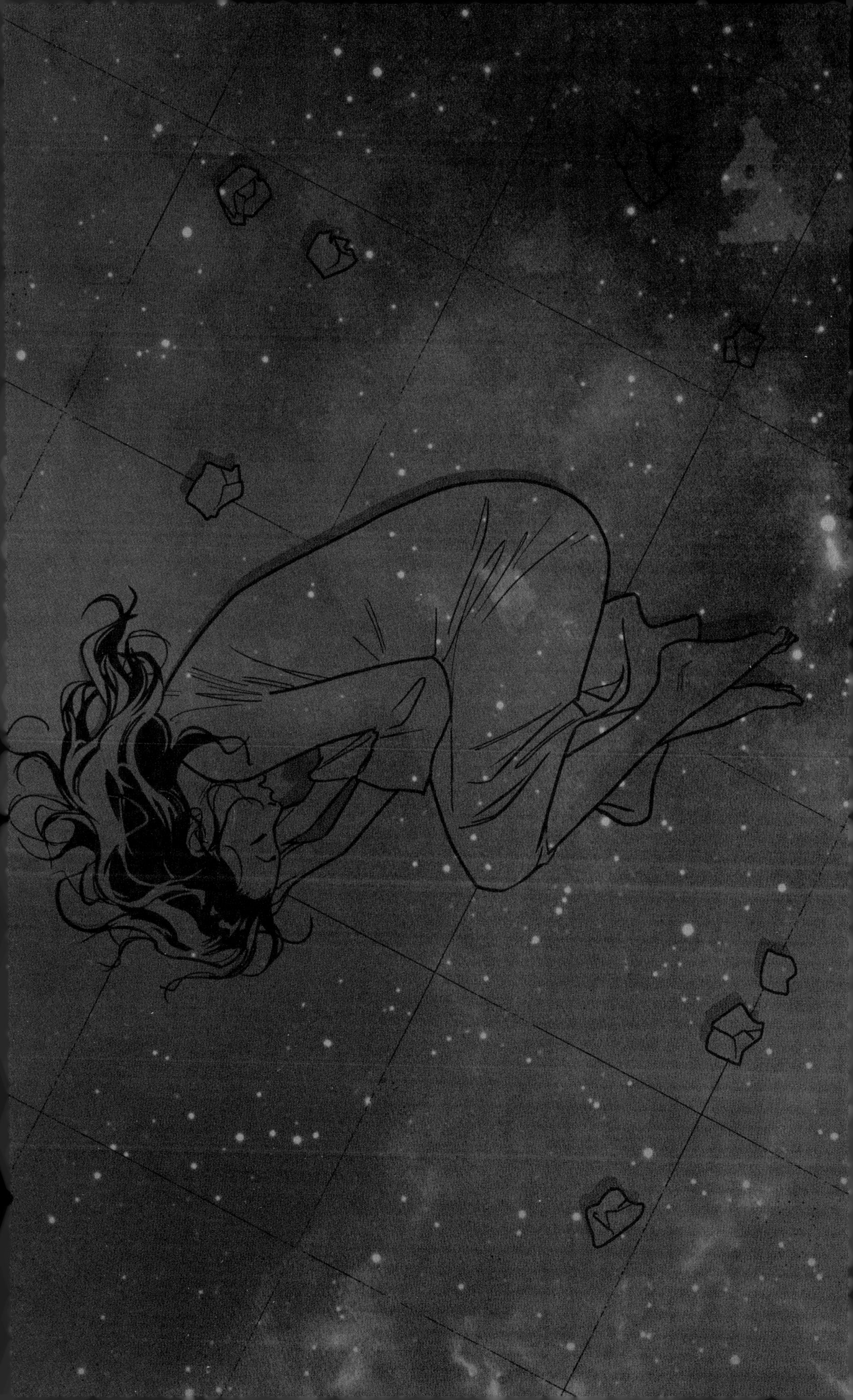

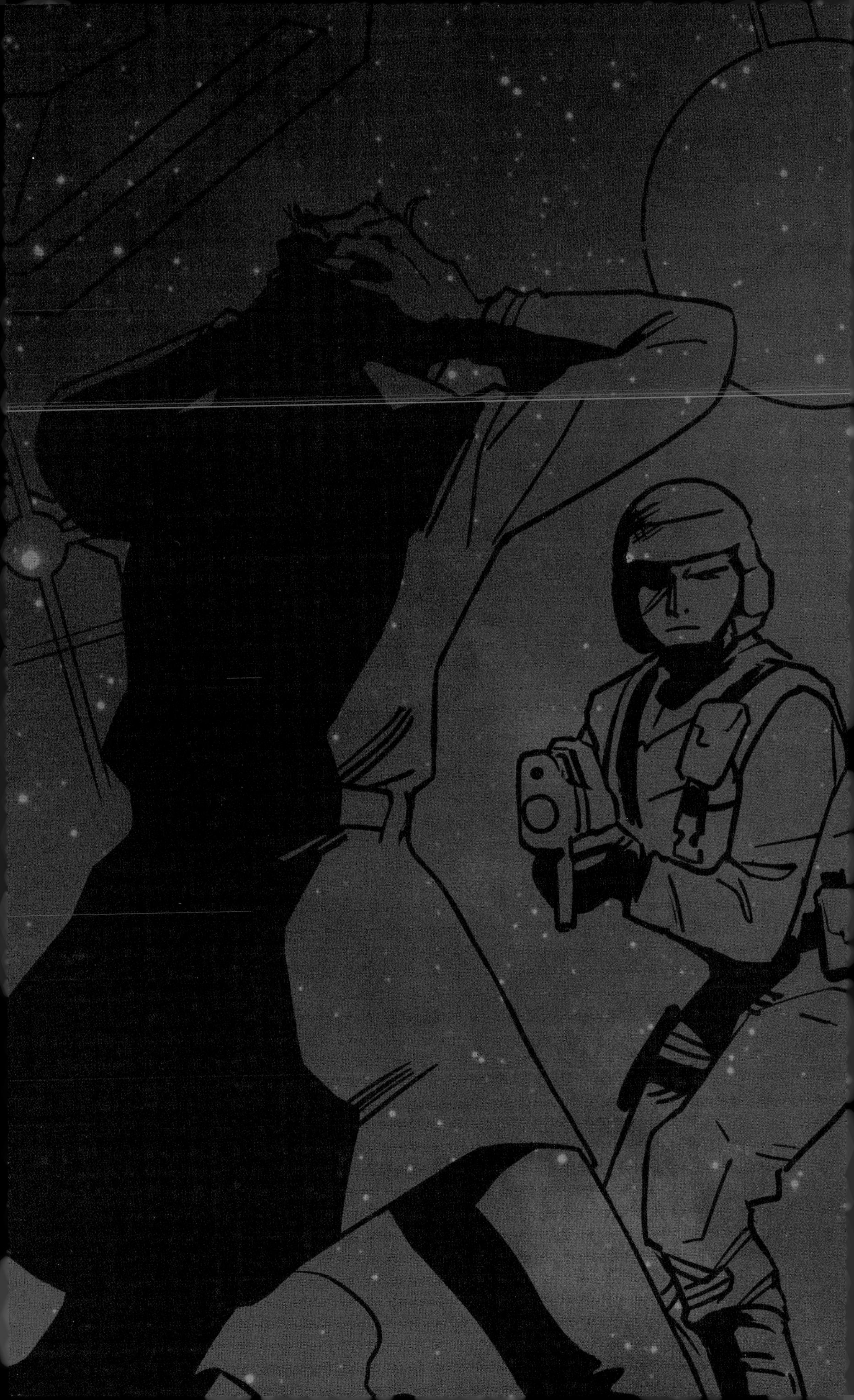

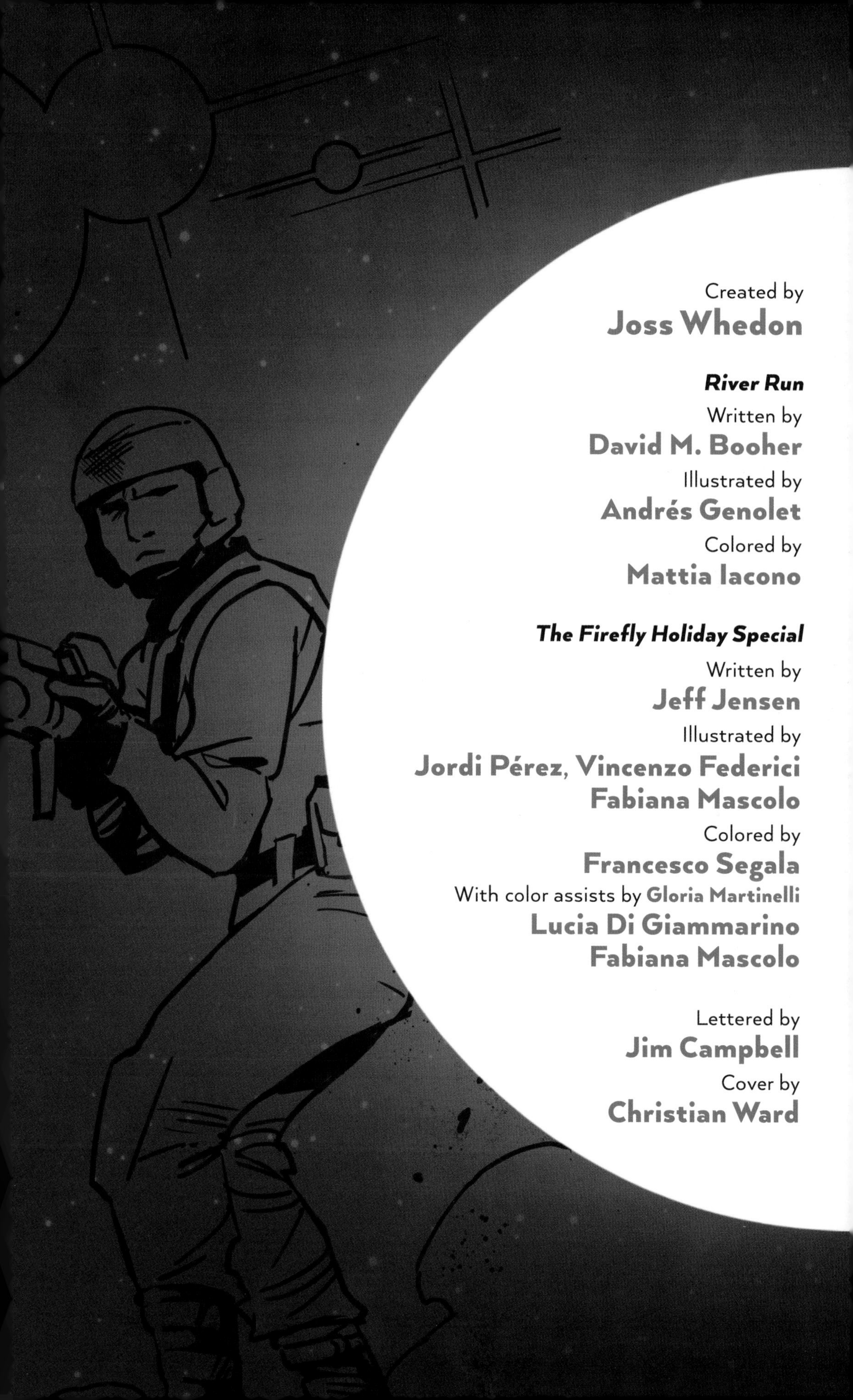

Created by
Joss Whedon

River Run

Written by
David M. Booher

Illustrated by
Andrés Genolet

Colored by
Mattia Iacono

The Firefly Holiday Special

Written by
Jeff Jensen

Illustrated by
Jordi Pérez, Vincenzo Federici
Fabiana Mascolo

Colored by
Francesco Segala

With color assists by **Gloria Martinelli**
Lucia Di Giammarino
Fabiana Mascolo

Lettered by
Jim Campbell

Cover by
Christian Ward

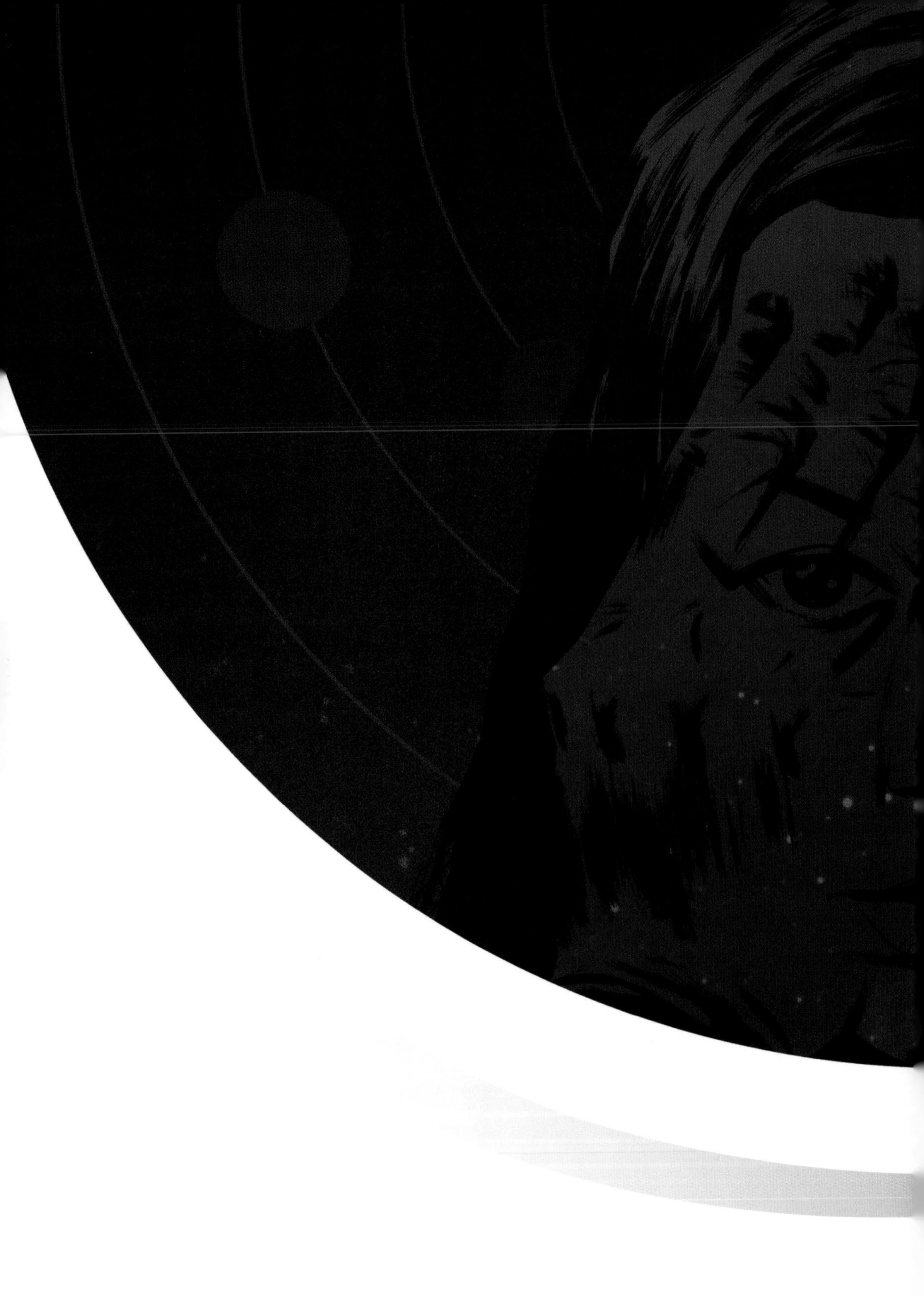

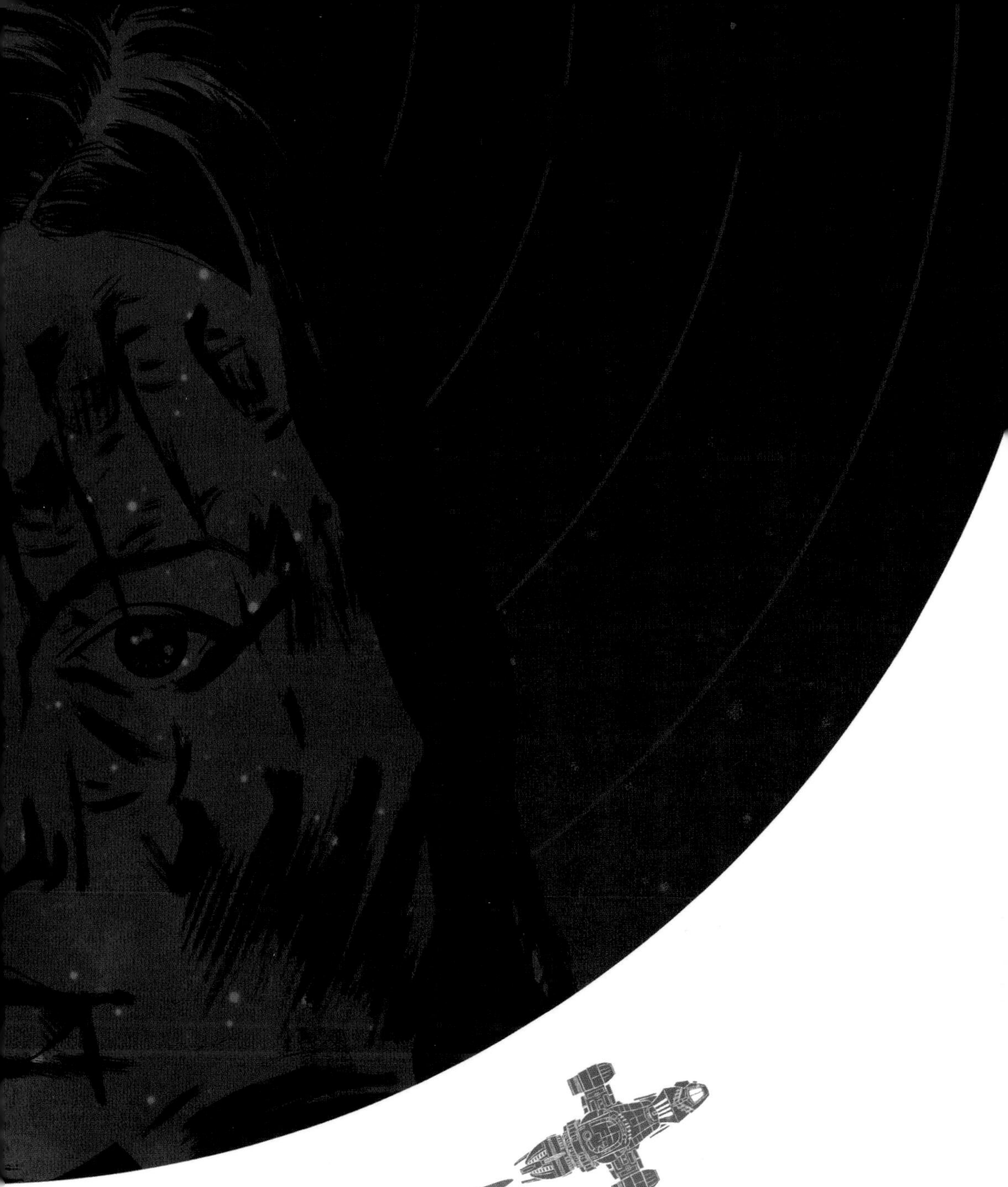

firefly™
RIVER RUN

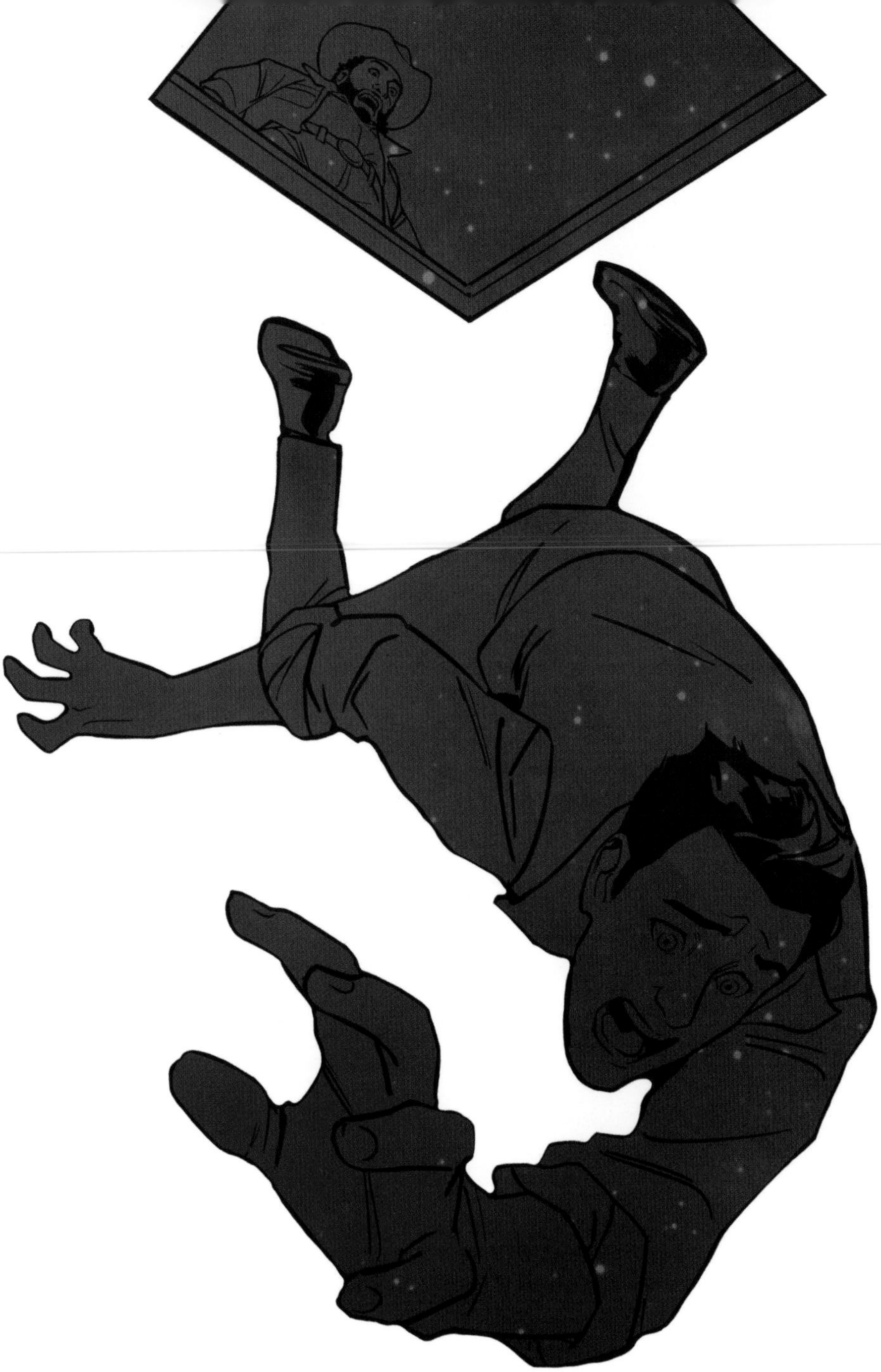

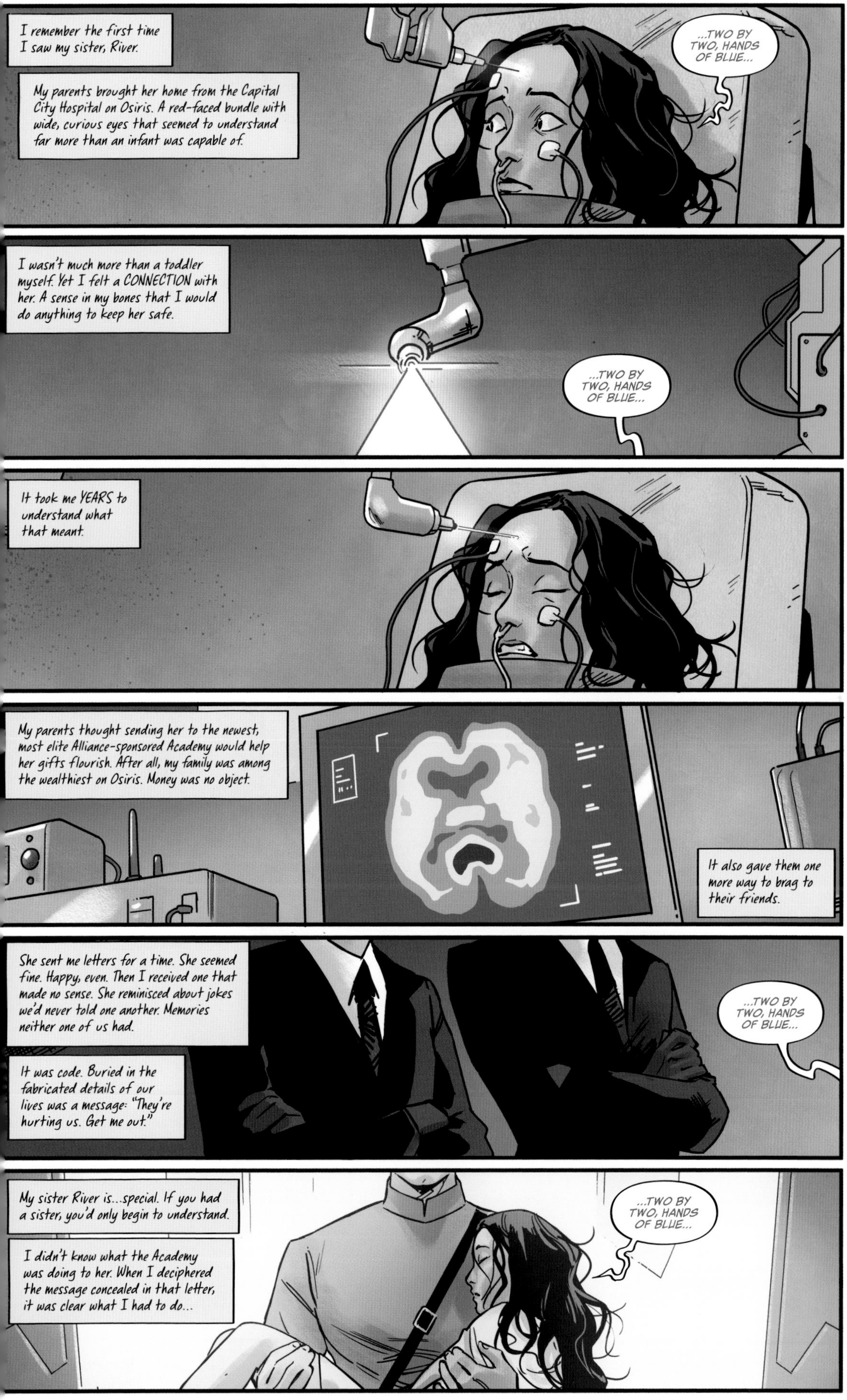
I remember the first time I saw my sister, River.
My parents brought her home from the Capital City Hospital on Osiris. A red-faced bundle with wide, curious eyes that seemed to understand far more than an infant was capable of.
...TWO BY TWO, HANDS OF BLUE...
I wasn't much more than a toddler myself. Yet I felt a CONNECTION with her. A sense in my bones that I would do anything to keep her safe.
...TWO BY TWO, HANDS OF BLUE...
It took me YEARS to understand what that meant.
My parents thought sending her to the newest, most elite Alliance-sponsored Academy would help her gifts flourish. After all, my family was among the wealthiest on Osiris. Money was no object.
It also gave them one more way to brag to their friends.
She sent me letters for a time. She seemed fine. Happy, even. Then I received one that made no sense. She reminisced about jokes we'd never told one another. Memories neither one of us had.
It was code. Buried in the fabricated details of our lives was a message: "They're hurting us. Get me out."
...TWO BY TWO, HANDS OF BLUE...
My sister River is...special. If you had a sister, you'd only begin to understand.
I didn't know what the Academy was doing to her. When I deciphered the message concealed in that letter, it was clear what I had to do...
...TWO BY TWO, HANDS OF BLUE...

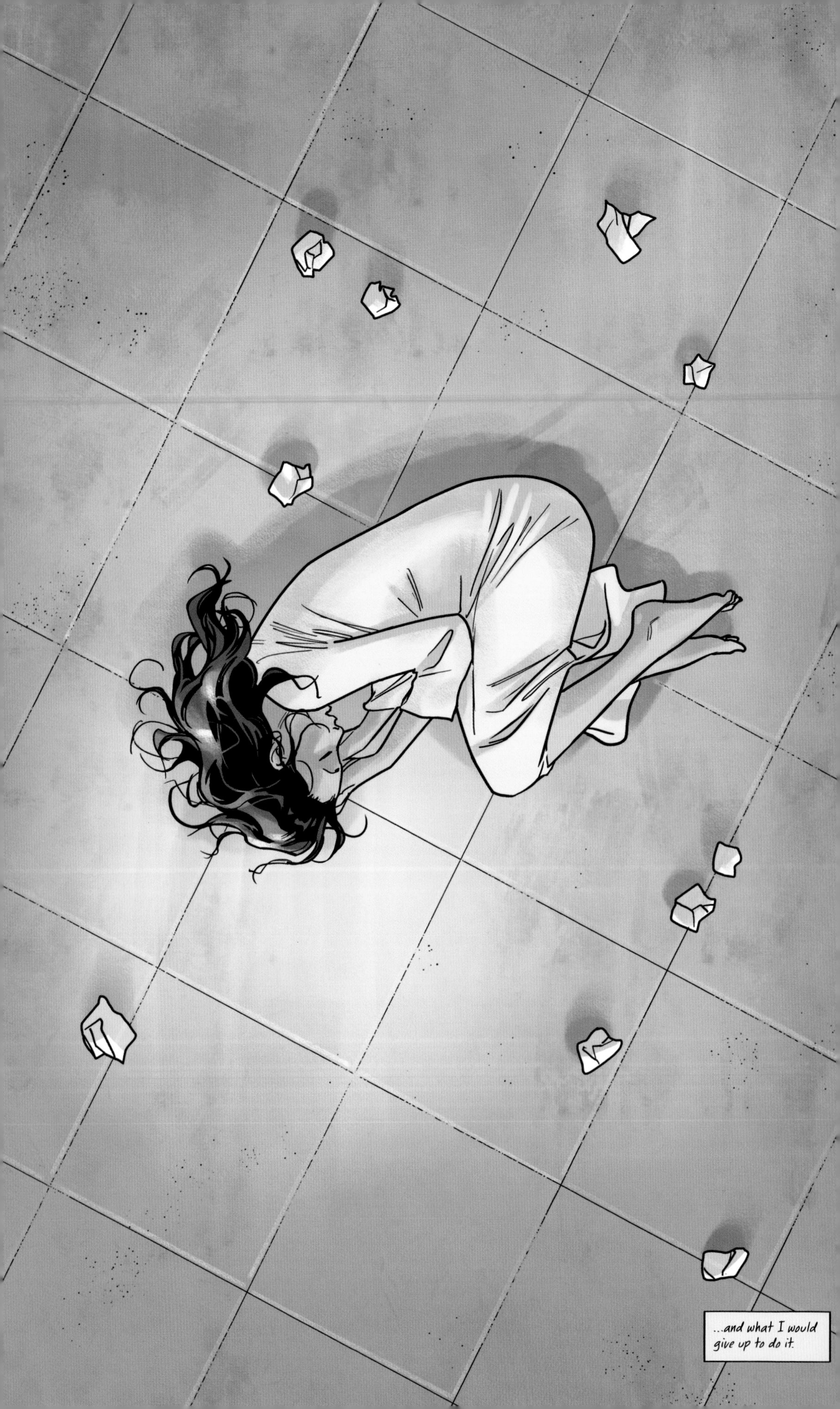
...and what I would give up to do it.

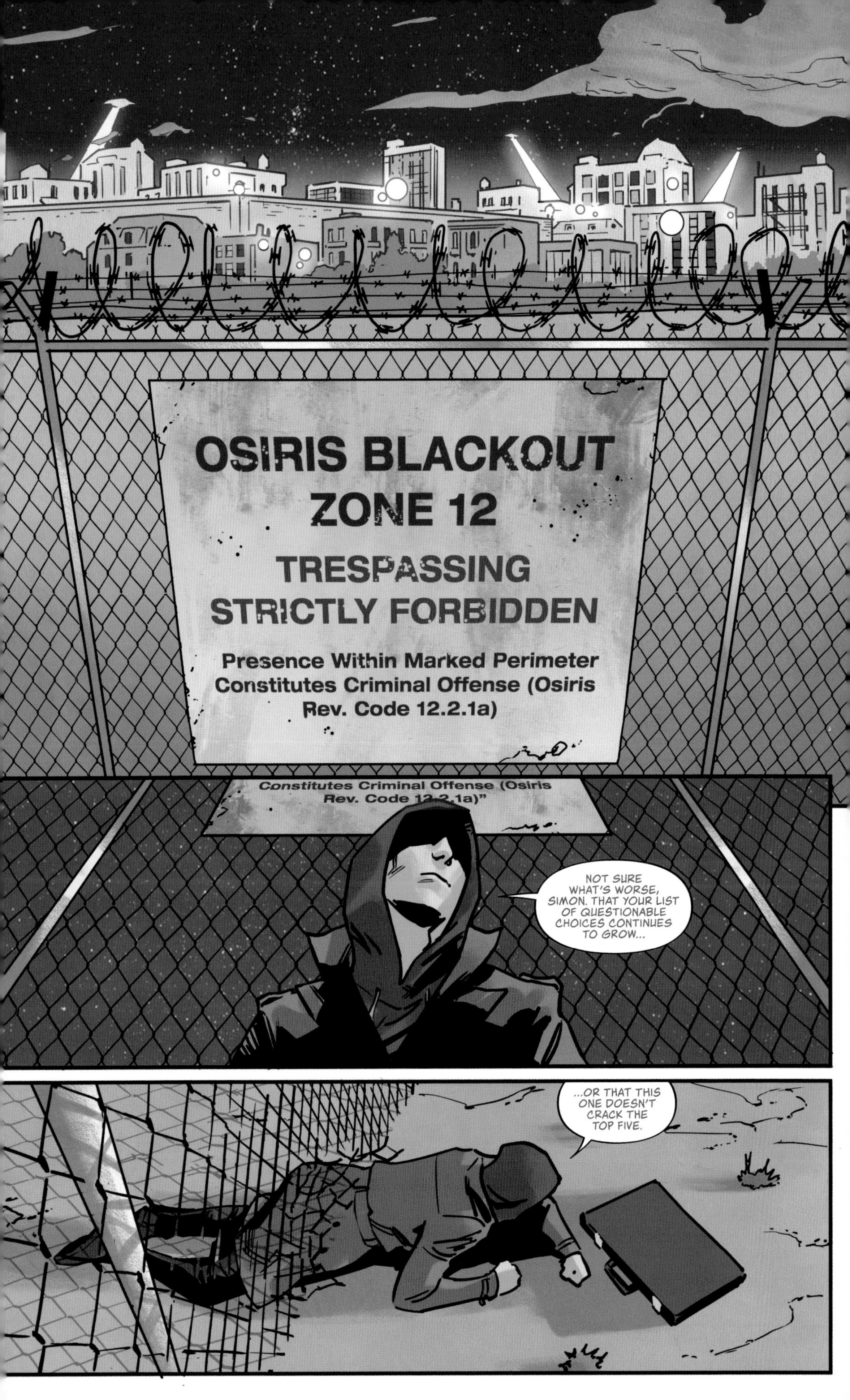
OSIRIS BLACKOUT
ZONE 12
TRESPASSING
STRICTLY FORBIDDEN
Presence Within Marked Perimeter Constitutes Criminal Offense (Osiris Rev. Code 12.2.1a)
Constitutes Criminal Offense (Osiris Rev. Code 12.2.1a)"
NOT SURE WHAT'S WORSE, SIMON. THAT YOUR LIST OF QUESTIONABLE CHOICES CONTINUES TO GROW...
...OR THAT THIS ONE DOESN'T CRACK THE TOP FIVE.

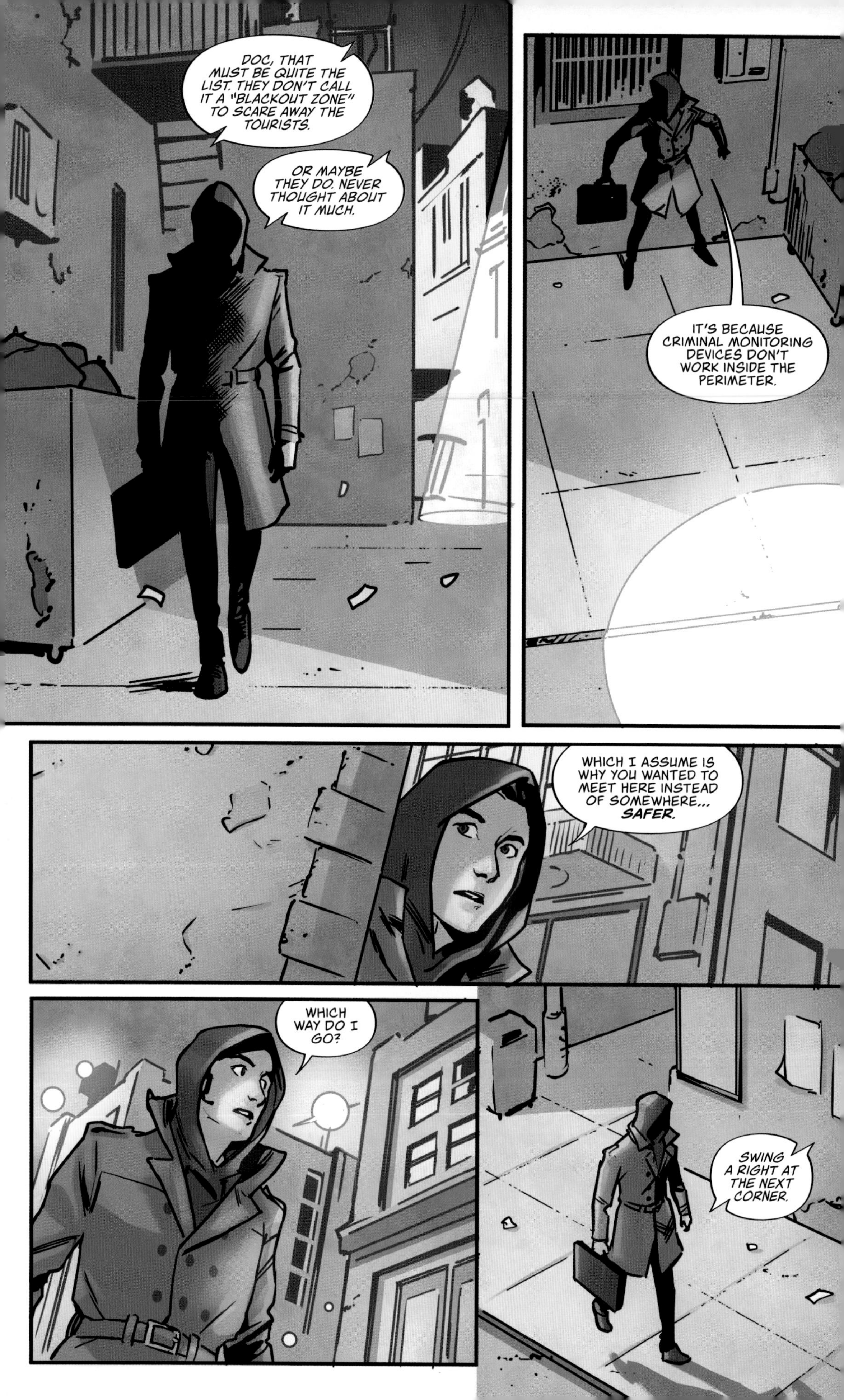
DOC, THAT MUST BE QUITE THE LIST. THEY DON'T CALL IT A "BLACKOUT ZONE" TO SCARE AWAY THE TOURISTS.
OR MAYBE THEY DO. NEVER THOUGHT ABOUT IT MUCH.
IT'S BECAUSE CRIMINAL MONITORING DEVICES DON'T WORK INSIDE THE PERIMETER.
WHICH I ASSUME IS WHY YOU WANTED TO MEET HERE INSTEAD OF SOMEWHERE... SAFER.
WHICH WAY DO I GO?
SWING A RIGHT AT THE NEXT CORNER.

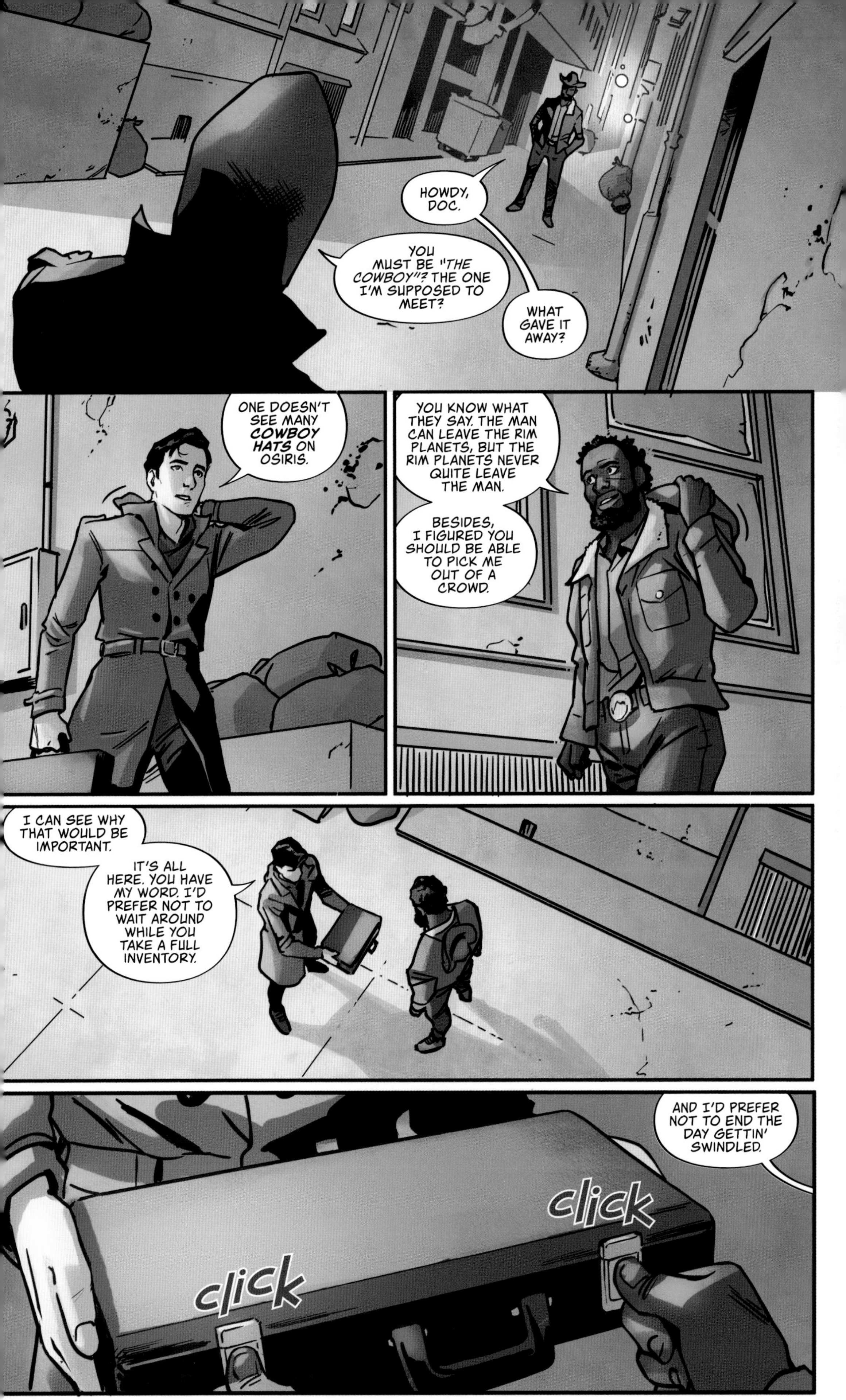
HOWDY, DOC.
YOU MUST BE "THE COWBOY"? THE ONE I'M SUPPOSED TO MEET?
WHAT GAVE IT AWAY?
ONE DOESN'T SEE MANY COWBOY HATS ON OSIRIS.
YOU KNOW WHAT THEY SAY. THE MAN CAN LEAVE THE RIM PLANETS, BUT THE RIM PLANETS NEVER QUITE LEAVE THE MAN.
BESIDES, I FIGURED YOU SHOULD BE ABLE TO PICK ME OUT OF A CROWD.
I CAN SEE WHY THAT WOULD BE IMPORTANT.
IT'S ALL HERE. YOU HAVE MY WORD. I'D PREFER NOT TO WAIT AROUND WHILE YOU TAKE A FULL INVENTORY.
AND I'D PREFER NOT TO END THE DAY GETTIN' SWINDLED.
click
click

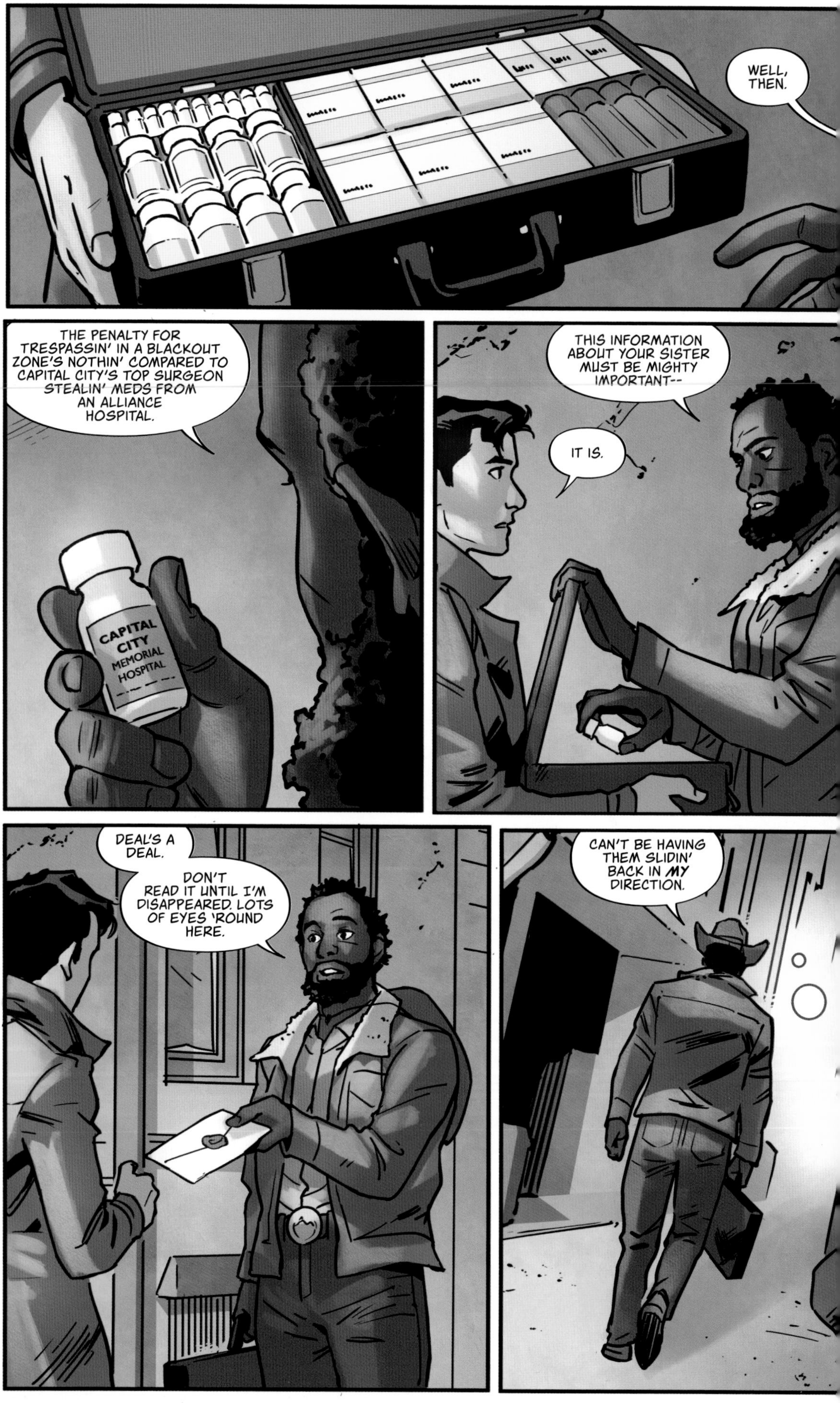
WELL, THEN.
THE PENALTY FOR TRESPASSIN' IN A BLACKOUT ZONE'S NOTHIN' COMPARED TO CAPITAL CITY'S TOP SURGEON STEALIN' MEDS FROM AN ALLIANCE HOSPITAL.
CAPITAL CITY MEMORIAL HOSPITAL
THIS INFORMATION ABOUT YOUR SISTER MUST BE MIGHTY IMPORTANT--
IT IS.
DEAL'S A DEAL.
DON'T READ IT UNTIL I'M DISAPPEARED. LOTS OF EYES 'ROUND HERE.
CAN'T BE HAVING THEM SLIDIN' BACK IN *MY* DIRECTION.

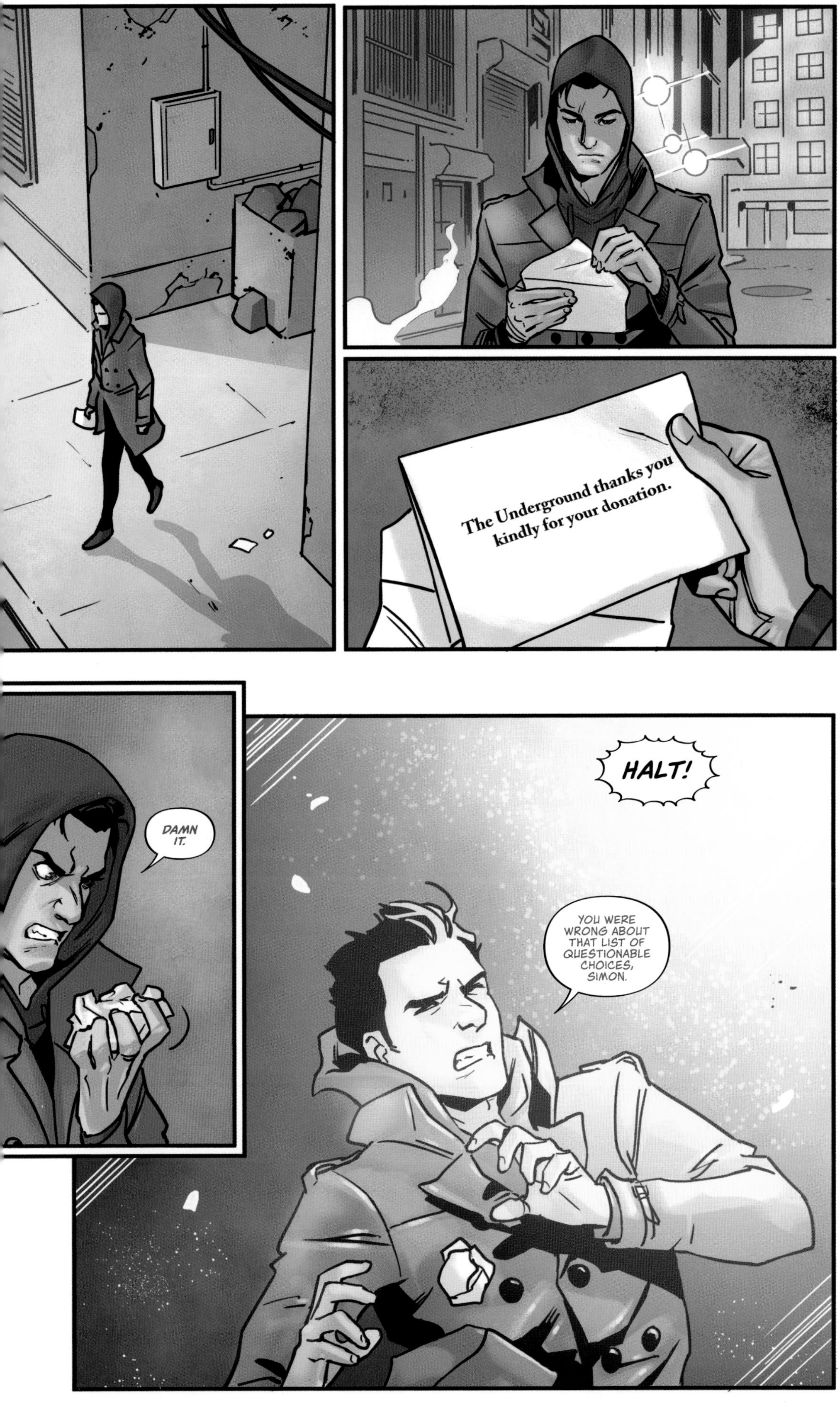

The Underground thanks you kindly for your donation.
DAMN IT.
HALT!
YOU WERE WRONG ABOUT THAT LIST OF QUESTIONABLE CHOICES, SIMON.

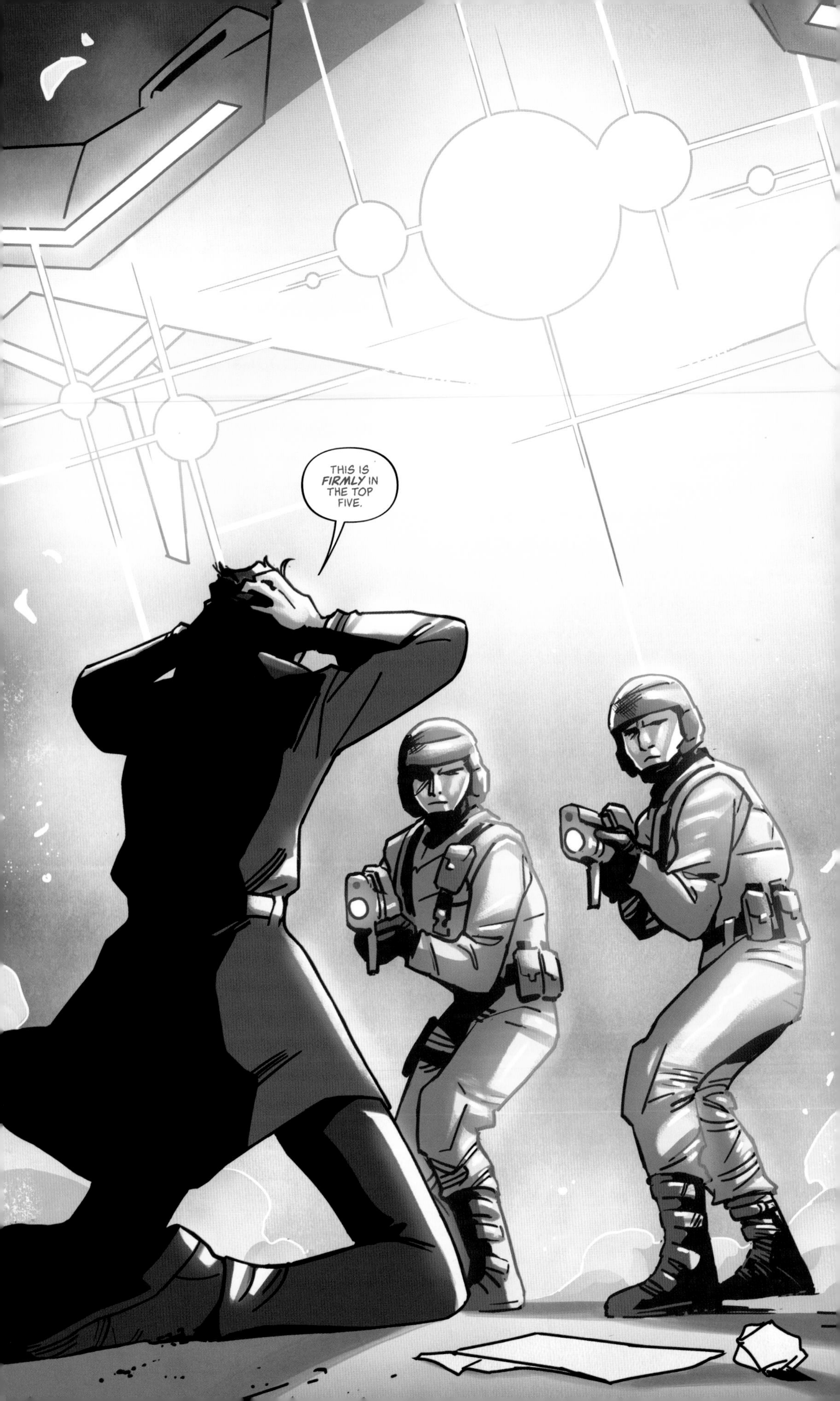
THIS IS *FIRMLY* IN THE TOP FIVE.

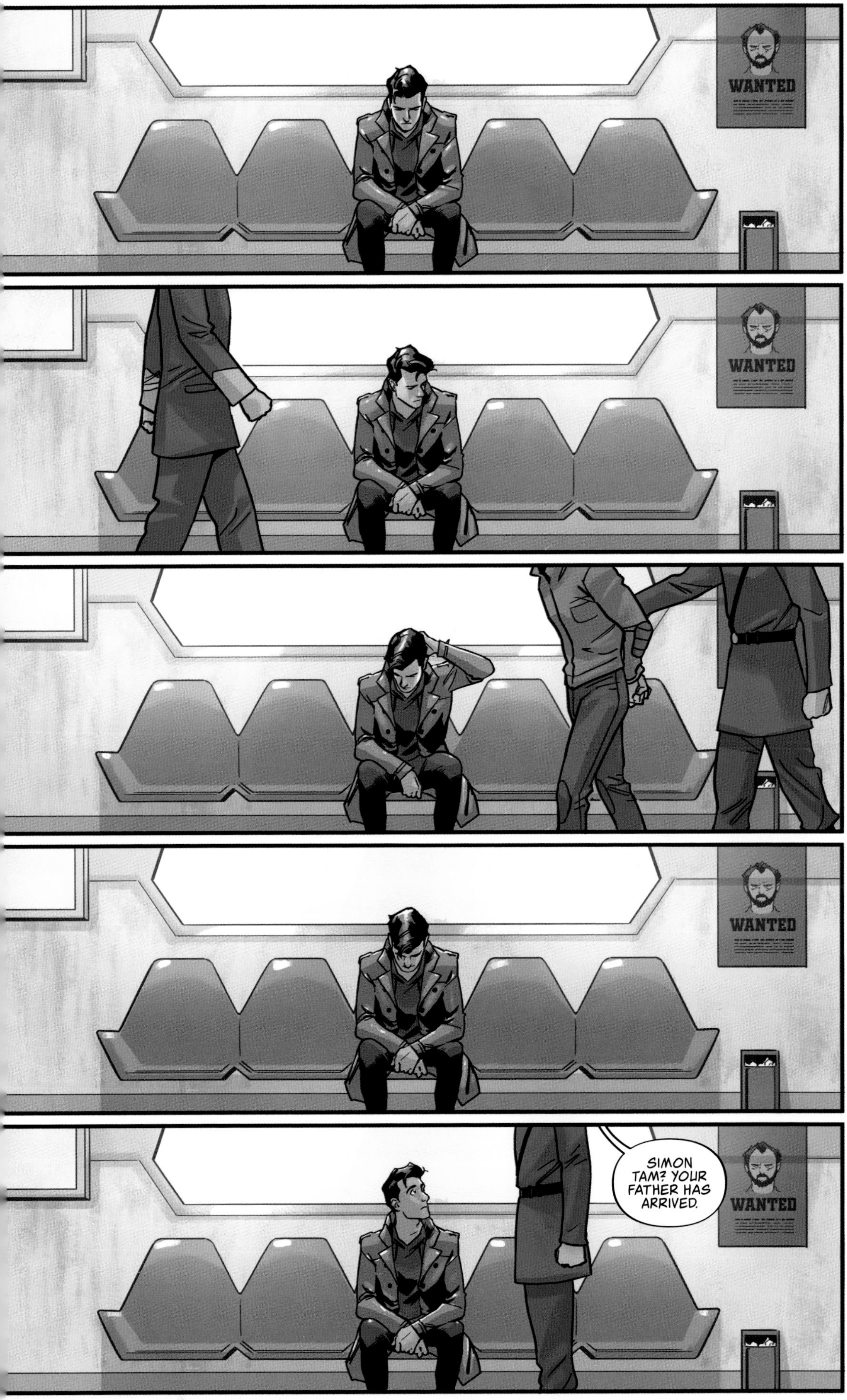
WANTED
WANTED
WANTED
SIMON TAM? YOUR FATHER HAS ARRIVED.
WANTED

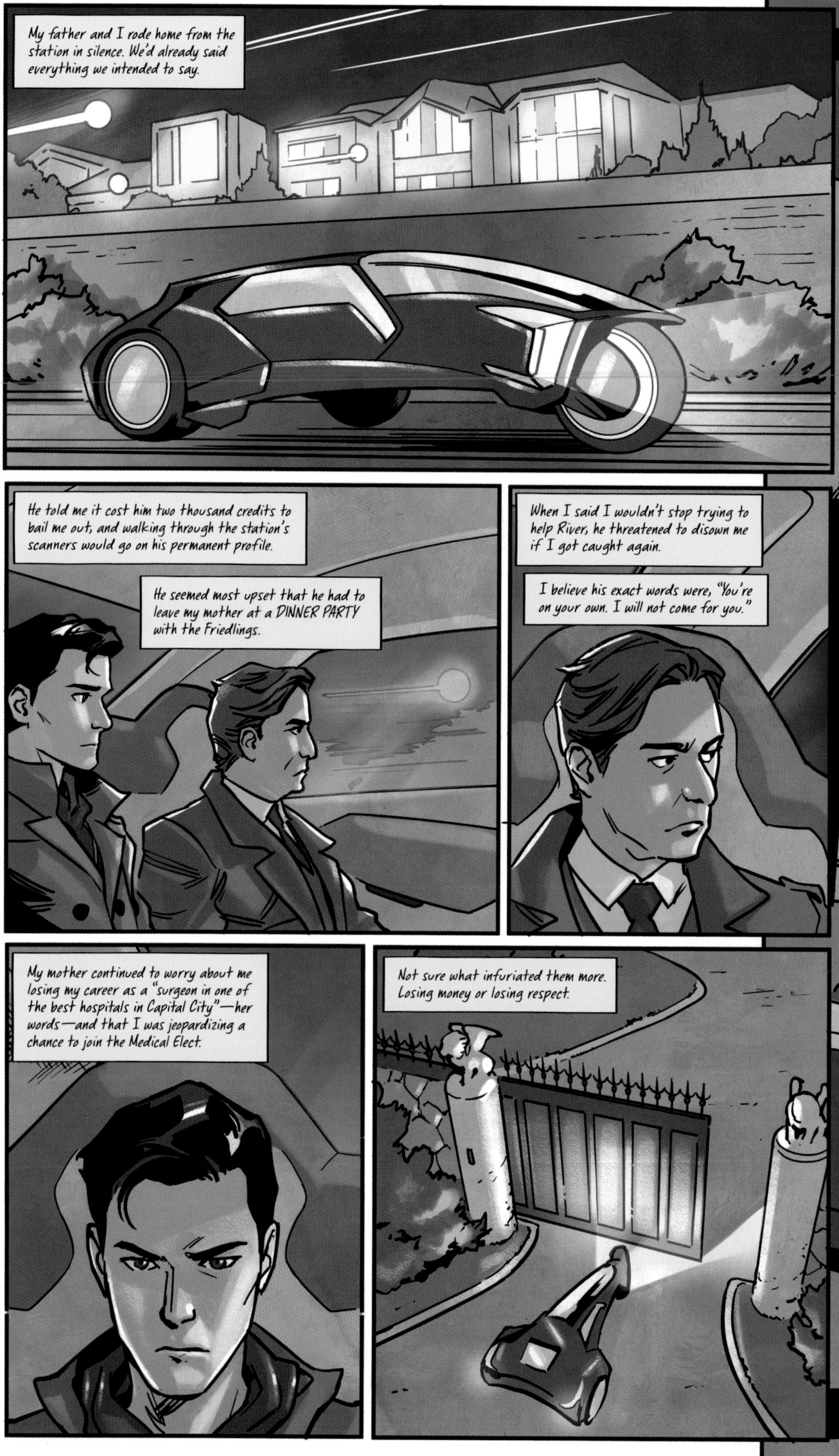
My father and I rode home from the station in silence. We'd already said everything we intended to say.
He told me it cost him two thousand credits to bail me out, and walking through the station's scanners would go on his permanent profile.
He seemed most upset that he had to leave my mother at a DINNER PARTY with the Friedlings.
When I said I wouldn't stop trying to help River, he threatened to disown me if I got caught again.
I believe his exact words were, "You're on your own. I will not come for you."
My mother continued to worry about me losing my career as a "surgeon in one of the best hospitals in Capital City"—her words—and that I was jeopardizing a chance to join the Medical Elect.
Not sure what infuriated them more. Losing money or losing respect.

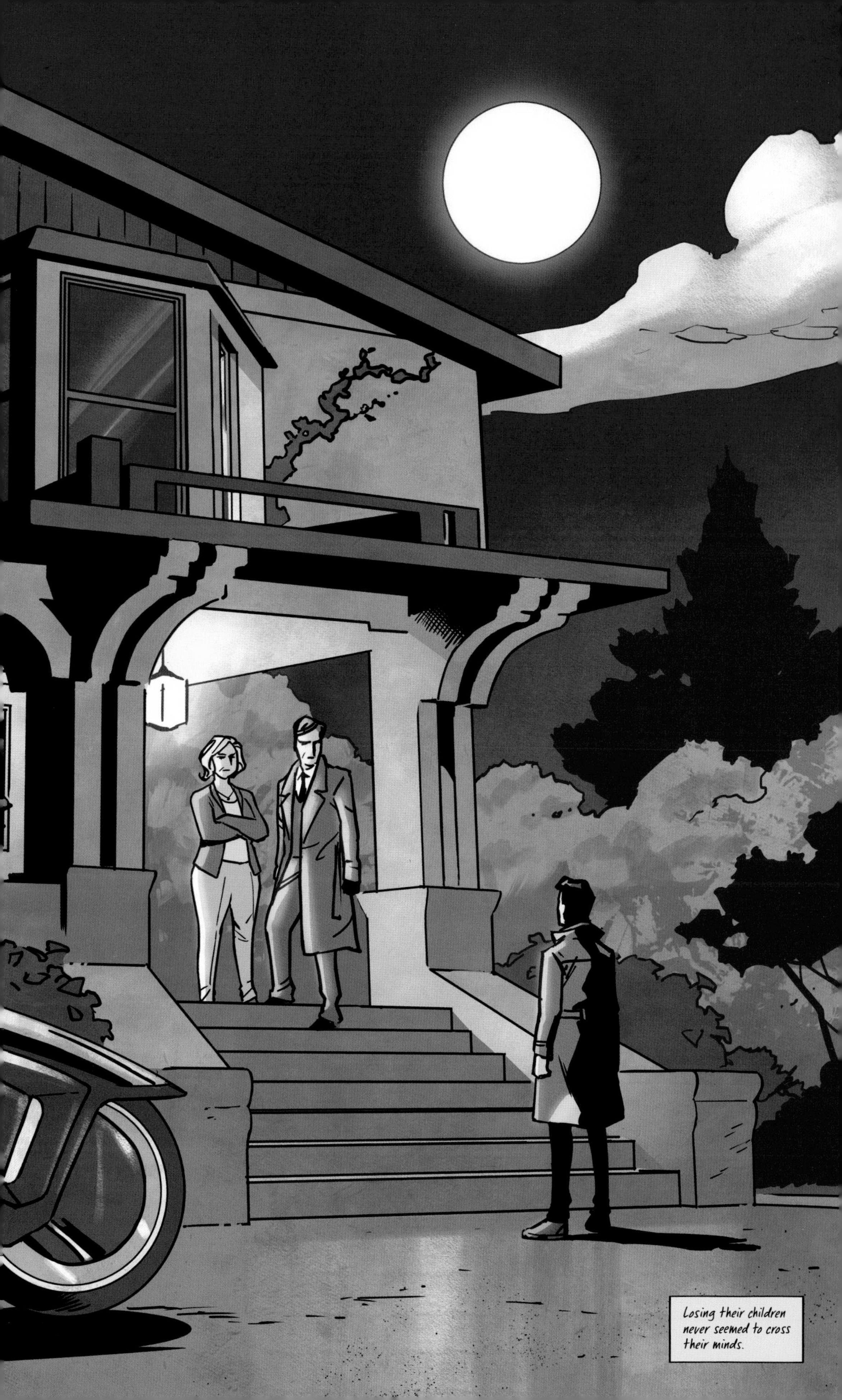
Losing their children never seemed to cross their minds.

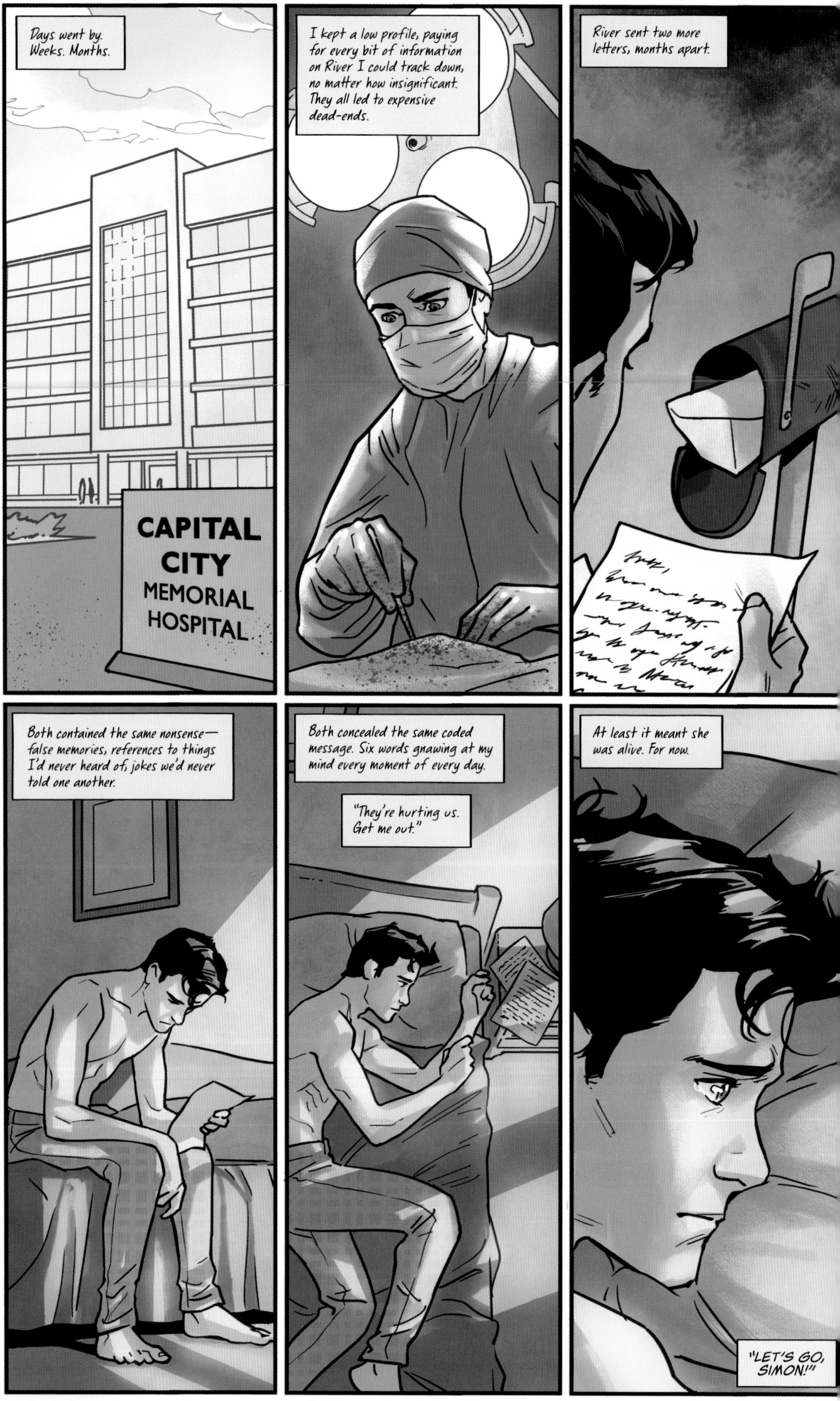
Days went by. Weeks. Months.
CAPITAL CITY MEMORIAL HOSPITAL
I kept a low profile, paying for every bit of information on River I could track down, no matter how insignificant. They all led to expensive dead-ends.
River sent two more letters, months apart.
Both contained the same nonsense—false memories, references to things I'd never heard of; jokes we'd never told one another.
Both concealed the same coded message. Six words gnawing at my mind every moment of every day.
"They're hurting us. Get me out."
At least it meant she was alive. For now.
"LET'S GO, SIMON!"

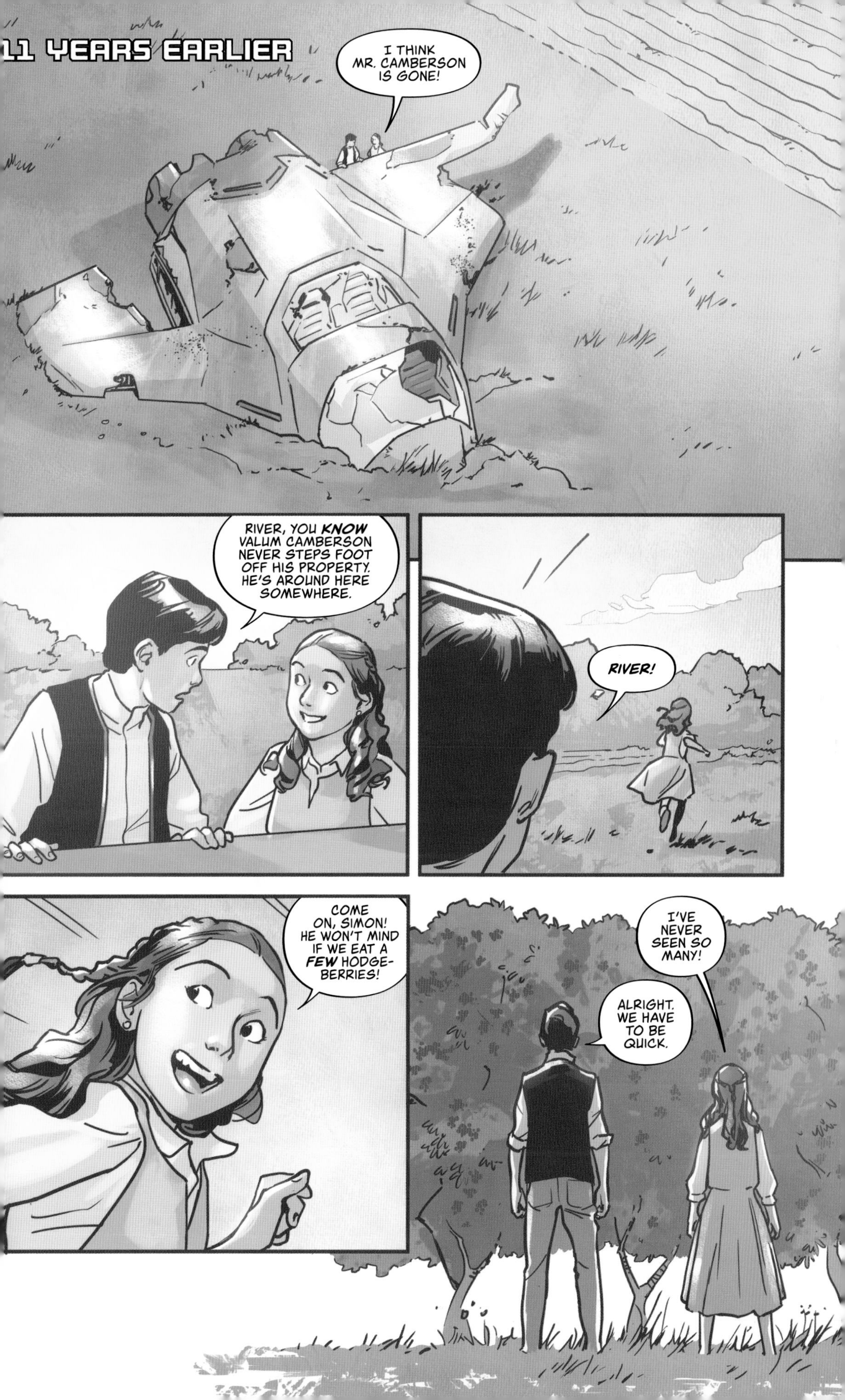
11 YEARS EARLIER
I THINK MR. CAMBERSON IS GONE!
RIVER, YOU KNOW VALUM CAMBERSON NEVER STEPS FOOT OFF HIS PROPERTY. HE'S AROUND HERE SOMEWHERE.
RIVER!
COME ON, SIMON! HE WON'T MIND IF WE EAT A FEW HODGE-BERRIES!
I'VE NEVER SEEN SO MANY!
ALRIGHT. WE HAVE TO BE QUICK.

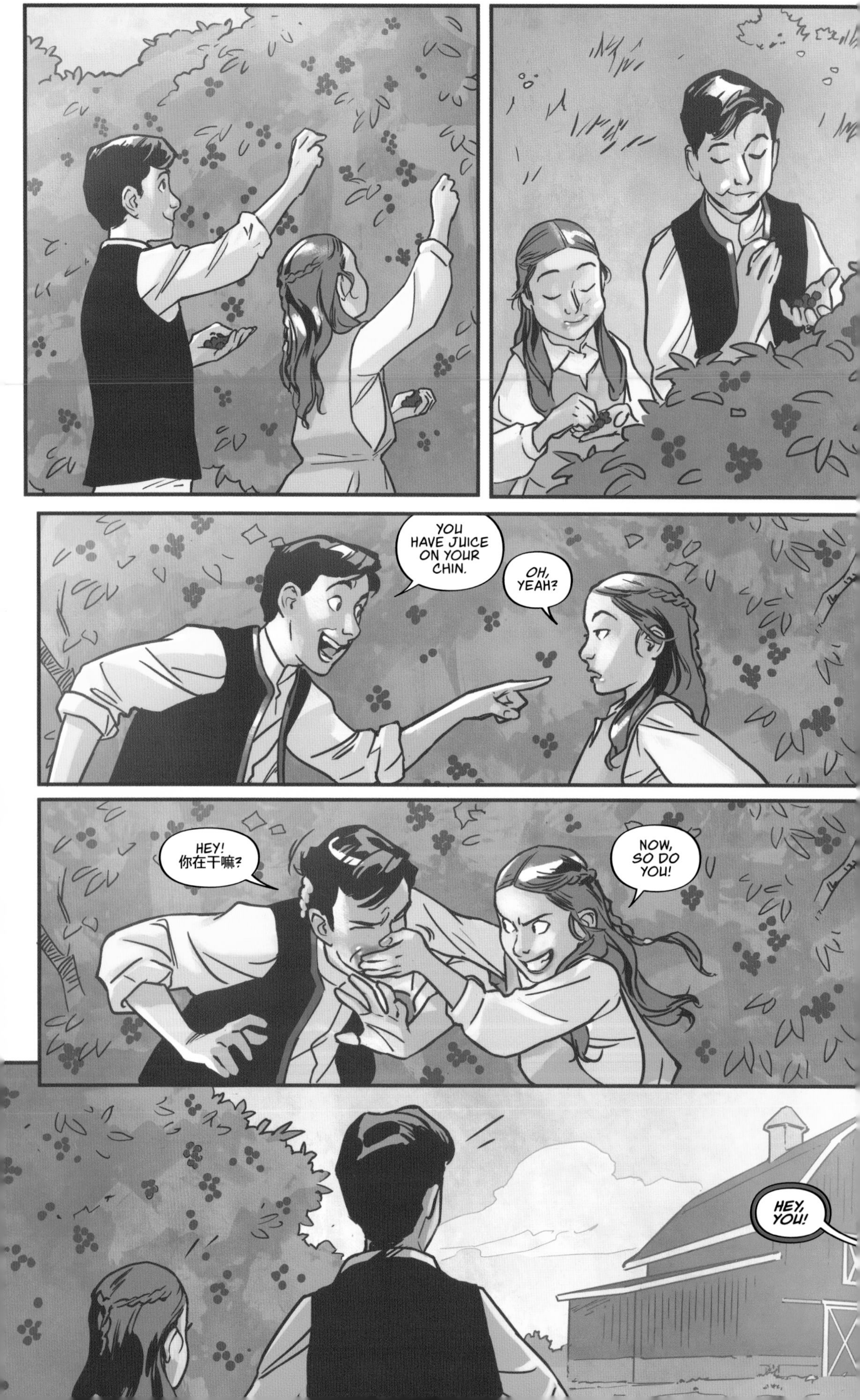

YOU HAVE JUICE ON YOUR CHIN.
OH, YEAH?
HEY! 你在干嘛?
NOW, SO DO YOU!
HEY, YOU!

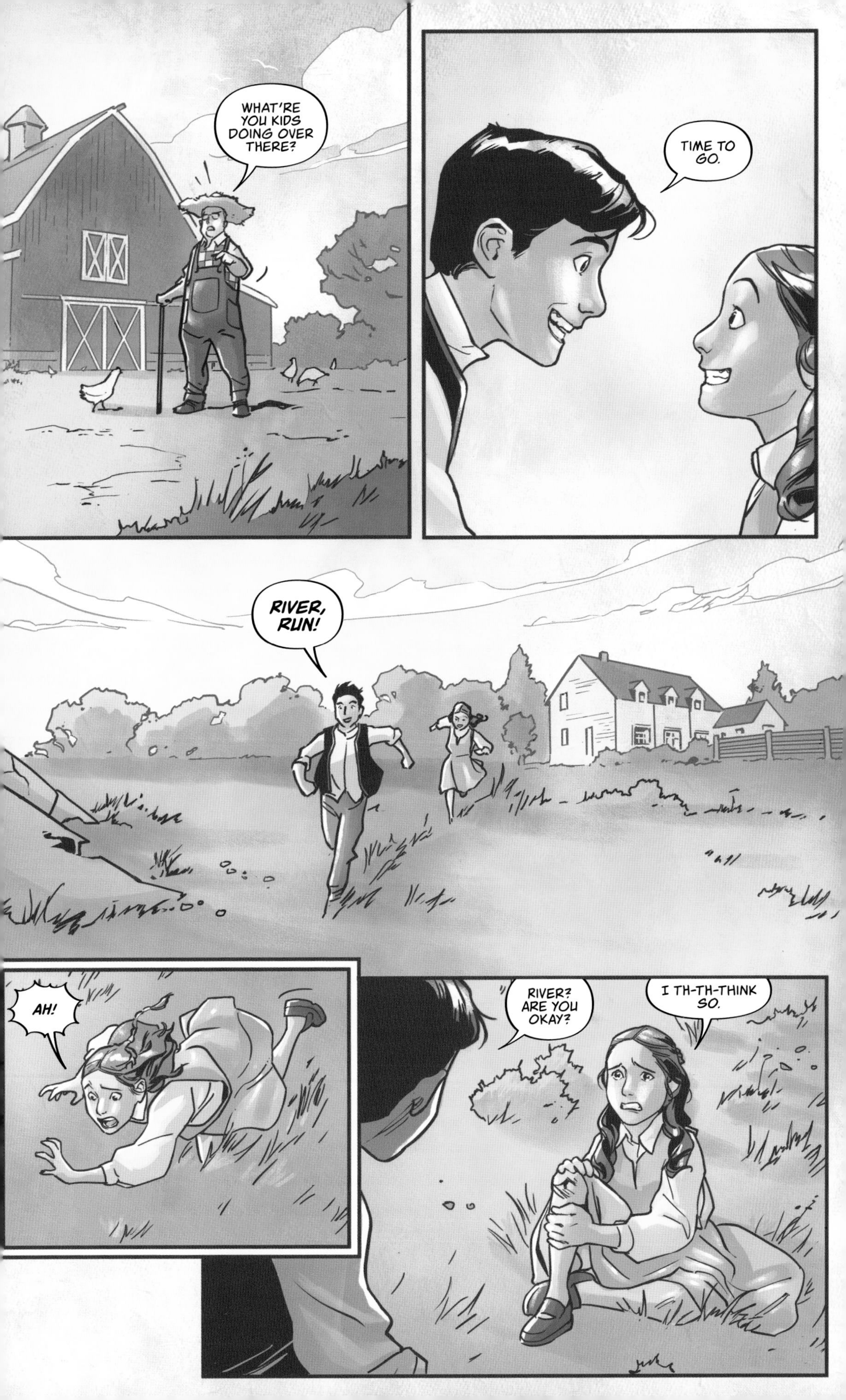
WHAT'RE YOU KIDS DOING OVER THERE?
TIME TO GO.
RIVER, RUN!
AH!
RIVER? ARE YOU OKAY?
I TH-TH-THINK SO.

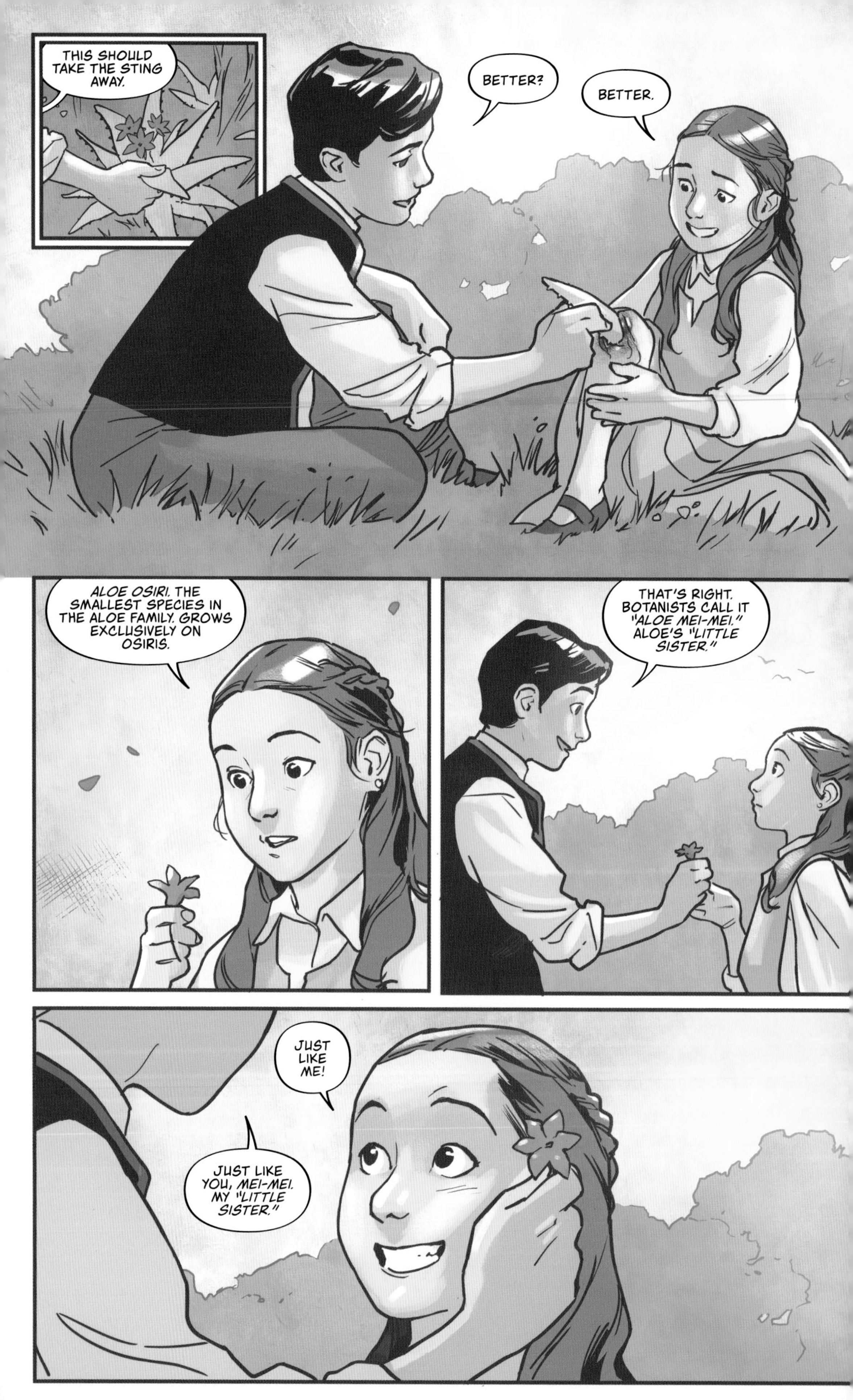
THIS SHOULD TAKE THE STING AWAY.
BETTER?
BETTER.
ALOE OSIRI. THE SMALLEST SPECIES IN THE ALOE FAMILY. GROWS EXCLUSIVELY ON OSIRIS.
THAT'S RIGHT. BOTANISTS CALL IT "ALOE MEI-MEI." ALOE'S "LITTLE SISTER."
JUST LIKE ME!
JUST LIKE YOU, MEI-MEI. MY "LITTLE SISTER."

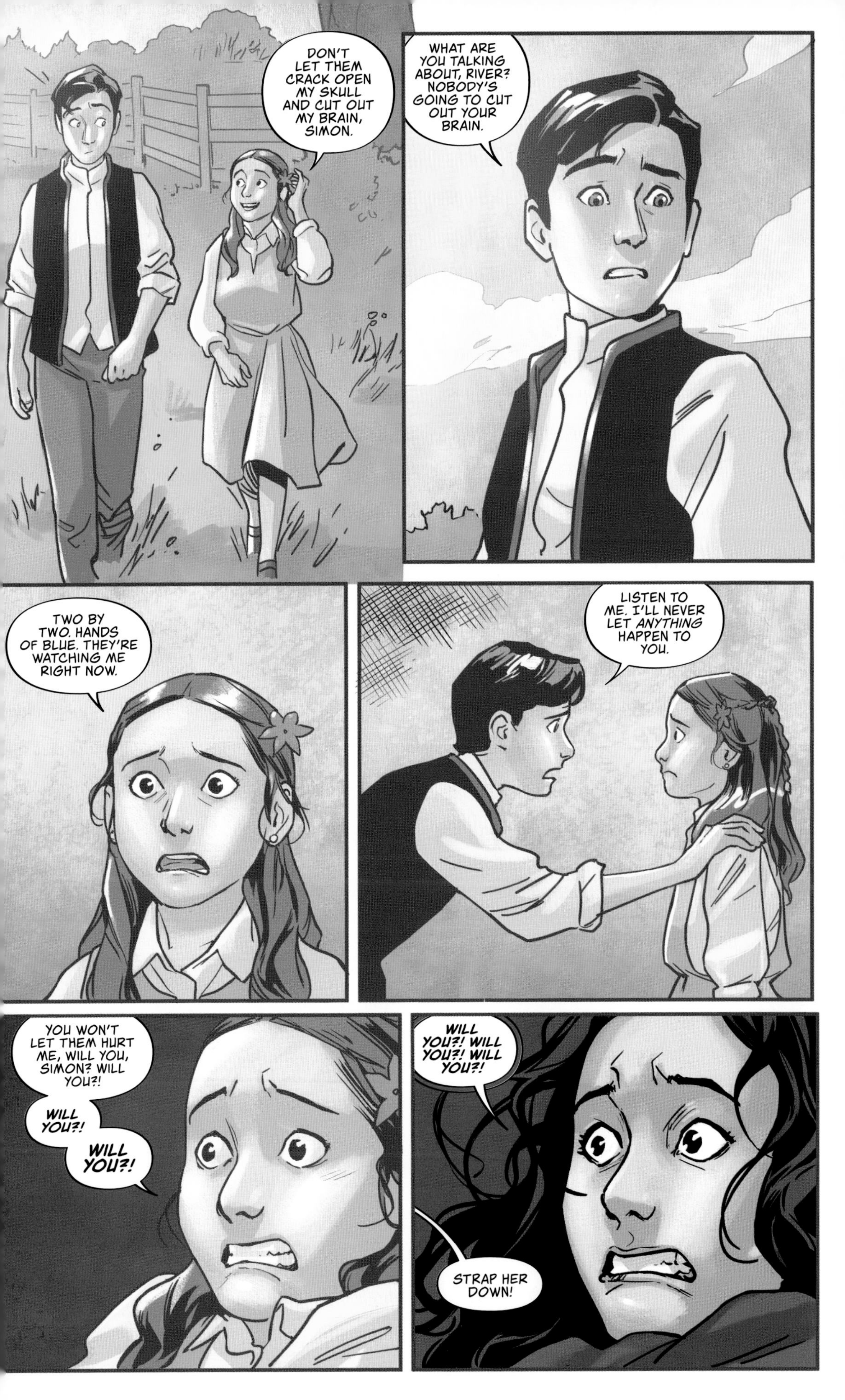
DON'T LET THEM CRACK OPEN MY SKULL AND CUT OUT MY BRAIN, SIMON.
WHAT ARE YOU TALKING ABOUT, RIVER? NOBODY'S GOING TO CUT OUT YOUR BRAIN.
TWO BY TWO. HANDS OF BLUE. THEY'RE WATCHING ME RIGHT NOW.
LISTEN TO ME. I'LL NEVER LET ANYTHING HAPPEN TO YOU.
YOU WON'T LET THEM HURT ME, WILL YOU, SIMON? WILL YOU?!
WILL YOU?!
WILL YOU?!
WILL YOU?! WILL YOU?! WILL YOU?!
STRAP HER DOWN!

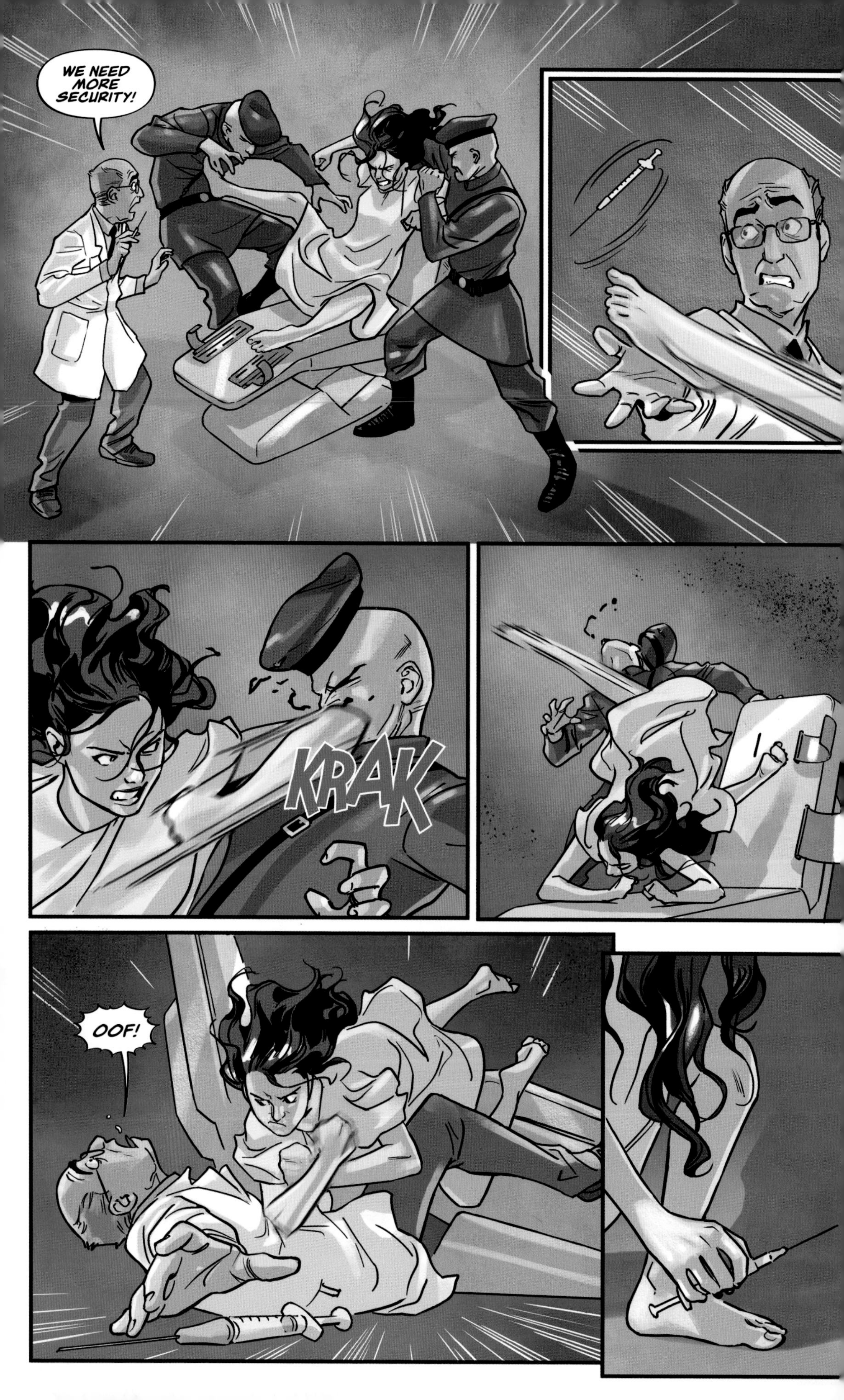
WE NEED MORE SECURITY!
KRAK
OOF!

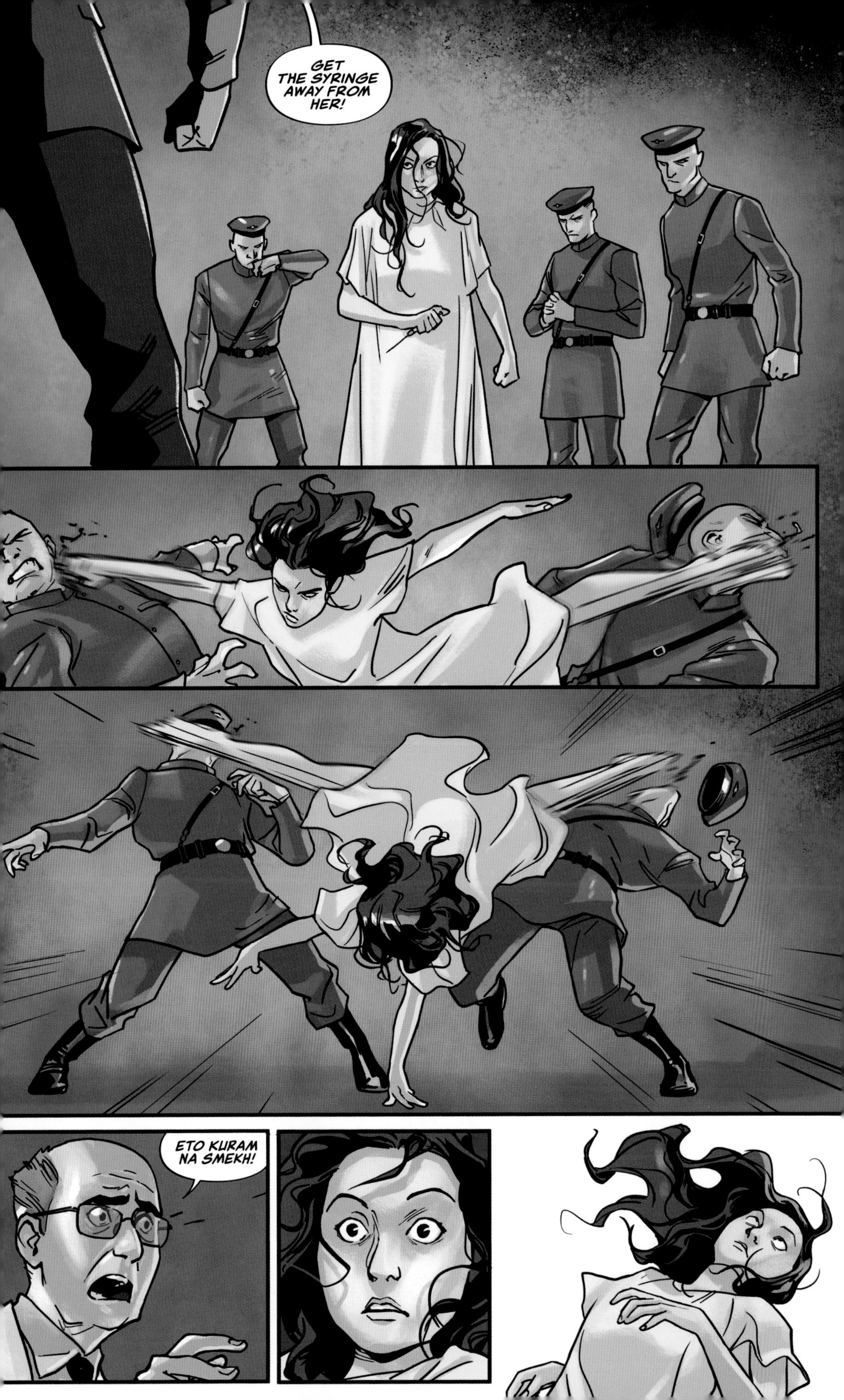
GET THE SYRINGE AWAY FROM HER!
ETO KURAM NA SMEKH!

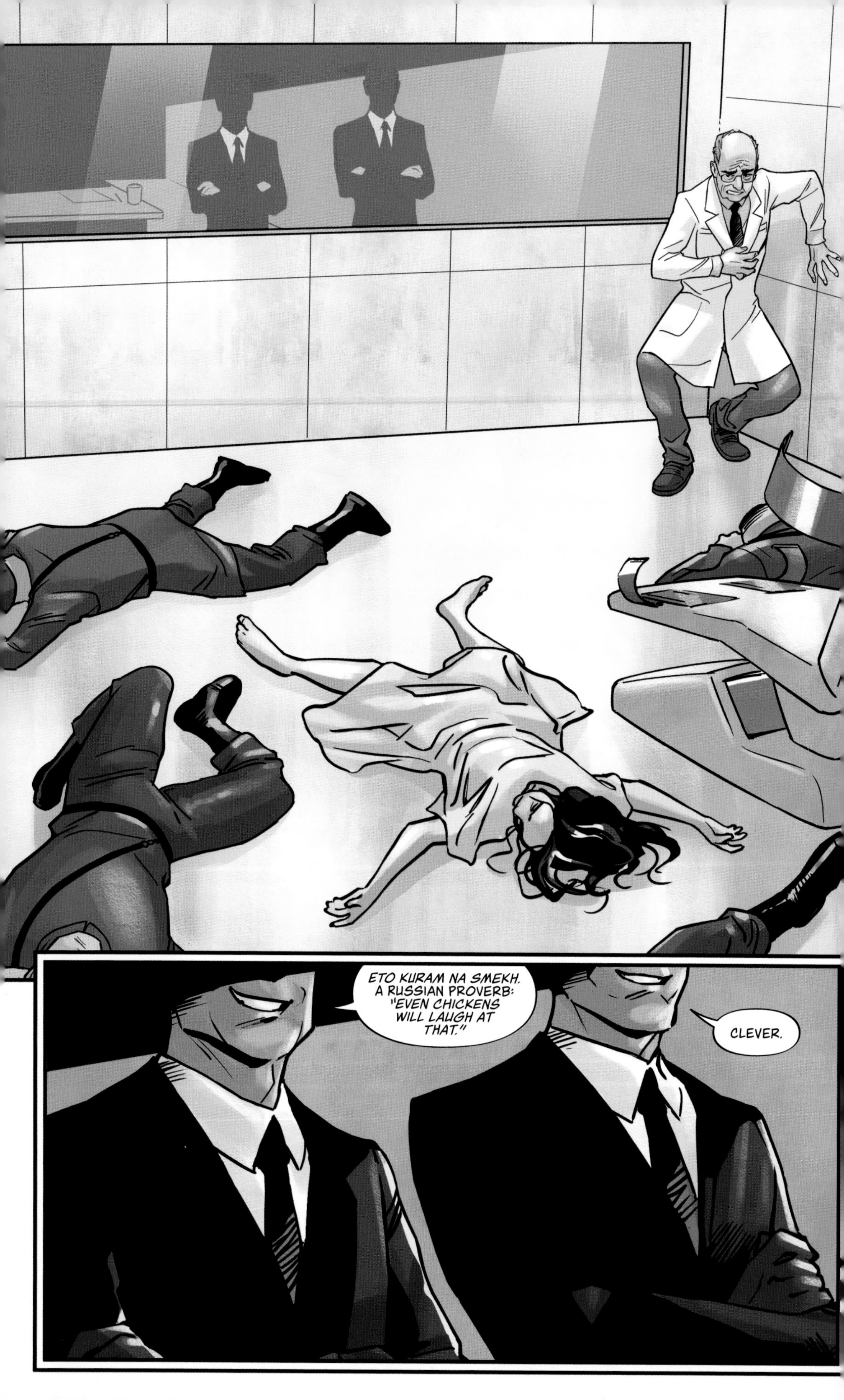
ETO KURAM NA SMEKH. A RUSSIAN PROVERB: "EVEN CHICKENS WILL LAUGH AT THAT."
CLEVER.

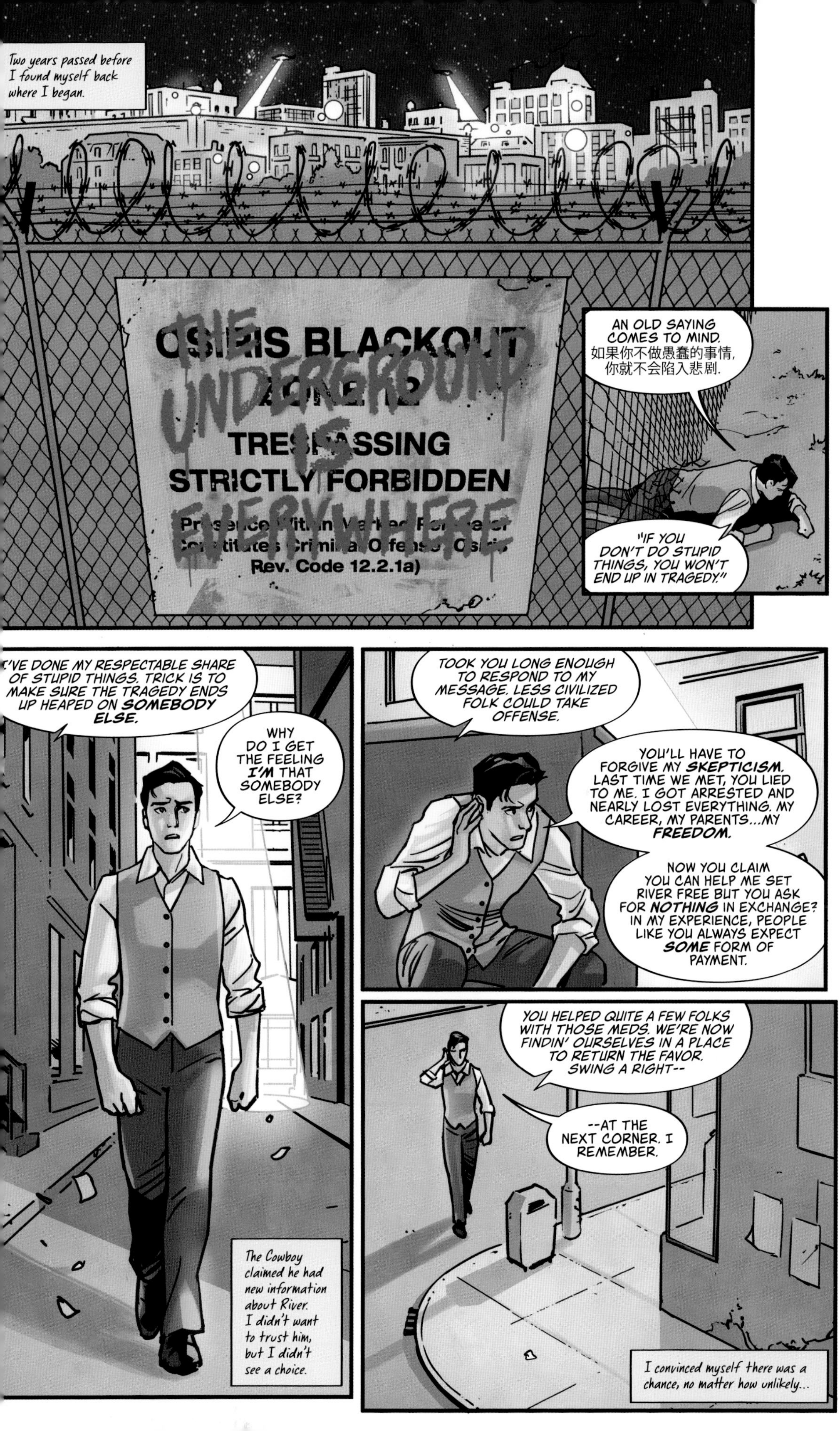

Two years passed before I found myself back where I began.
OSIRIS BLACKOUT
TRESPASSING
STRICTLY FORBIDDEN
Rev. Code 12.2.1a)
THE UNDERGROUND IS EVERYWHERE
AN OLD SAYING COMES TO MIND. 如果你不做愚蠢的事情,你就不会陷入悲剧.
"IF YOU DON'T DO STUPID THINGS, YOU WON'T END UP IN TRAGEDY."
I'VE DONE MY RESPECTABLE SHARE OF STUPID THINGS. TRICK IS TO MAKE SURE THE TRAGEDY ENDS UP HEAPED ON SOMEBODY ELSE.
WHY DO I GET THE FEELING I'M THAT SOMEBODY ELSE?
The Cowboy claimed he had new information about River. I didn't want to trust him, but I didn't see a choice.
TOOK YOU LONG ENOUGH TO RESPOND TO MY MESSAGE. LESS CIVILIZED FOLK COULD TAKE OFFENSE.
YOU'LL HAVE TO FORGIVE MY SKEPTICISM. LAST TIME WE MET, YOU LIED TO ME. I GOT ARRESTED AND NEARLY LOST EVERYTHING. MY CAREER, MY PARENTS...MY FREEDOM.
NOW YOU CLAIM YOU CAN HELP ME SET RIVER FREE BUT YOU ASK FOR NOTHING IN EXCHANGE? IN MY EXPERIENCE, PEOPLE LIKE YOU ALWAYS EXPECT SOME FORM OF PAYMENT.
YOU HELPED QUITE A FEW FOLKS WITH THOSE MEDS. WE'RE NOW FINDIN' OURSELVES IN A PLACE TO RETURN THE FAVOR. SWING A RIGHT--
--AT THE NEXT CORNER. I REMEMBER.
I convinced myself there was a chance, no matter how unlikely...

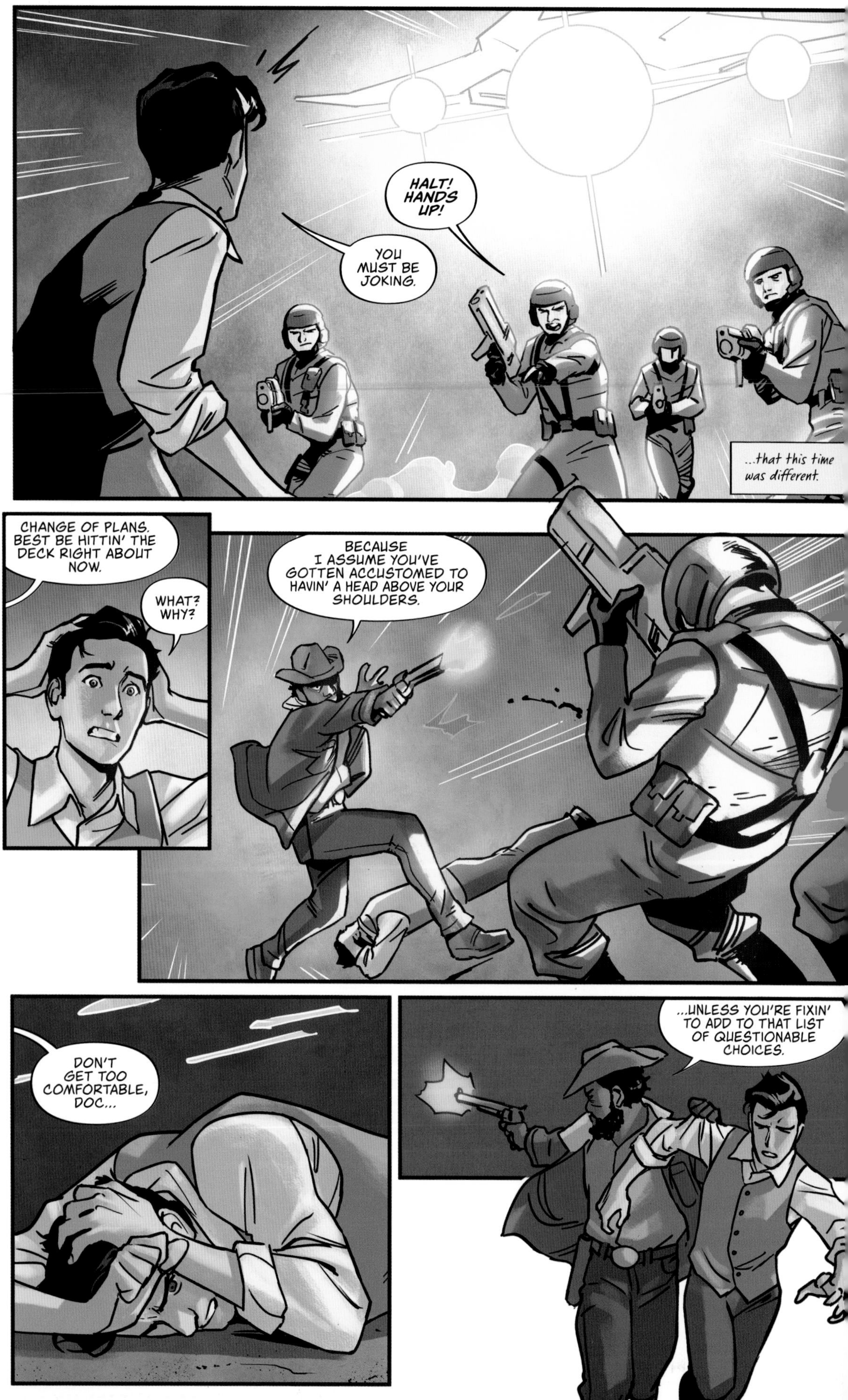
HALT! HANDS UP!
YOU MUST BE JOKING.
...that this time was different.
CHANGE OF PLANS. BEST BE HITTIN' THE DECK RIGHT ABOUT NOW.
WHAT? WHY?
BECAUSE I ASSUME YOU'VE GOTTEN ACCUSTOMED TO HAVIN' A HEAD ABOVE YOUR SHOULDERS.
DON'T GET TOO COMFORTABLE, DOC...
...UNLESS YOU'RE FIXIN' TO ADD TO THAT LIST OF QUESTIONABLE CHOICES.

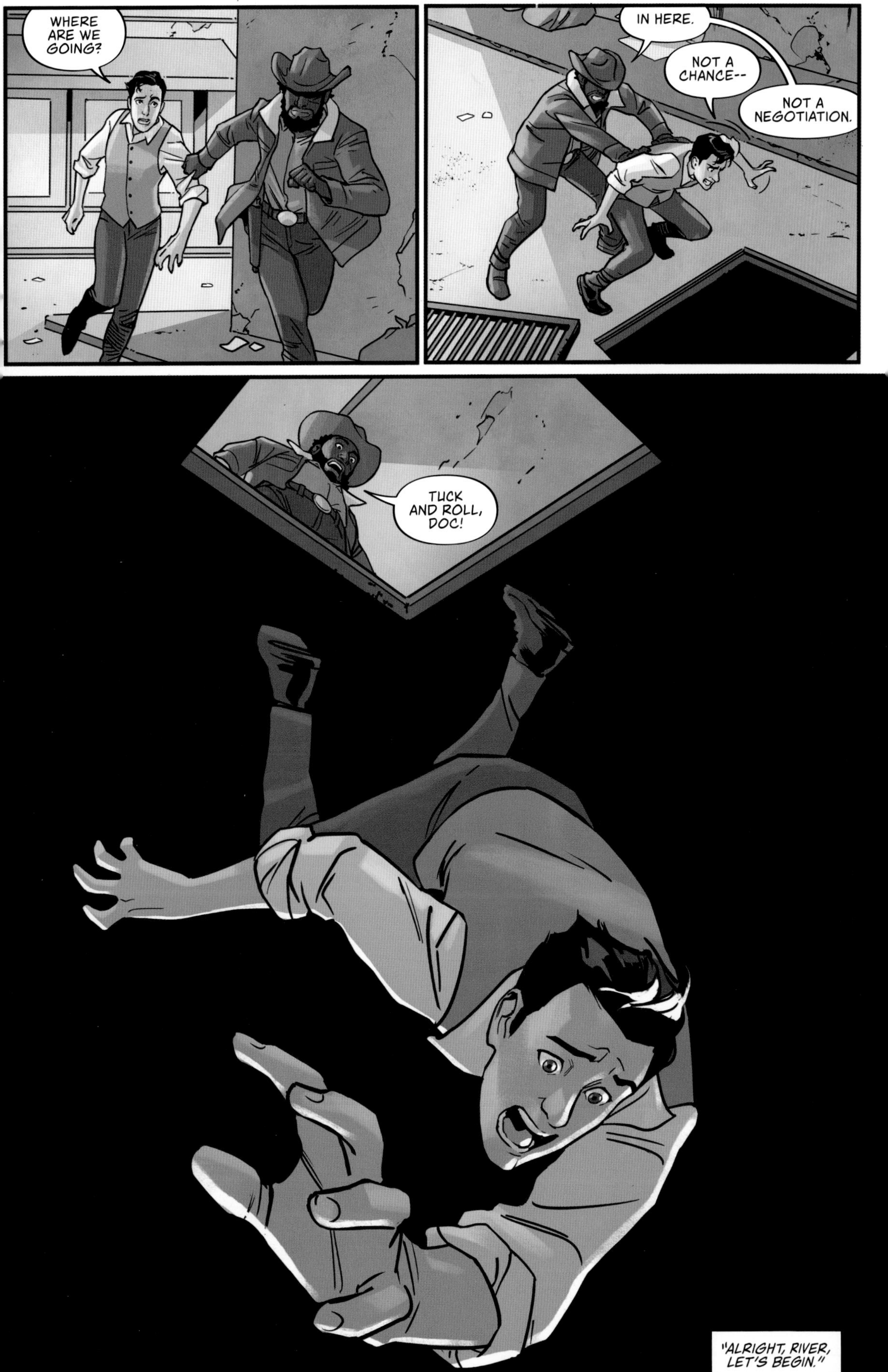
WHERE ARE WE GOING?
IN HERE.
NOT A CHANCE--
NOT A NEGOTIATION.
TUCK AND ROLL, DOC!
"ALRIGHT, RIVER, LET'S BEGIN."

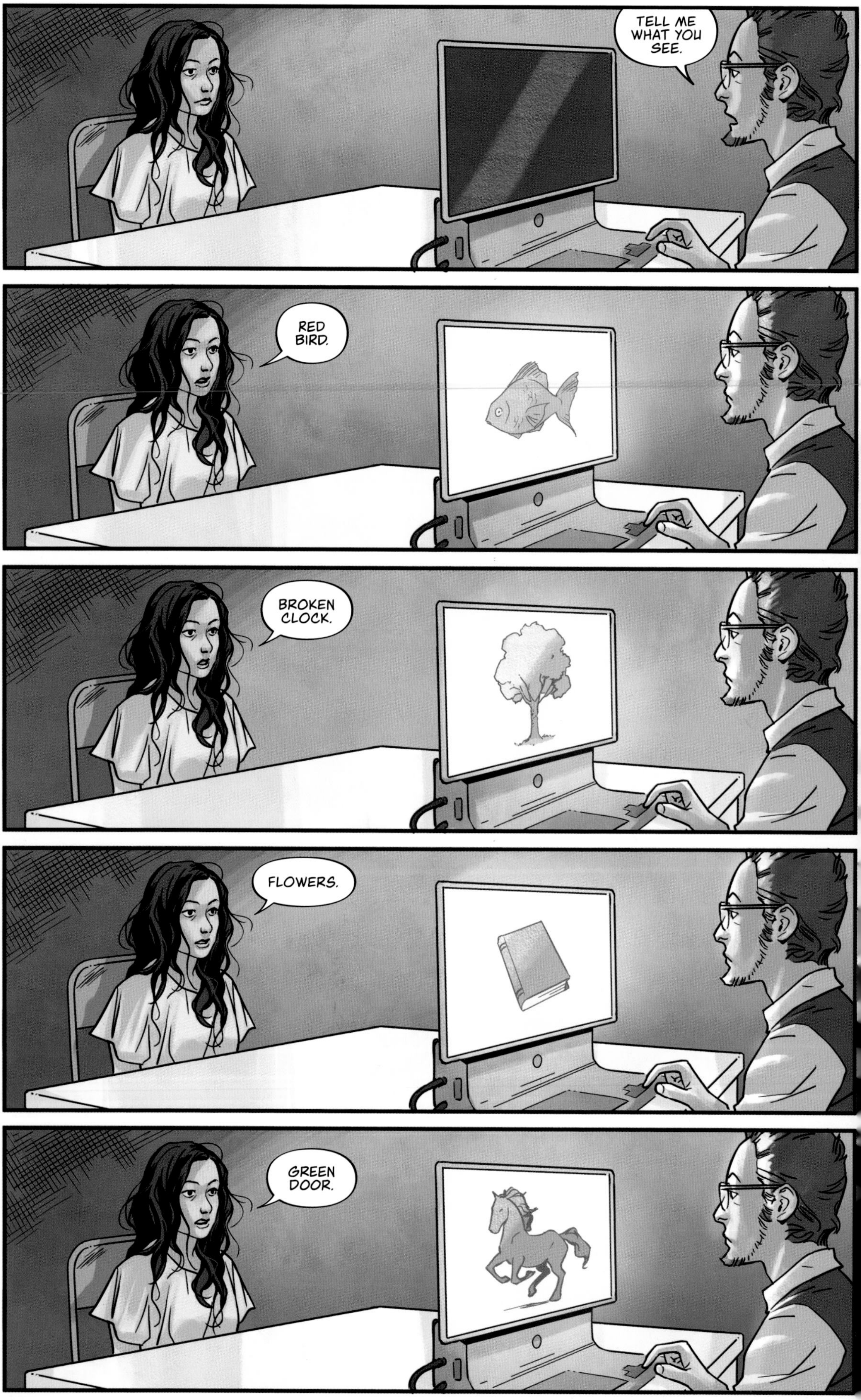
TELL ME WHAT YOU SEE.
RED BIRD.
BROKEN CLOCK.
FLOWERS.
GREEN DOOR.

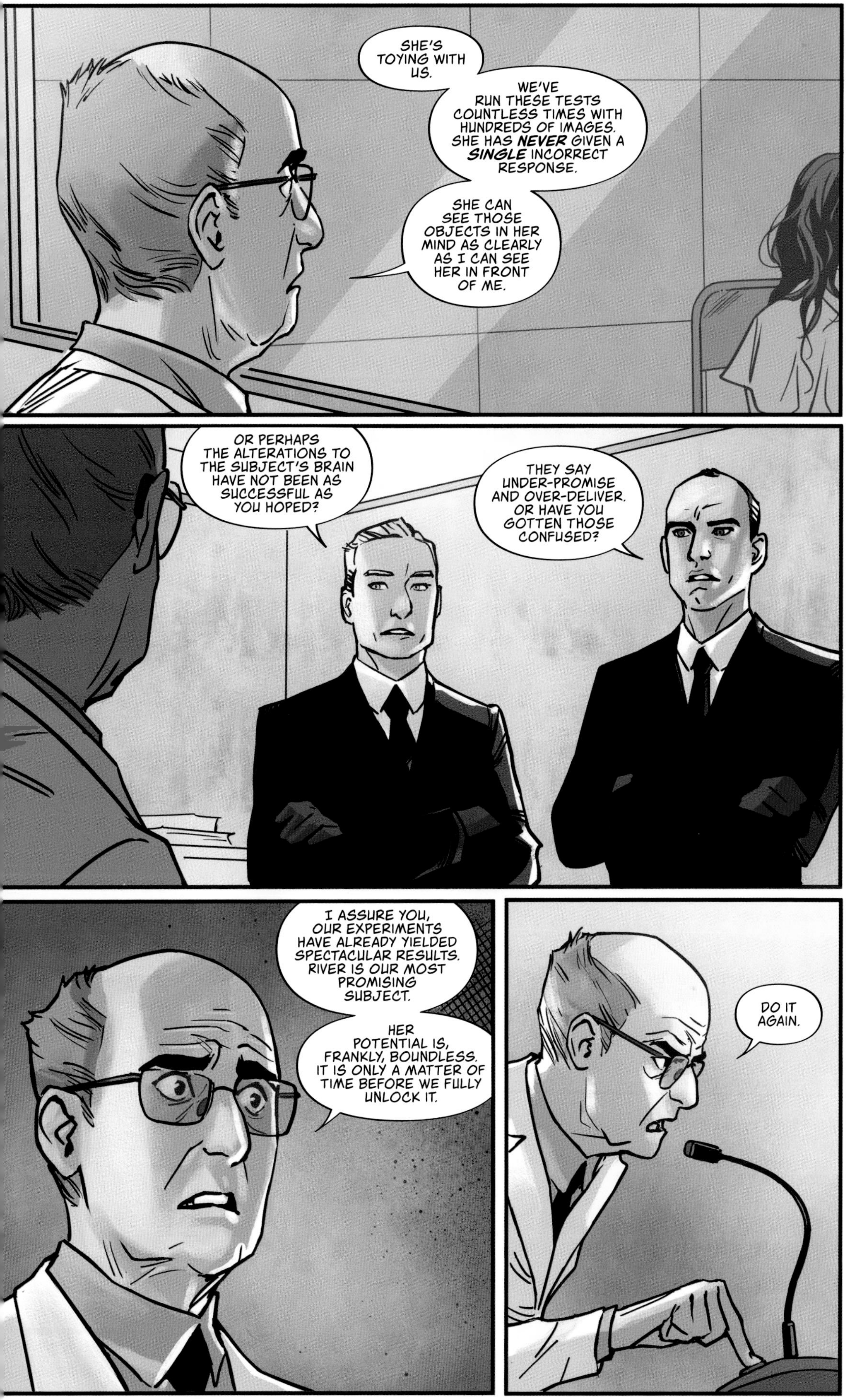
SHE'S TOYING WITH US.
WE'VE RUN THESE TESTS COUNTLESS TIMES WITH HUNDREDS OF IMAGES. SHE HAS NEVER GIVEN A SINGLE INCORRECT RESPONSE.
SHE CAN SEE THOSE OBJECTS IN HER MIND AS CLEARLY AS I CAN SEE HER IN FRONT OF ME.
OR PERHAPS THE ALTERATIONS TO THE SUBJECT'S BRAIN HAVE NOT BEEN AS SUCCESSFUL AS YOU HOPED?
THEY SAY UNDER-PROMISE AND OVER-DELIVER. OR HAVE YOU GOTTEN THOSE CONFUSED?
I ASSURE YOU, OUR EXPERIMENTS HAVE ALREADY YIELDED SPECTACULAR RESULTS. RIVER IS OUR MOST PROMISING SUBJECT.
HER POTENTIAL IS, FRANKLY, BOUNDLESS. IT IS ONLY A MATTER OF TIME BEFORE WE FULLY UNLOCK IT.
DO IT AGAIN.

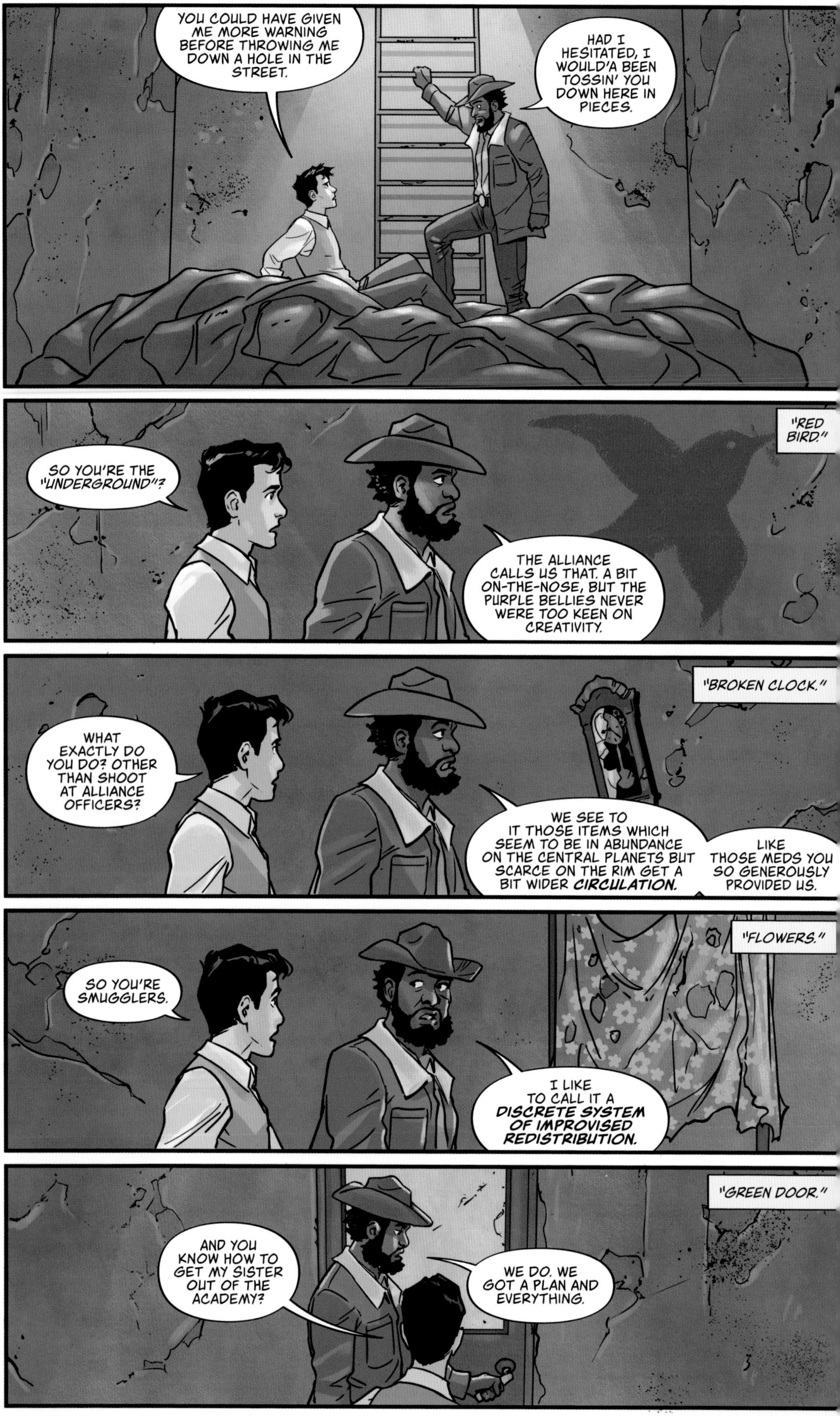
YOU COULD HAVE GIVEN ME MORE WARNING BEFORE THROWING ME DOWN A HOLE IN THE STREET.
HAD I HESITATED, I WOULD'A BEEN TOSSIN' YOU DOWN HERE IN PIECES.
"RED BIRD."
SO YOU'RE THE "UNDERGROUND"?
THE ALLIANCE CALLS US THAT. A BIT ON-THE-NOSE, BUT THE PURPLE BELLIES NEVER WERE TOO KEEN ON CREATIVITY.
"BROKEN CLOCK."
WHAT EXACTLY DO YOU DO? OTHER THAN SHOOT AT ALLIANCE OFFICERS?
WE SEE TO IT THOSE ITEMS WHICH SEEM TO BE IN ABUNDANCE ON THE CENTRAL PLANETS BUT SCARCE ON THE RIM GET A BIT WIDER *CIRCULATION.*
LIKE THOSE MEDS YOU SO GENEROUSLY PROVIDED US.
"FLOWERS."
SO YOU'RE SMUGGLERS.
I LIKE TO CALL IT A *DISCRETE SYSTEM OF IMPROVISED REDISTRIBUTION.*
"GREEN DOOR."
AND YOU KNOW HOW TO GET MY SISTER OUT OF THE ACADEMY?
WE DO. WE GOT A PLAN AND EVERYTHING.

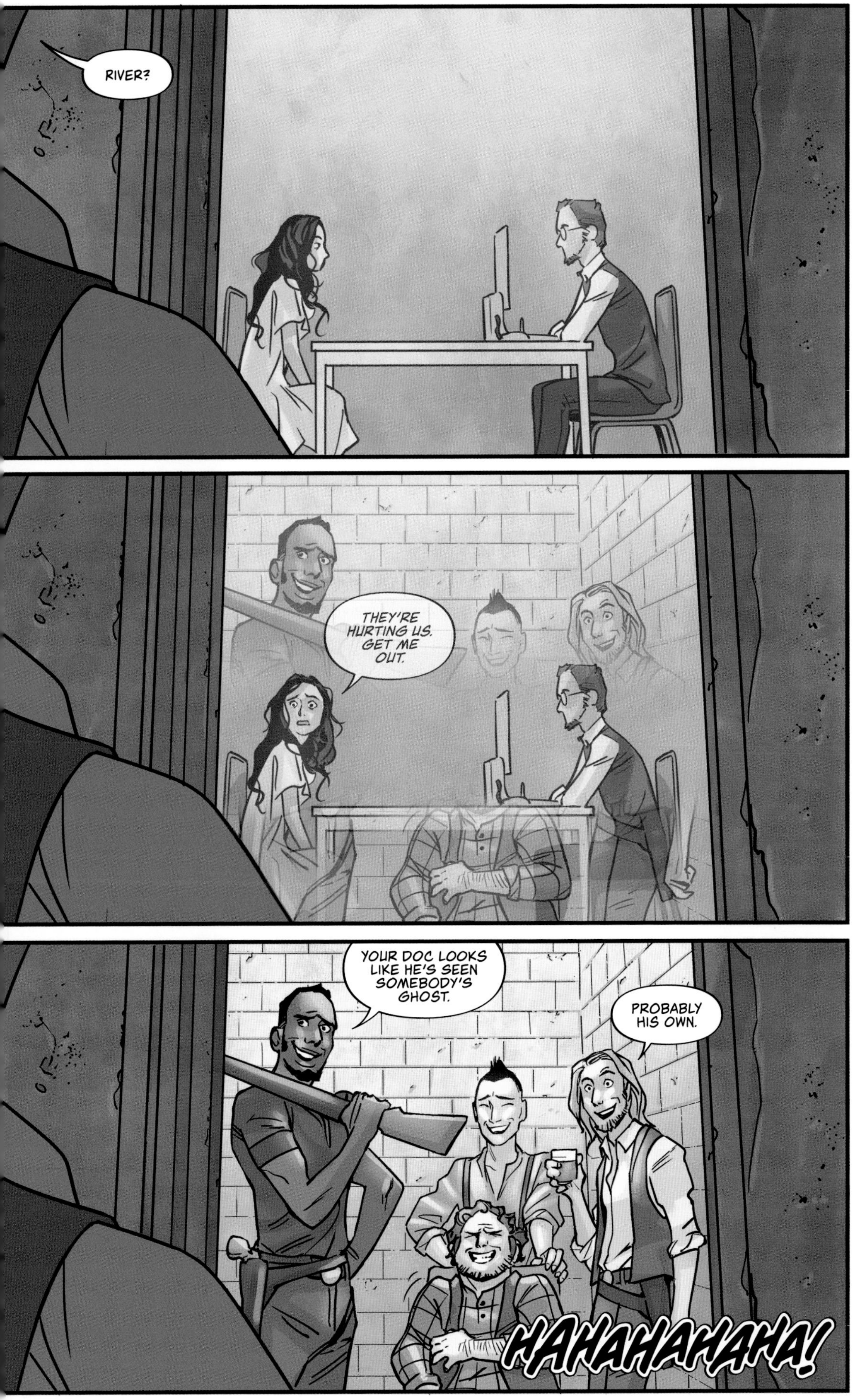
RIVER?
THEY'RE HURTING US. GET ME OUT.
YOUR DOC LOOKS LIKE HE'S SEEN SOMEBODY'S GHOST.
PROBABLY HIS OWN.
HAHAHAHAHAHA!

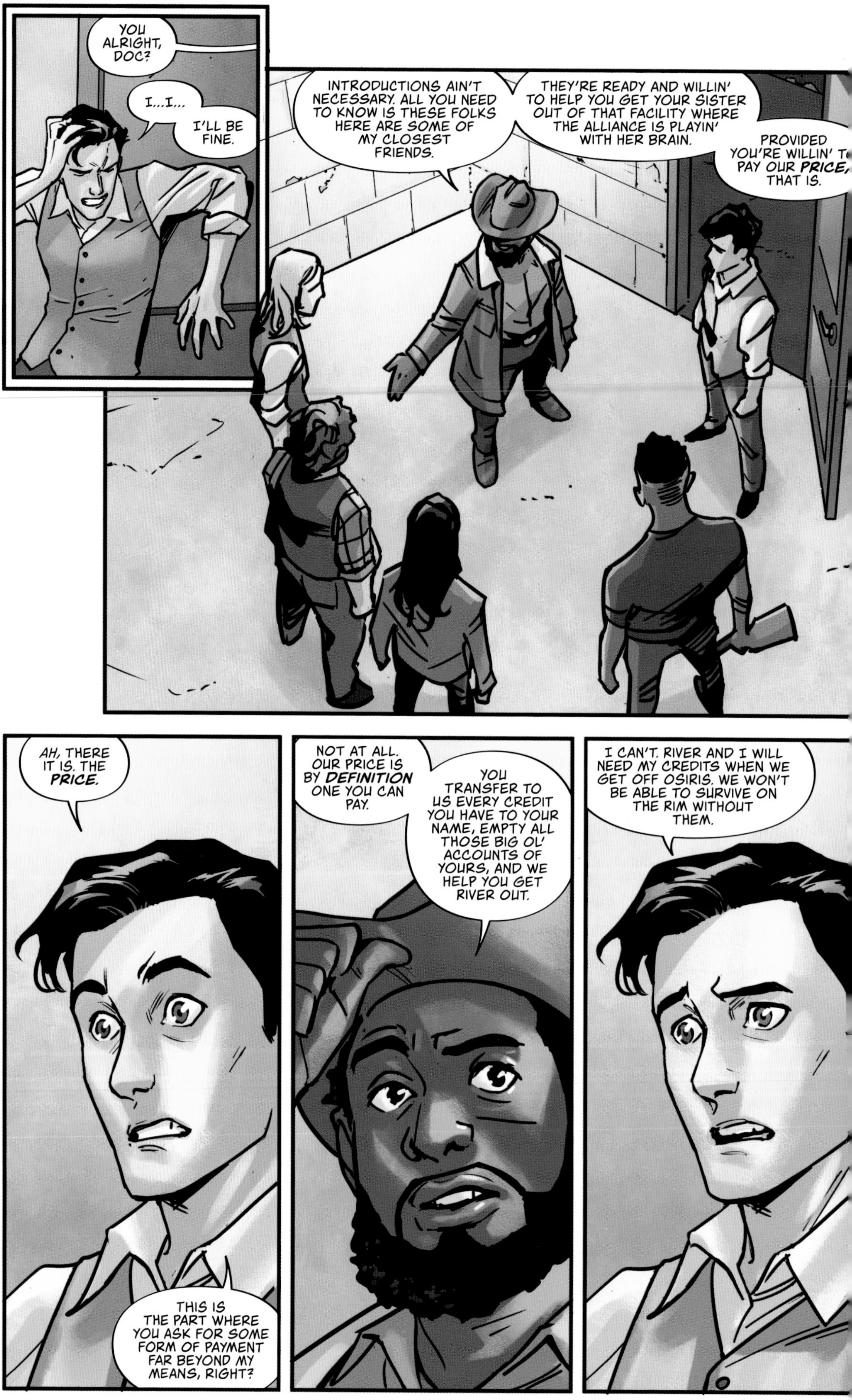
YOU ALRIGHT, DOC?
I...I...
I'LL BE FINE.
INTRODUCTIONS AIN'T NECESSARY. ALL YOU NEED TO KNOW IS THESE FOLKS HERE ARE SOME OF MY CLOSEST FRIENDS.
THEY'RE READY AND WILLIN' TO HELP YOU GET YOUR SISTER OUT OF THAT FACILITY WHERE THE ALLIANCE IS PLAYIN' WITH HER BRAIN.
PROVIDED YOU'RE WILLIN' T PAY OUR PRICE, THAT IS.
AH, THERE IT IS. THE PRICE.
THIS IS THE PART WHERE YOU ASK FOR SOME FORM OF PAYMENT FAR BEYOND MY MEANS, RIGHT?
NOT AT ALL. OUR PRICE IS BY DEFINITION ONE YOU CAN PAY.
YOU TRANSFER TO US EVERY CREDIT YOU HAVE TO YOUR NAME, EMPTY ALL THOSE BIG OL' ACCOUNTS OF YOURS, AND WE HELP YOU GET RIVER OUT.
I CAN'T. RIVER AND I WILL NEED MY CREDITS WHEN WE GET OFF OSIRIS. WE WON'T BE ABLE TO SURVIVE ON THE RIM WITHOUT THEM.

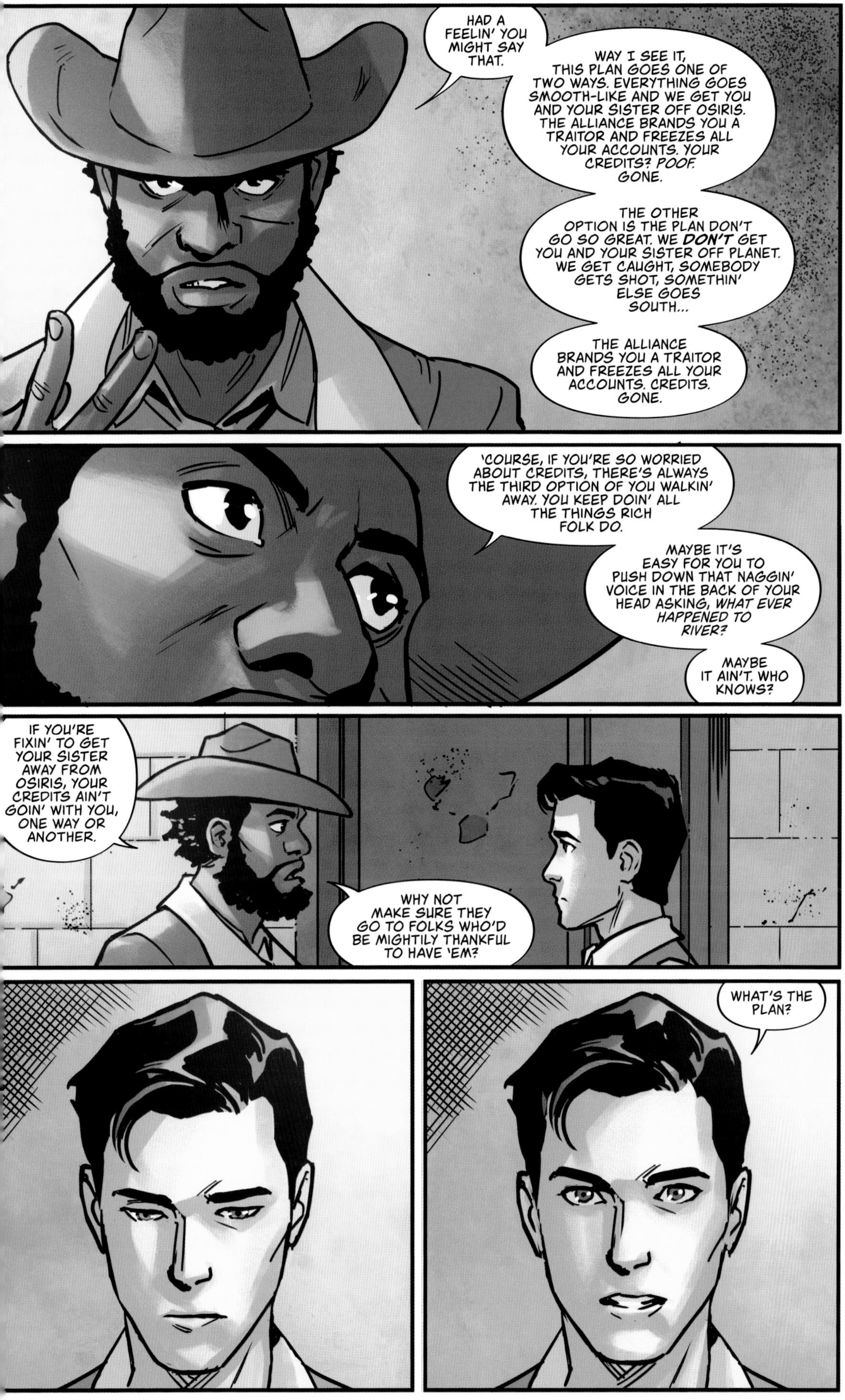
HAD A FEELIN' YOU MIGHT SAY THAT.
WAY I SEE IT, THIS PLAN GOES ONE OF TWO WAYS. EVERYTHING GOES SMOOTH-LIKE AND WE GET YOU AND YOUR SISTER OFF OSIRIS. THE ALLIANCE BRANDS YOU A TRAITOR AND FREEZES ALL YOUR ACCOUNTS. YOUR CREDITS? *POOF.* GONE.
THE OTHER OPTION IS THE PLAN DON'T GO SO GREAT. WE ***DON'T*** GET YOU AND YOUR SISTER OFF PLANET. WE GET CAUGHT, SOMEBODY GETS SHOT, SOMETHIN' ELSE GOES SOUTH...
THE ALLIANCE BRANDS YOU A TRAITOR AND FREEZES ALL YOUR ACCOUNTS. CREDITS. GONE.
'COURSE, IF YOU'RE SO WORRIED ABOUT CREDITS, THERE'S ALWAYS THE THIRD OPTION OF YOU WALKIN' AWAY. YOU KEEP DOIN' ALL THE THINGS RICH FOLK DO.
MAYBE IT'S EASY FOR YOU TO PUSH DOWN THAT NAGGIN' VOICE IN THE BACK OF YOUR HEAD ASKING, *WHAT EVER HAPPENED TO RIVER?*
MAYBE IT AIN'T. WHO KNOWS?
IF YOU'RE FIXIN' TO GET YOUR SISTER AWAY FROM OSIRIS, YOUR CREDITS AIN'T GOIN' WITH YOU, ONE WAY OR ANOTHER.
WHY NOT MAKE SURE THEY GO TO FOLKS WHO'D BE MIGHTILY THANKFUL TO HAVE 'EM?
WHAT'S THE PLAN?

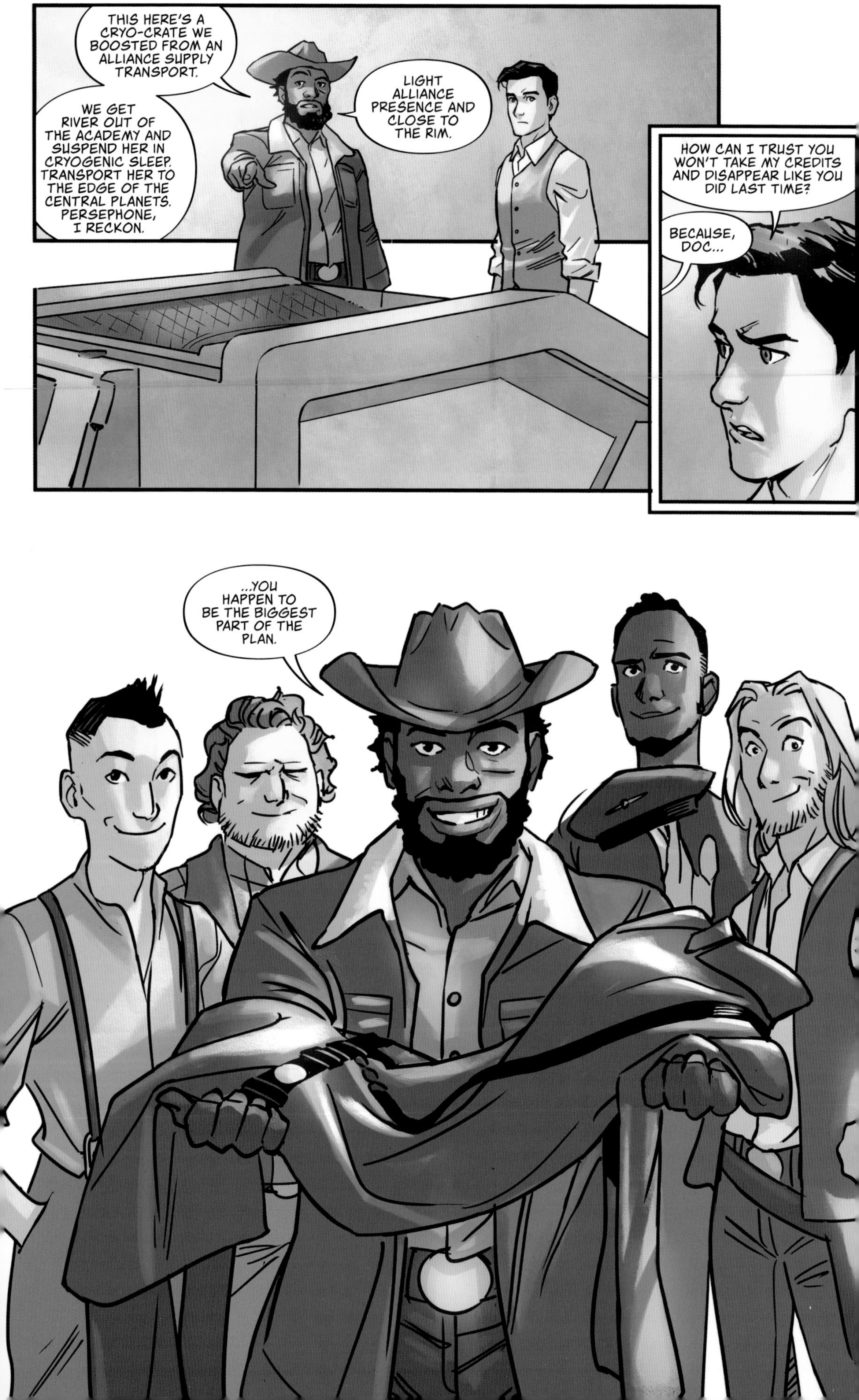
THIS HERE'S A CRYO-CRATE WE BOOSTED FROM AN ALLIANCE SUPPLY TRANSPORT.
WE GET RIVER OUT OF THE ACADEMY AND SUSPEND HER IN CRYOGENIC SLEEP. TRANSPORT HER TO THE EDGE OF THE CENTRAL PLANETS. PERSEPHONE, I RECKON.
LIGHT ALLIANCE PRESENCE AND CLOSE TO THE RIM.
HOW CAN I TRUST YOU WON'T TAKE MY CREDITS AND DISAPPEAR LIKE YOU DID LAST TIME?
BECAUSE, DOC...
...YOU HAPPEN TO BE THE BIGGEST PART OF THE PLAN.

I did what the Cowboy asked. I started making credit transfers to the list of accounts he had given me.

I spread them over a week to delay Alliance detection.

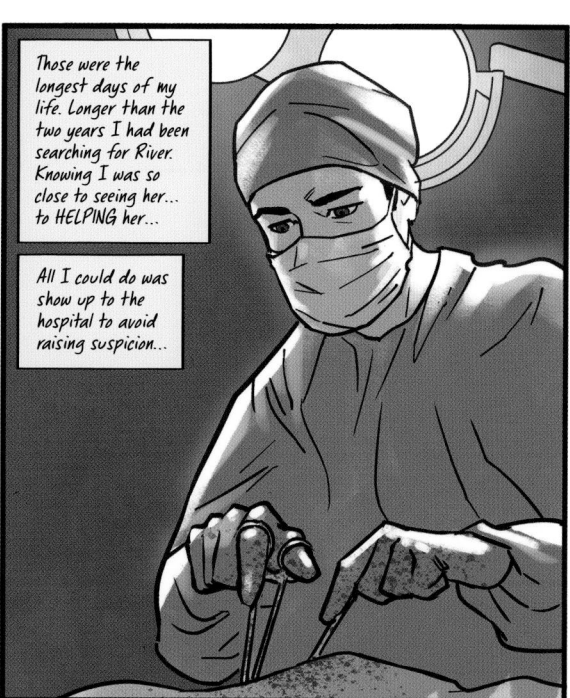

Those were the longest days of my life. Longer than the two years I had been searching for River. Knowing I was so close to seeing her... to HELPING her...

All I could do was show up to the hospital to avoid raising suspicion...

...while going over the plan a thousand times in my head.

I thought it would be difficult pretending my life wasn't about to change forever...

...until I realized it already had.

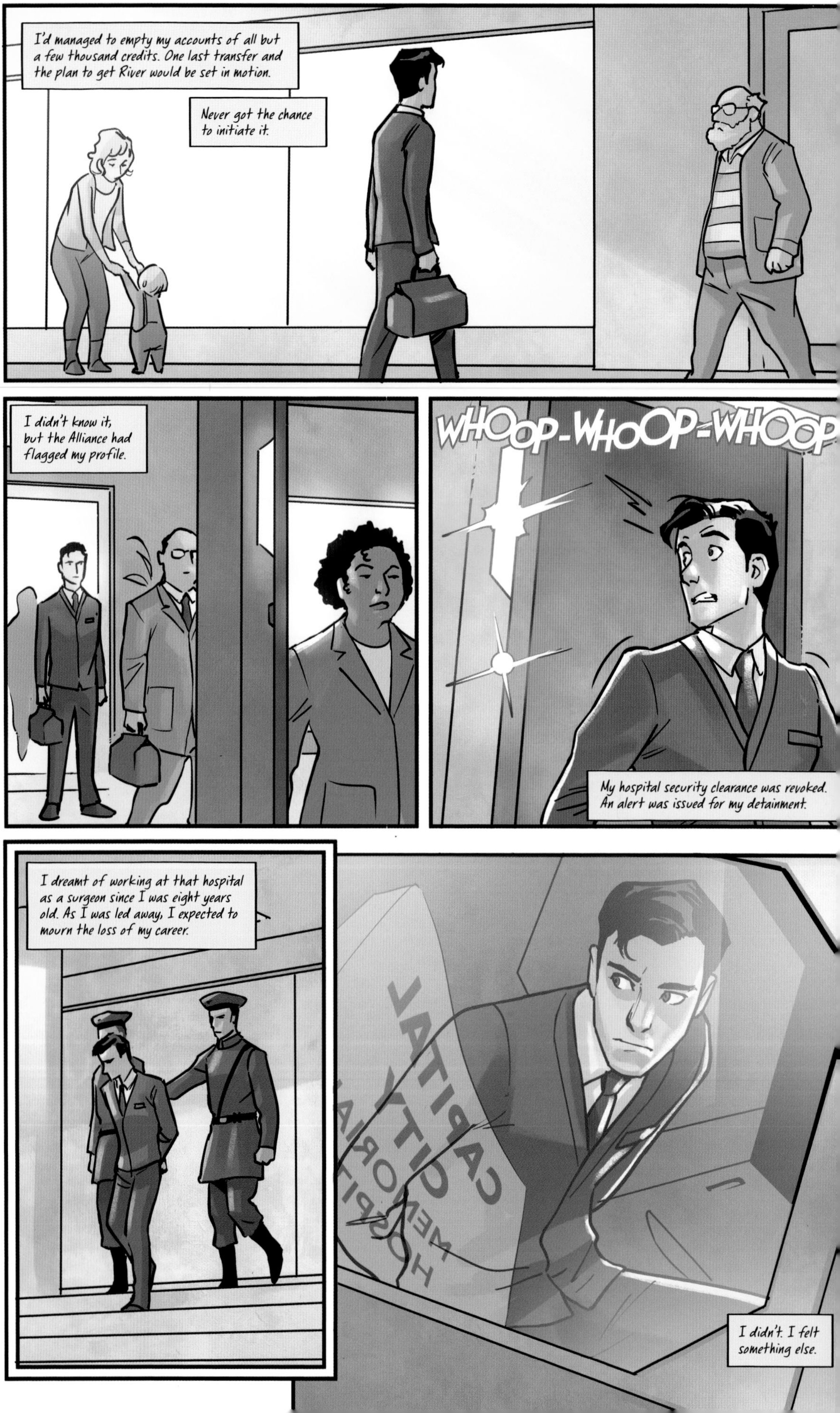
I'd managed to empty my accounts of all but a few thousand credits. One last transfer and the plan to get River would be set in motion.
Never got the chance to initiate it.
I didn't know it, but the Alliance had flagged my profile.
WHOOP-WHOOP-WHOOP
My hospital security clearance was revoked. An alert was issued for my detainment.
I dreamt of working at that hospital as a surgeon since I was eight years old. As I was led away, I expected to mourn the loss of my career.
CAPITAL CITY MEMORIAL HOSPITAL
I didn't. I felt something else.

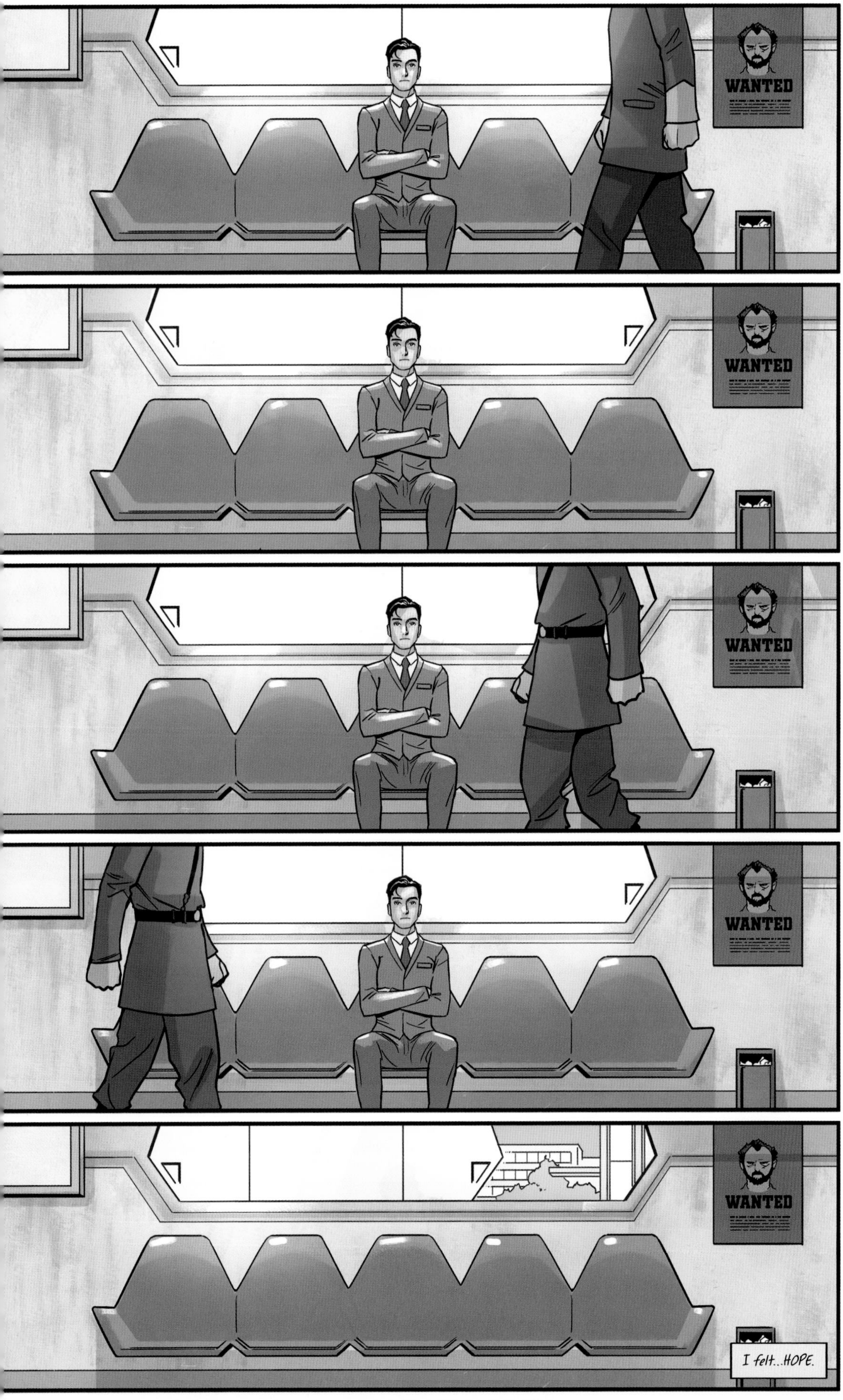
WANTED
WANTED
WANTED
WANTED
WANTED
I felt...HOPE.

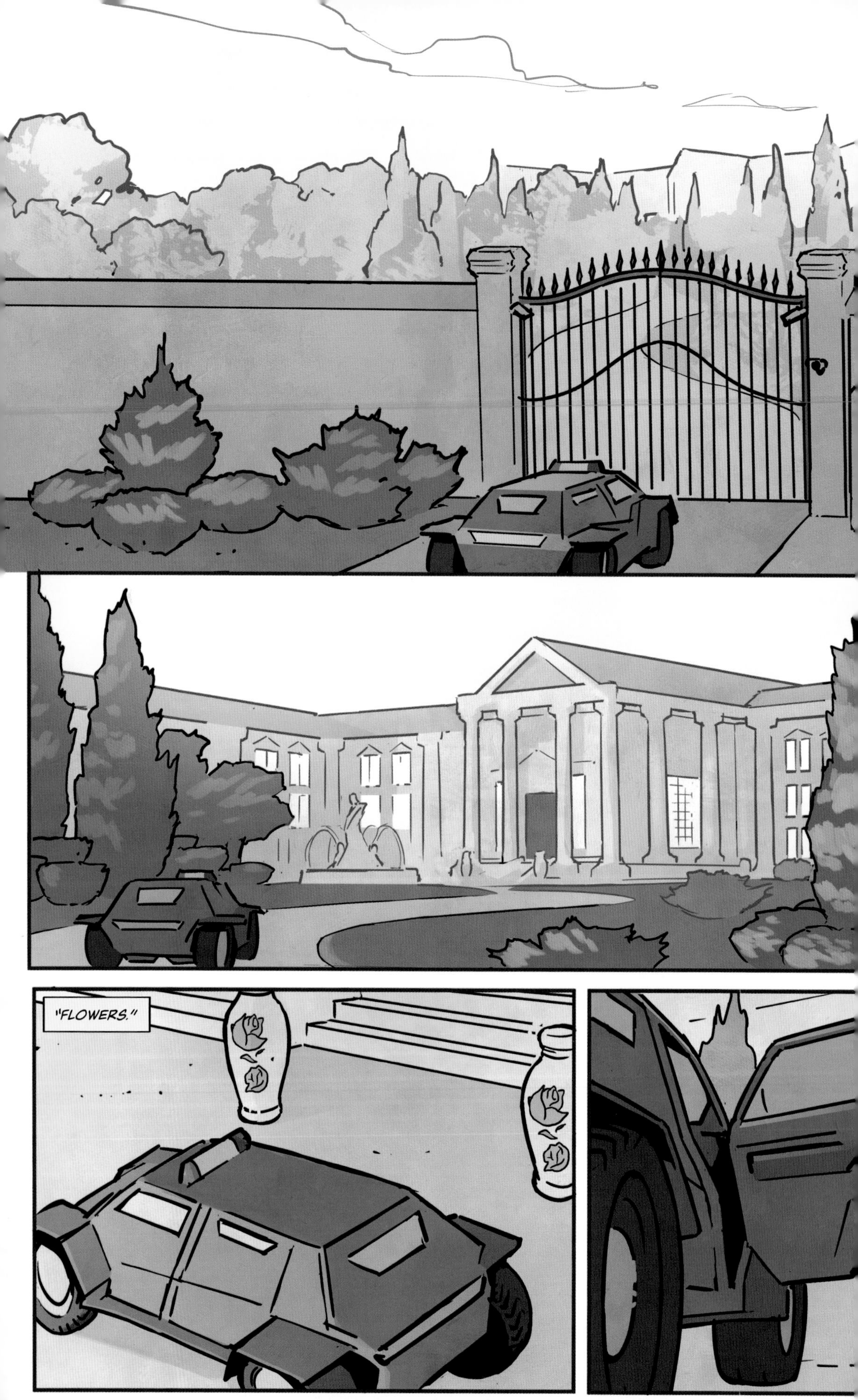
"FLOWERS."

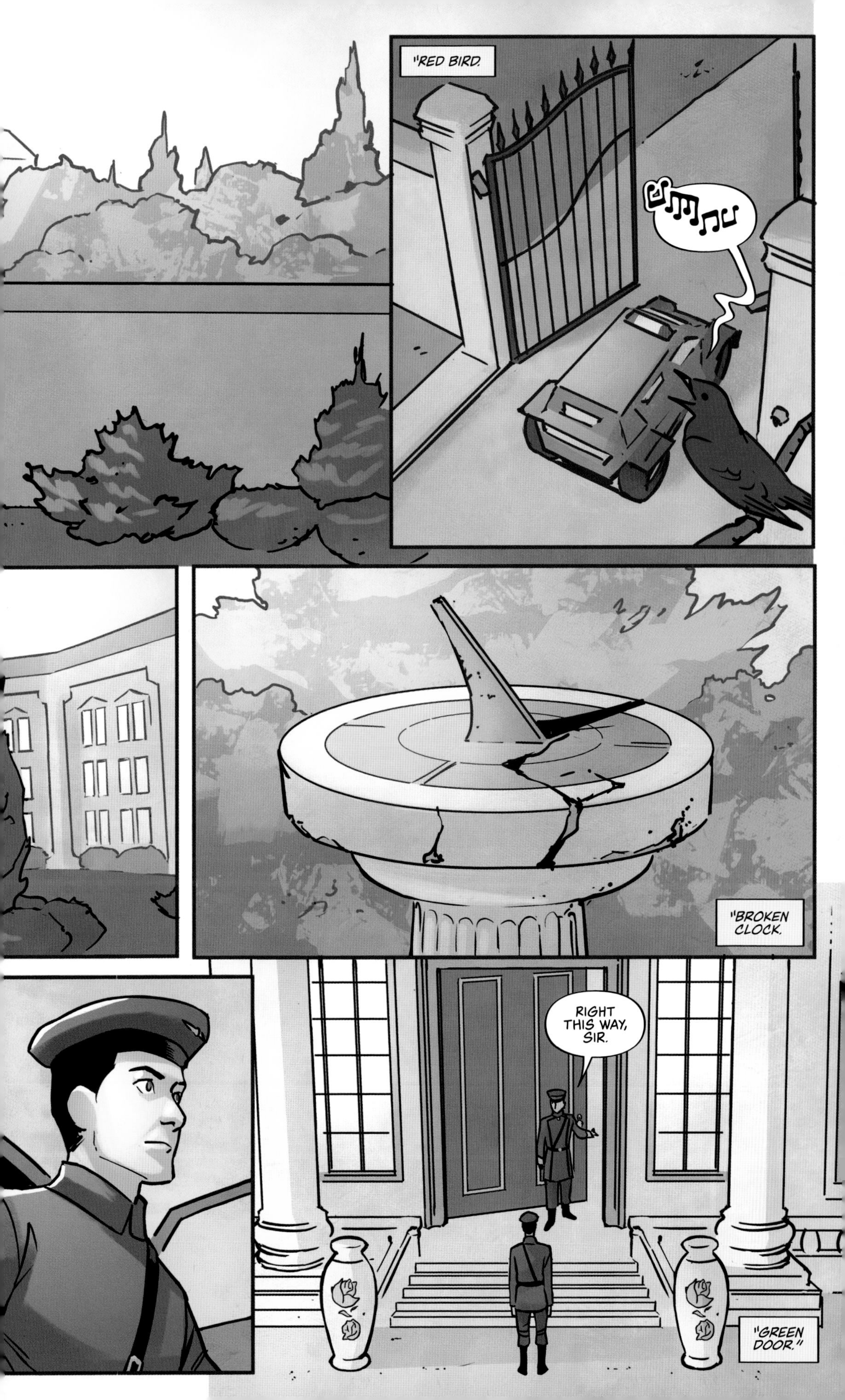
"RED BIRD.
"BROKEN CLOCK.
RIGHT THIS WAY, SIR.
"GREEN DOOR."

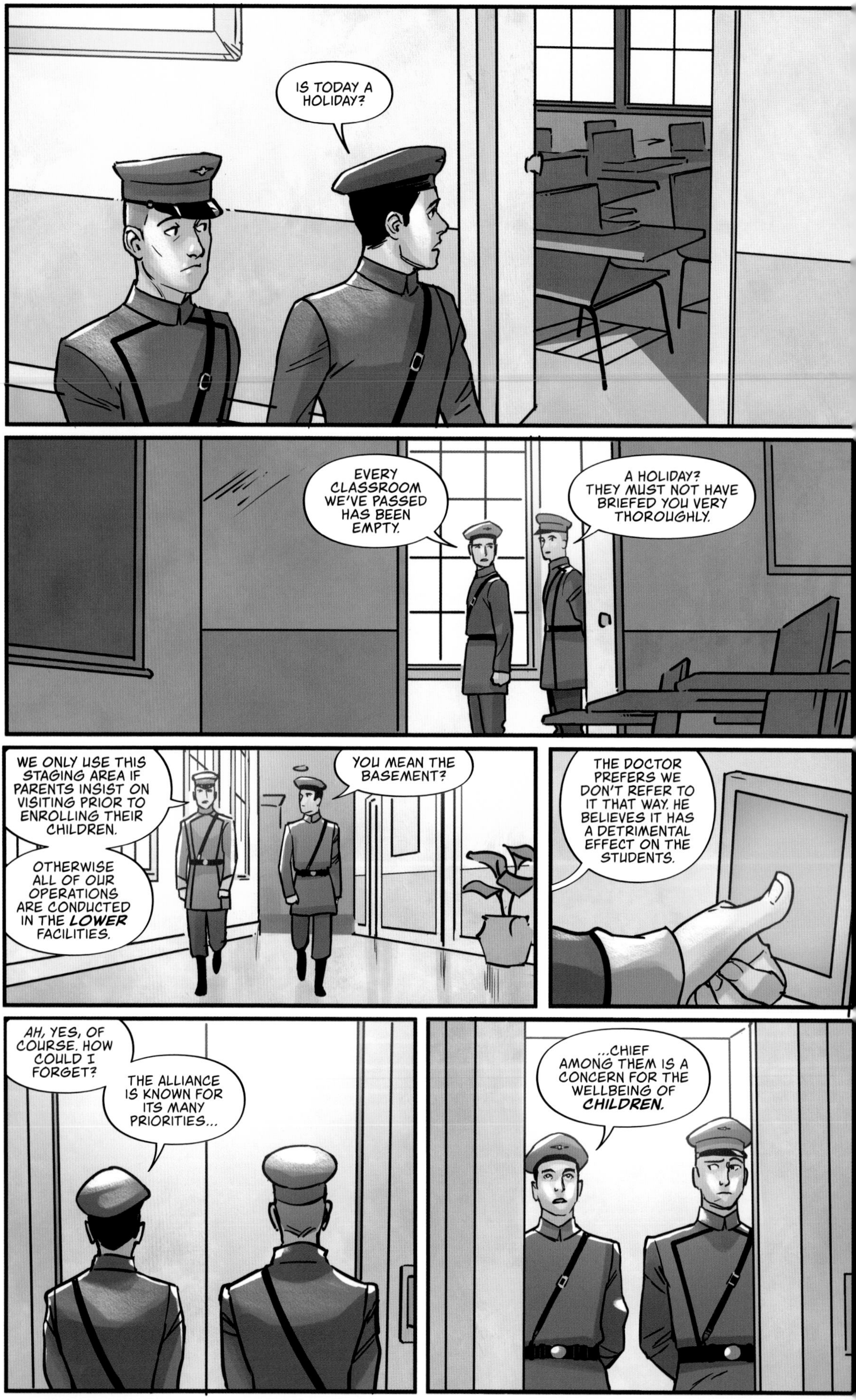
IS TODAY A HOLIDAY?
EVERY CLASSROOM WE'VE PASSED HAS BEEN EMPTY.
A HOLIDAY? THEY MUST NOT HAVE BRIEFED YOU VERY THOROUGHLY.
WE ONLY USE THIS STAGING AREA IF PARENTS INSIST ON VISITING PRIOR TO ENROLLING THEIR CHILDREN.
OTHERWISE ALL OF OUR OPERATIONS ARE CONDUCTED IN THE *LOWER* FACILITIES.
YOU MEAN THE BASEMENT?
THE DOCTOR PREFERS WE DON'T REFER TO IT THAT WAY. HE BELIEVES IT HAS A DETRIMENTAL EFFECT ON THE STUDENTS.
AH, YES, OF COURSE. HOW COULD I FORGET?
THE ALLIANCE IS KNOWN FOR ITS MANY PRIORITIES...
...CHIEF AMONG THEM IS A CONCERN FOR THE WELLBEING OF ***CHILDREN.***

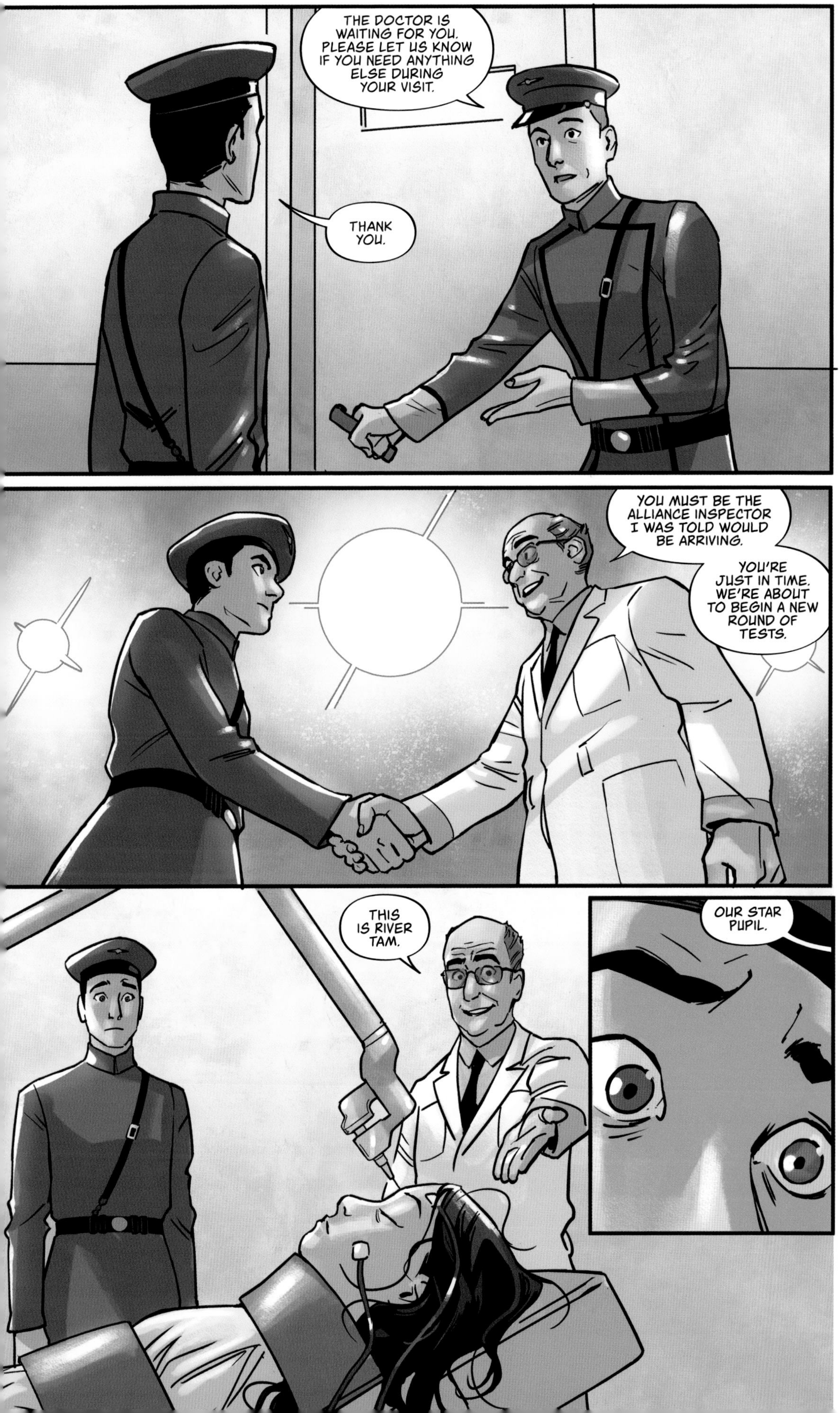
THE DOCTOR IS WAITING FOR YOU. PLEASE LET US KNOW IF YOU NEED ANYTHING ELSE DURING YOUR VISIT.
THANK YOU.
YOU MUST BE THE ALLIANCE INSPECTOR I WAS TOLD WOULD BE ARRIVING.
YOU'RE JUST IN TIME. WE'RE ABOUT TO BEGIN A NEW ROUND OF TESTS.
THIS IS RIVER TAM.
OUR STAR PUPIL.

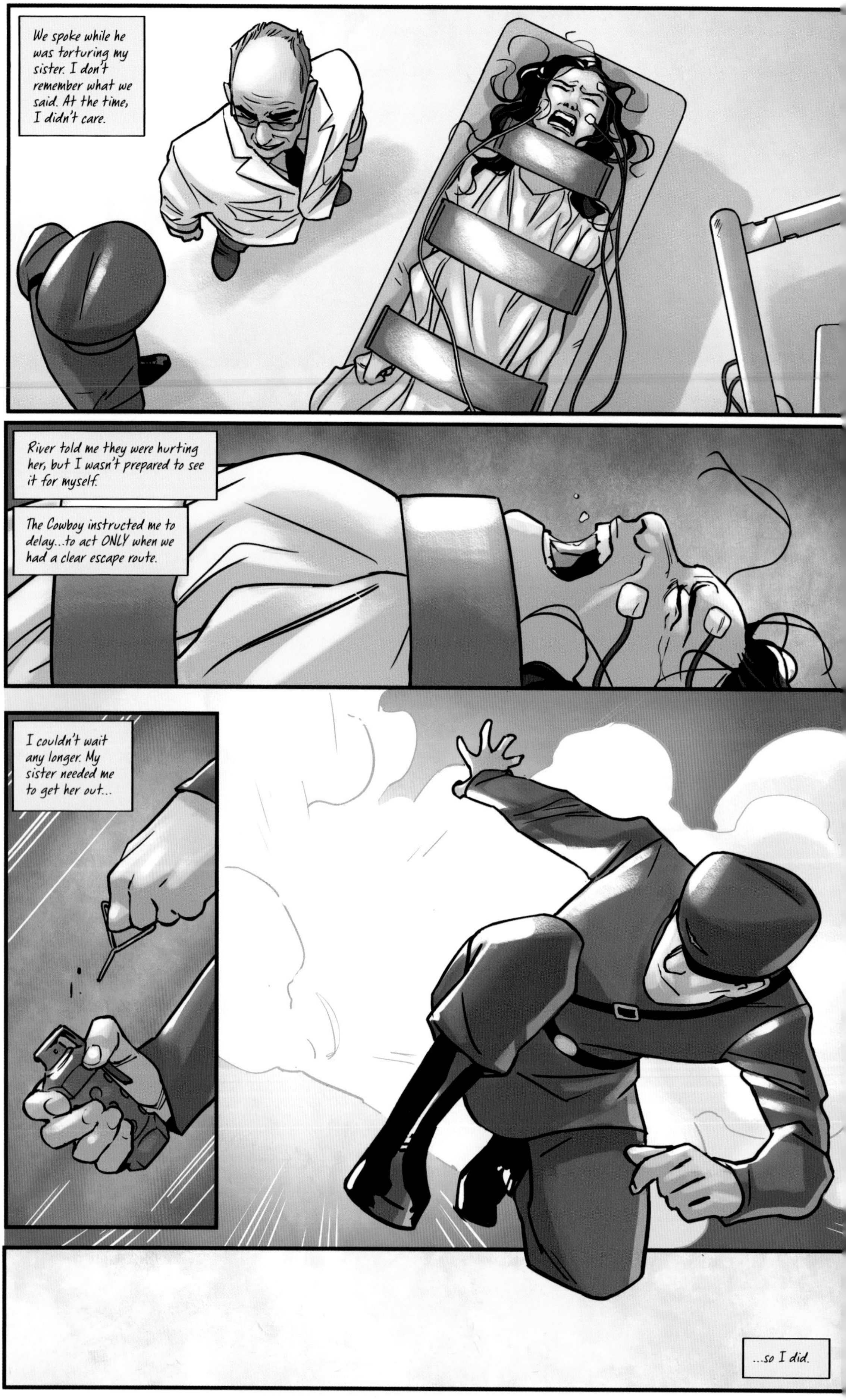
We spoke while he was torturing my sister. I don't remember what we said. At the time, I didn't care.
River told me they were hurting her, but I wasn't prepared to see it for myself.
The Cowboy instructed me to delay...to act ONLY when we had a clear escape route.
I couldn't wait any longer. My sister needed me to get her out...
...so I did.

NO, SIMON! NO! I DON'T WANT TO GO TO SLEEP!
IT'S OKAY, RIVER! YOU HAVE TO GO INTO CRYO SO WE CAN GET YOU OFF OSIRIS.
I HEAR THEIR VOICES IN MY DREAMS. THEY STILL WANT TO HURT ME.
TWO BY TWO. HANDS OF BLUE.
I'M SORRY IT TOOK ME SO LONG TO FIND YOU. I'M HERE NOW AND I'M NOT LEAVING YOU AGAIN.
I'M GOING TO PROTECT YOU.
"I KNOW THEY WERE HURTING YOU, MEI-MEI..."
beep

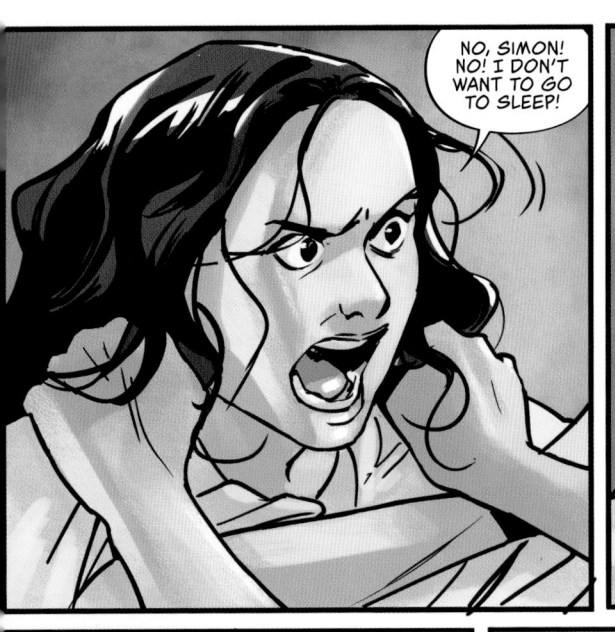

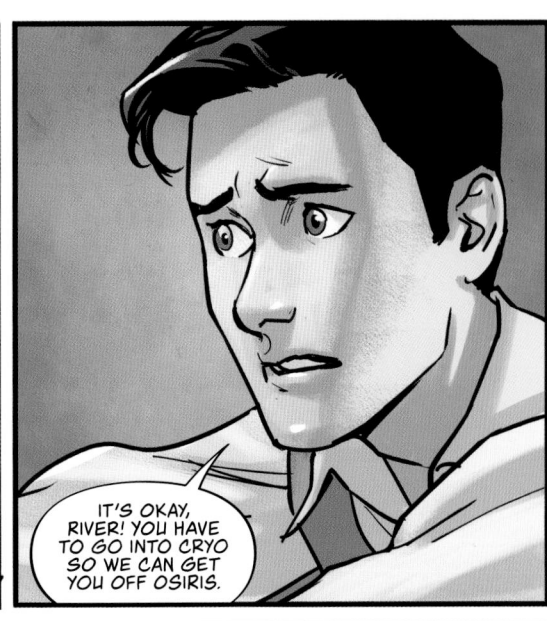

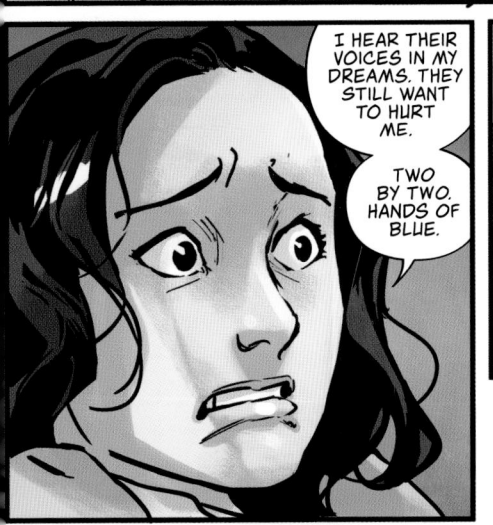

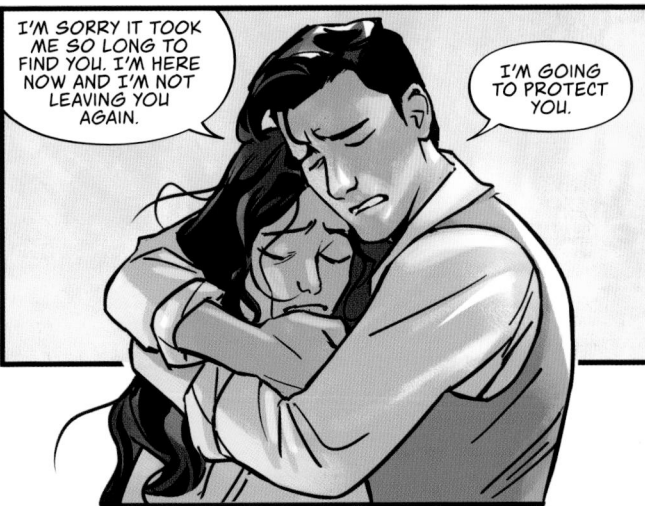

"...BUT I WON'T LET THEM HURT YOU ANYMORE."

THE END.

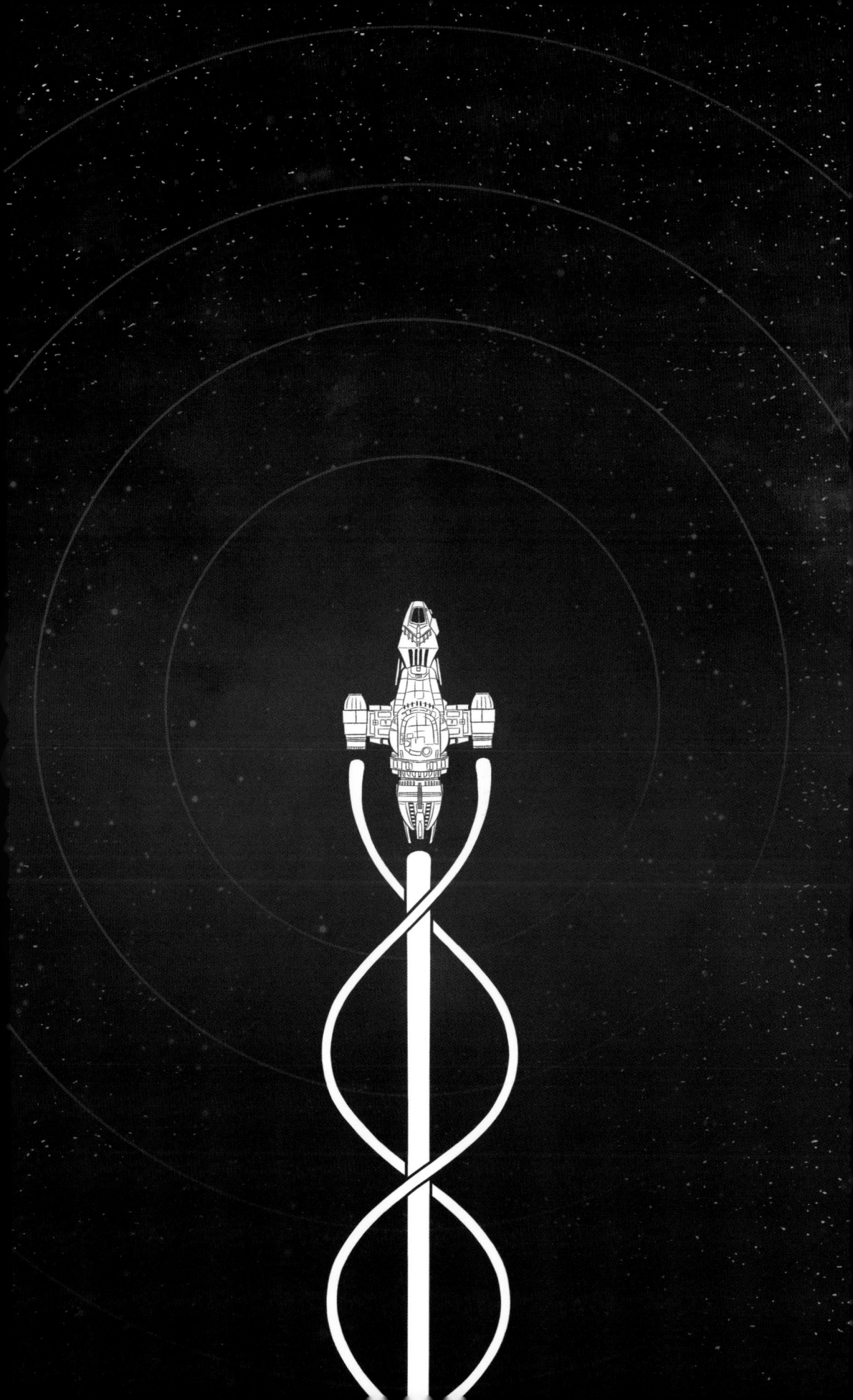

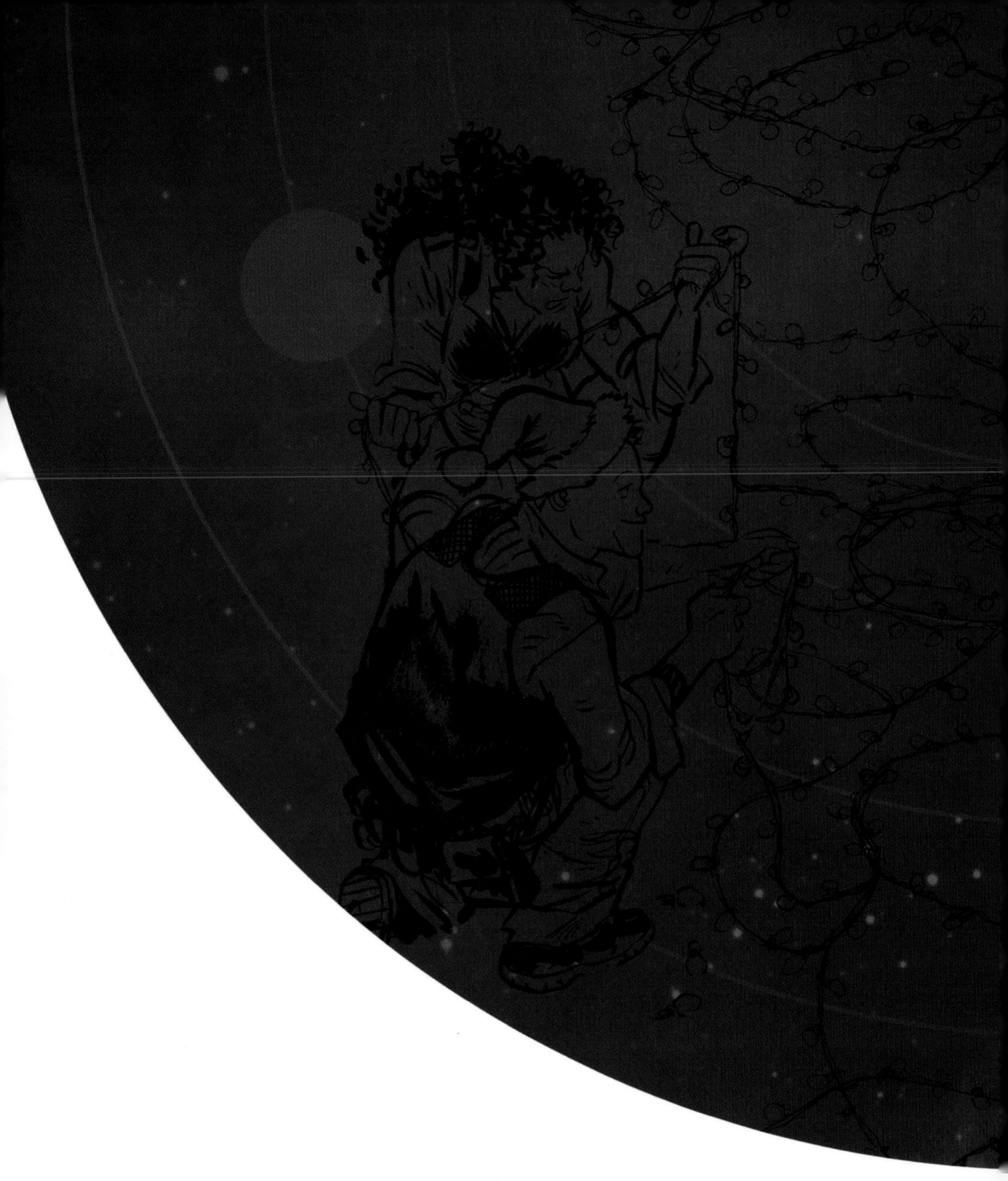

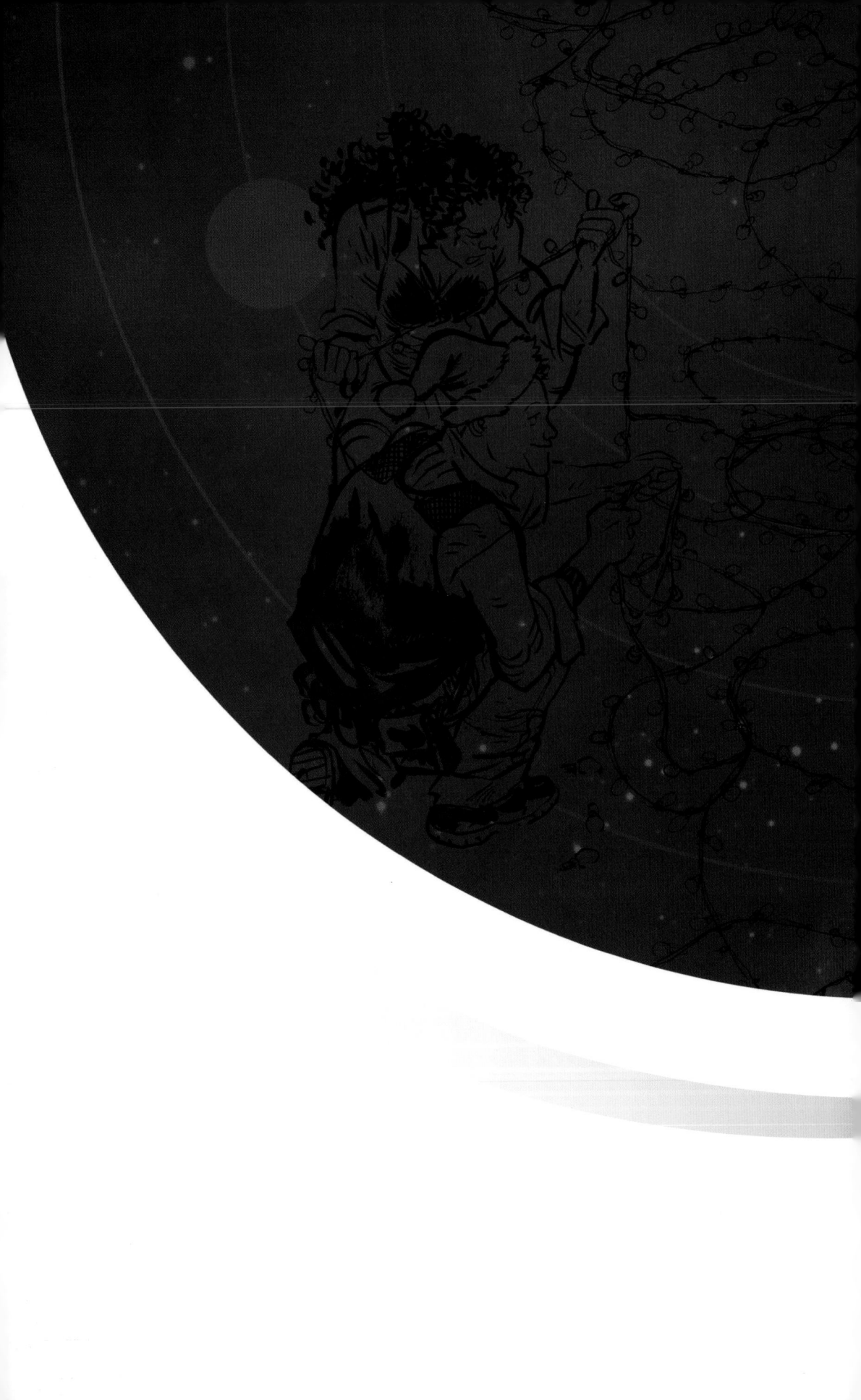

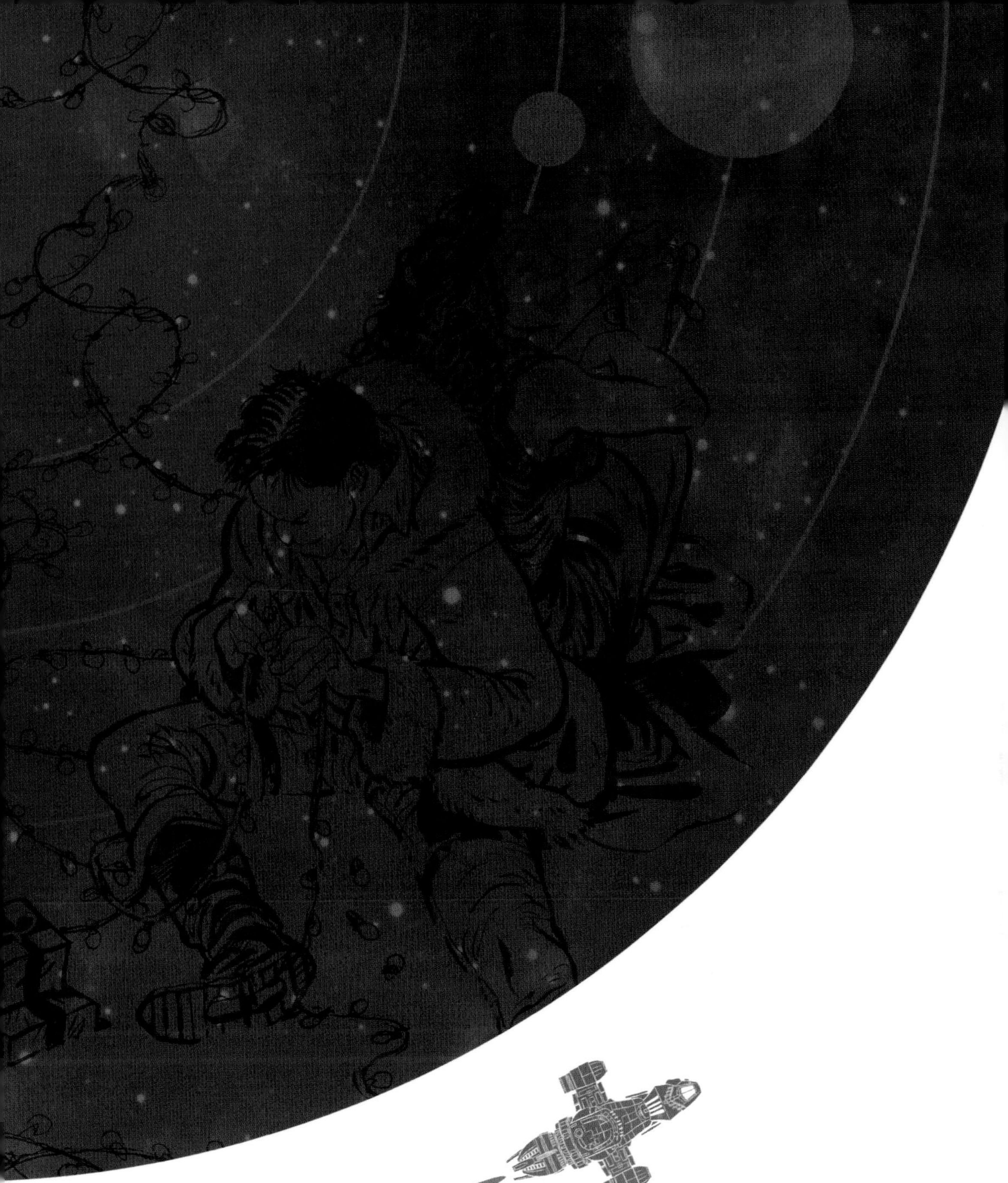

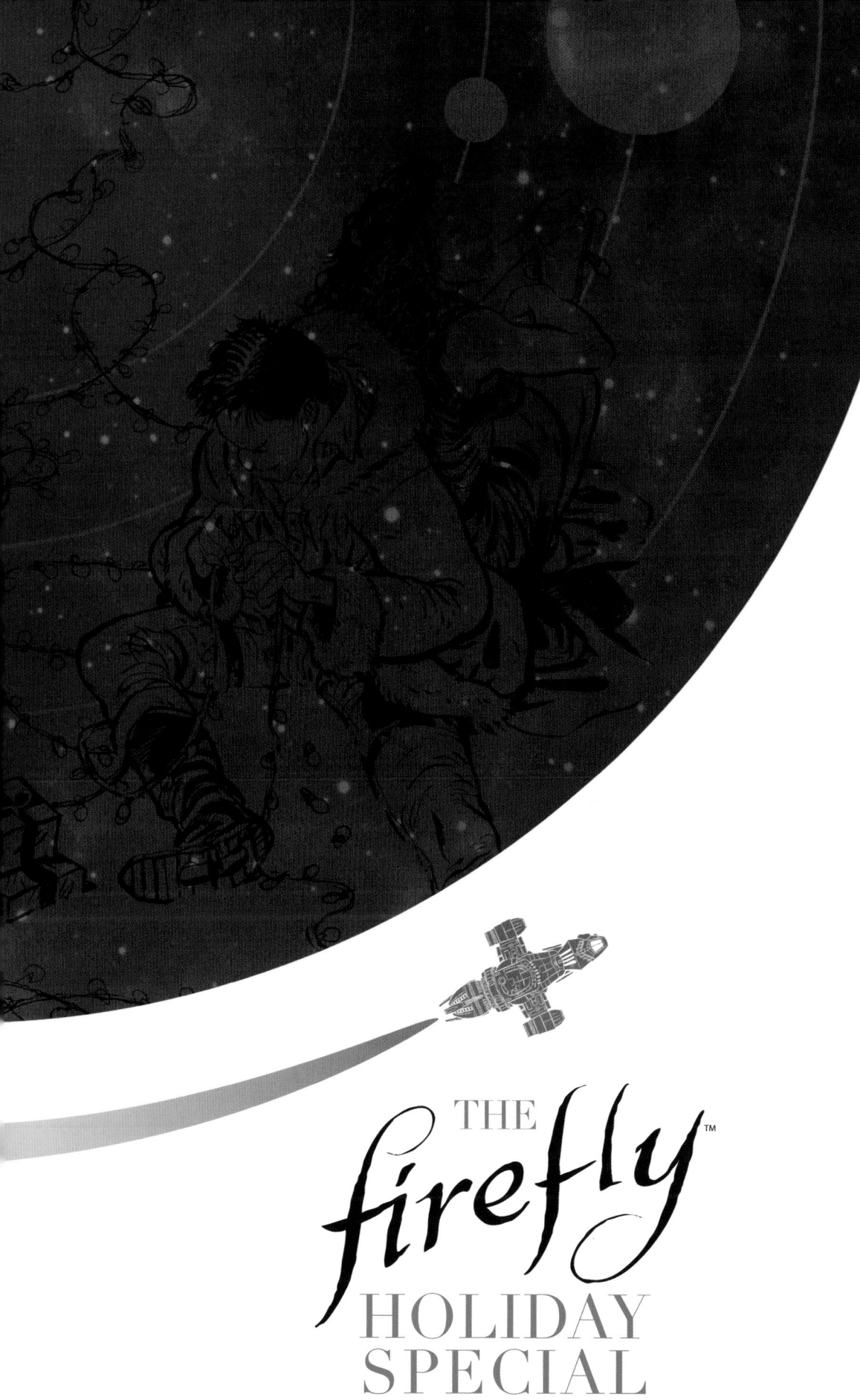

THE firefly™ HOLIDAY SPECIAL

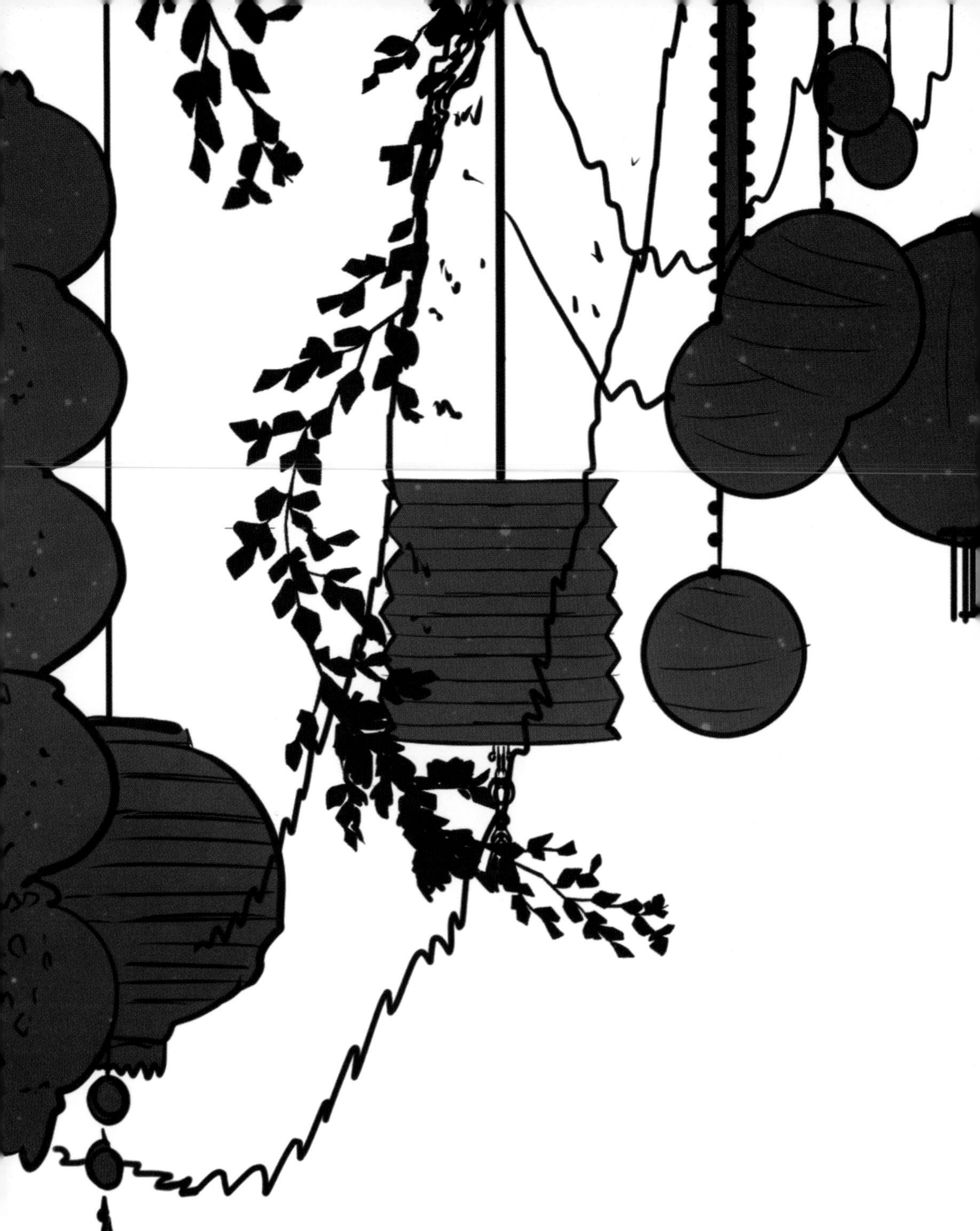

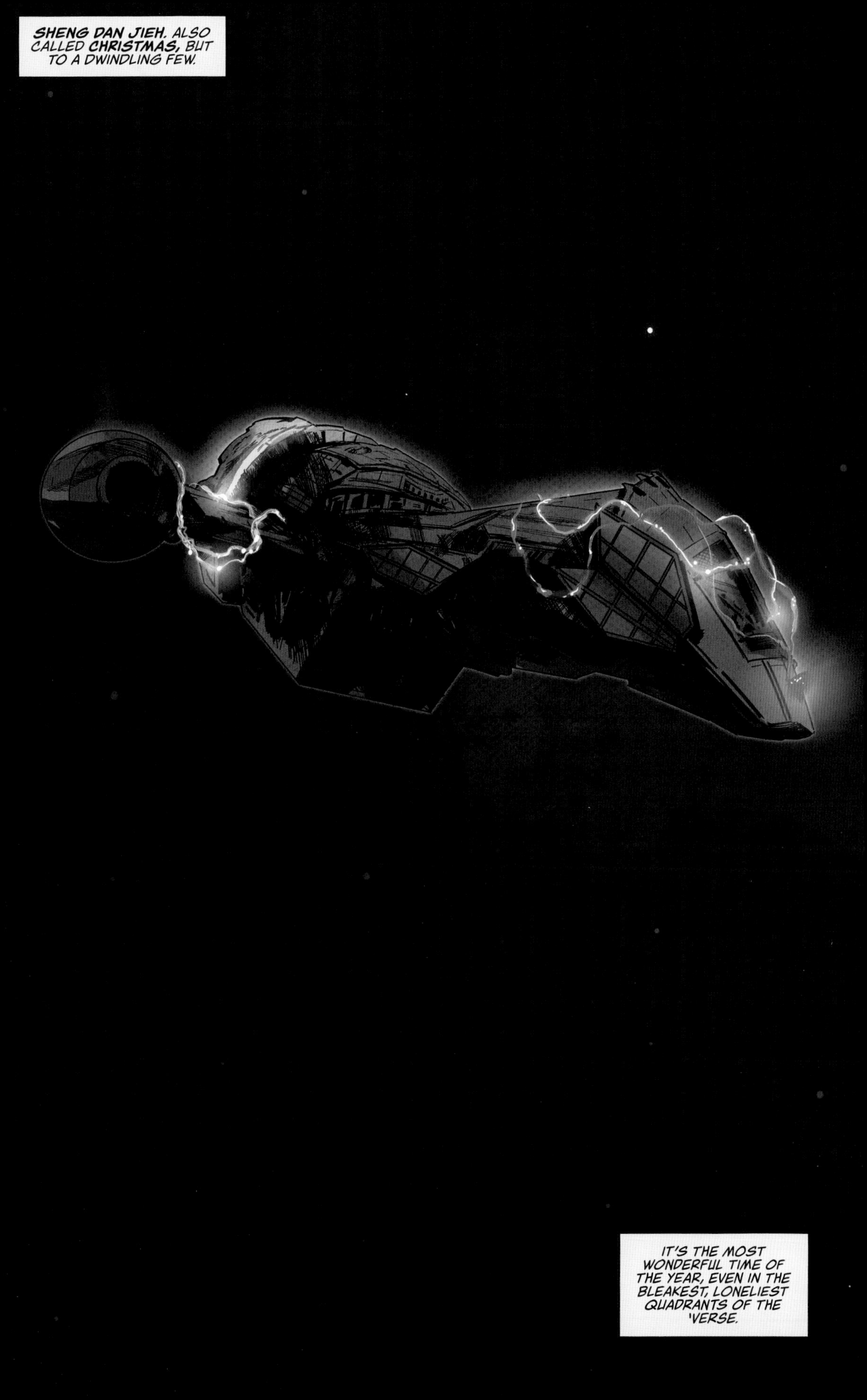
SHENG DAN JIEH. ALSO CALLED CHRISTMAS, BUT TO A DWINDLING FEW.
IT'S THE MOST WONDERFUL TIME OF THE YEAR, EVEN IN THE BLEAKEST, LONELIEST QUADRANTS OF THE 'VERSE.

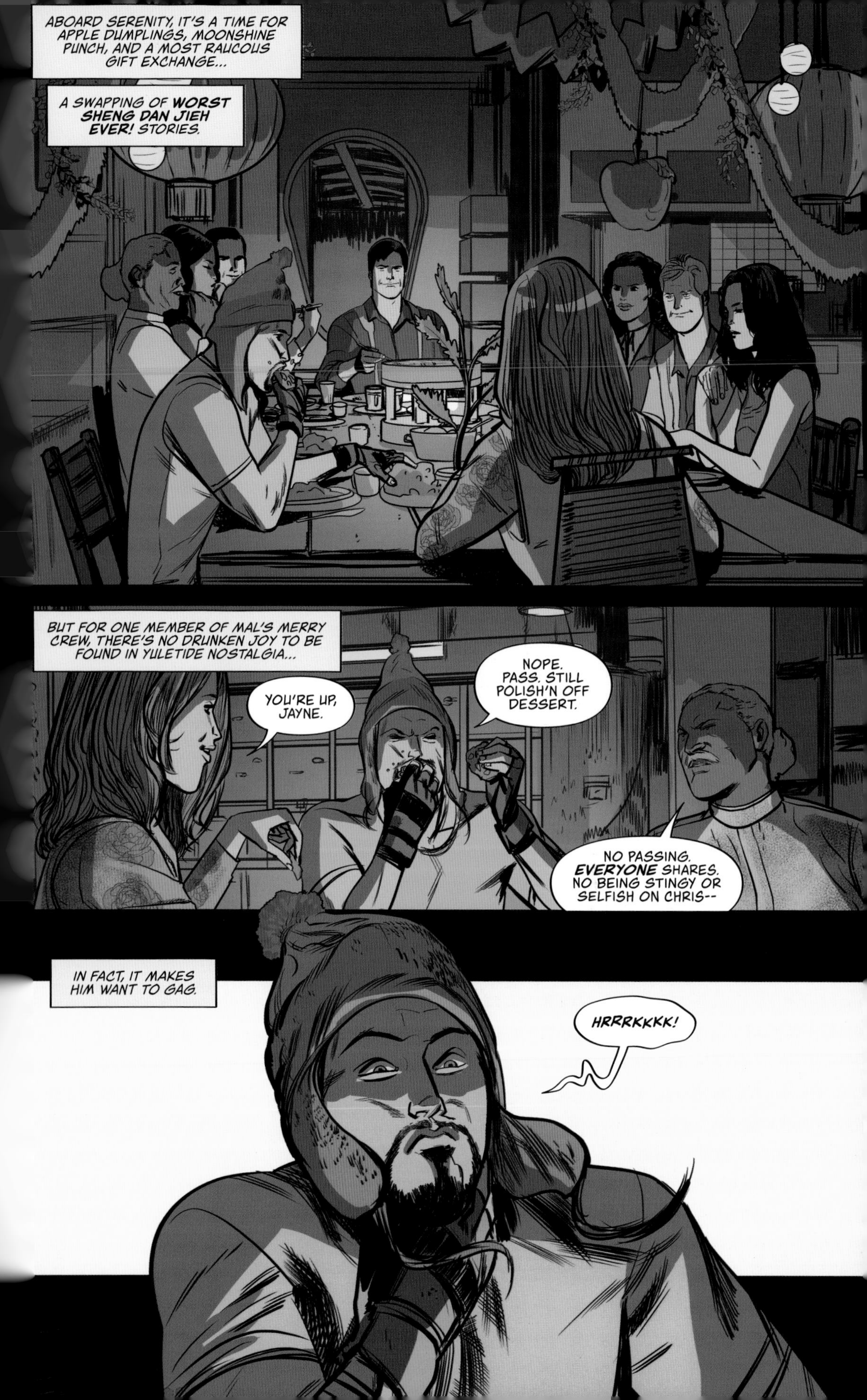
ABOARD SERENITY, IT'S A TIME FOR APPLE DUMPLINGS, MOONSHINE PUNCH, AND A MOST RAUCOUS GIFT EXCHANGE...
A SWAPPING OF **WORST SHENG DAN JIEH EVER!** STORIES.
BUT FOR ONE MEMBER OF MAL'S MERRY CREW, THERE'S NO DRUNKEN JOY TO BE FOUND IN YULETIDE NOSTALGIA...
YOU'RE UP, JAYNE.
NOPE. PASS. STILL POLISH'N OFF DESSERT.
NO PASSING. **EVERYONE** SHARES. NO BEING STINGY OR SELFISH ON CHRIS--
IN FACT, IT MAKES HIM WANT TO GAG.
HRRRKKKK!

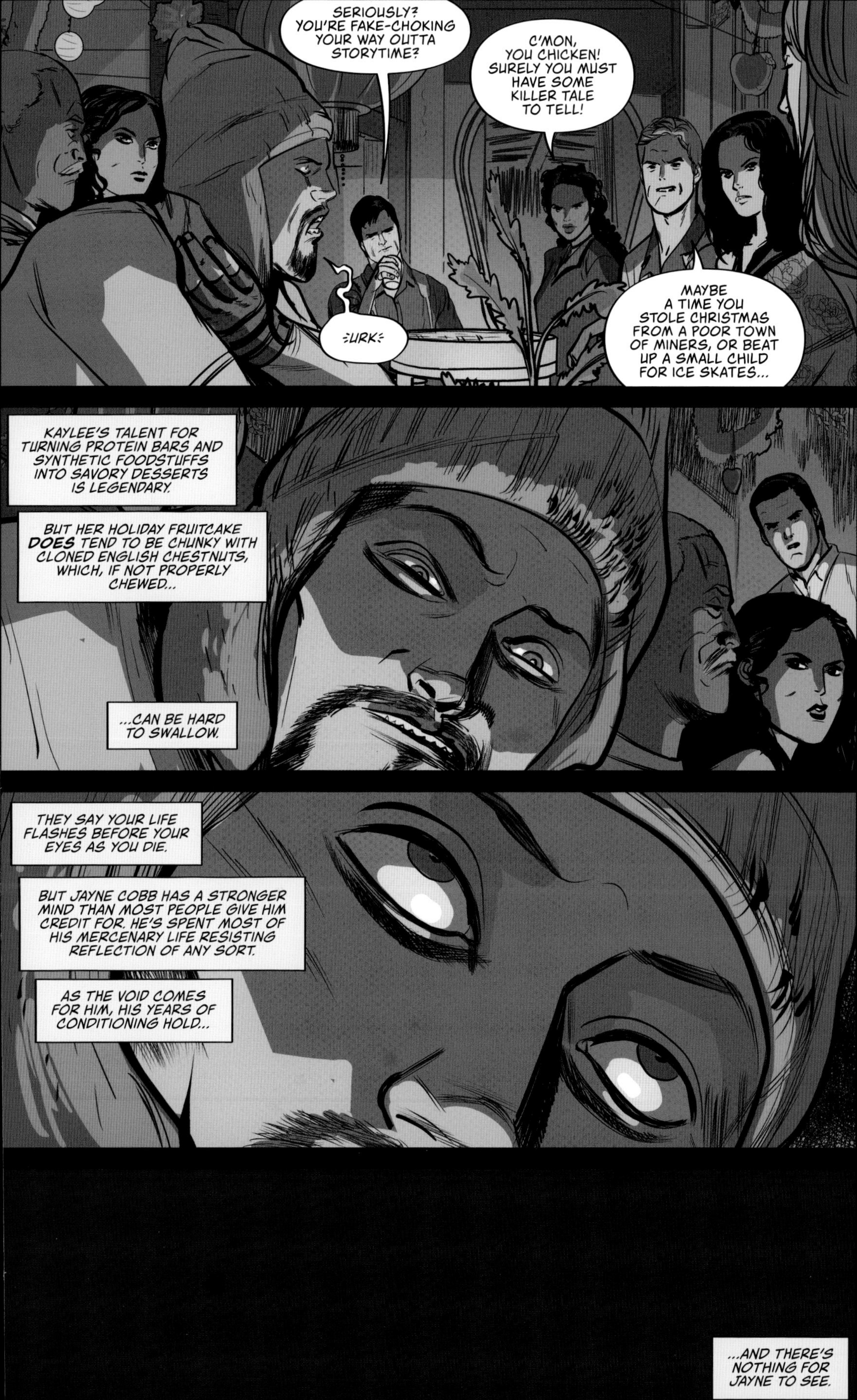

SERIOUSLY? YOU'RE FAKE-CHOKING YOUR WAY OUTTA STORYTIME?
C'MON, YOU CHICKEN! SURELY YOU MUST HAVE SOME KILLER TALE TO TELL!
URK
MAYBE A TIME YOU STOLE CHRISTMAS FROM A POOR TOWN OF MINERS, OR BEAT UP A SMALL CHILD FOR ICE SKATES...
KAYLEE'S TALENT FOR TURNING PROTEIN BARS AND SYNTHETIC FOODSTUFFS INTO SAVORY DESSERTS IS LEGENDARY.
BUT HER HOLIDAY FRUITCAKE DOES TEND TO BE CHUNKY WITH CLONED ENGLISH CHESTNUTS, WHICH, IF NOT PROPERLY CHEWED...
...CAN BE HARD TO SWALLOW.
THEY SAY YOUR LIFE FLASHES BEFORE YOUR EYES AS YOU DIE.
BUT JAYNE COBB HAS A STRONGER MIND THAN MOST PEOPLE GIVE HIM CREDIT FOR. HE'S SPENT MOST OF HIS MERCENARY LIFE RESISTING REFLECTION OF ANY SORT.
AS THE VOID COMES FOR HIM, HIS YEARS OF CONDITIONING HOLD...
...AND THERE'S NOTHING FOR JAYNE TO SEE.

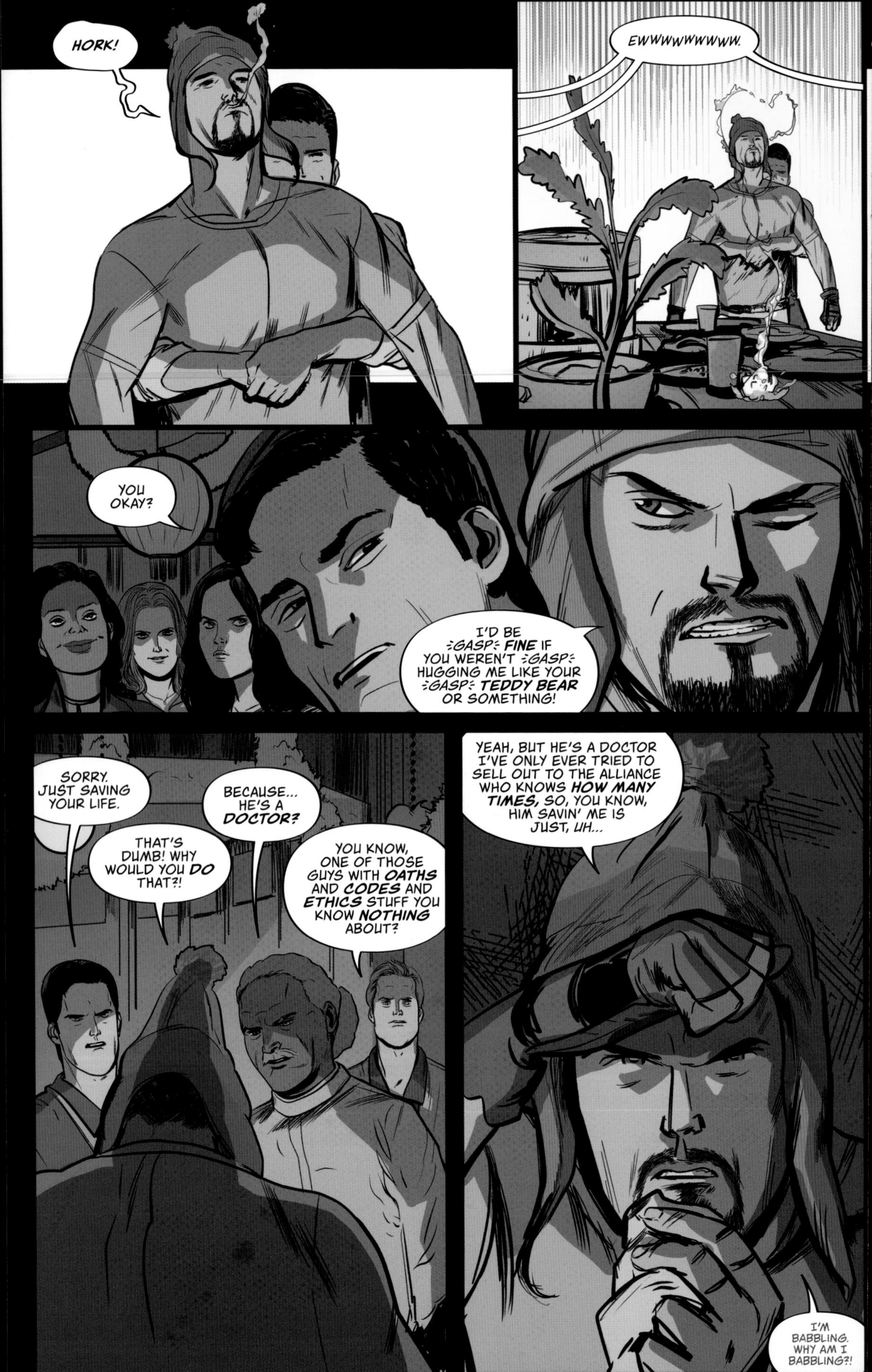
HORK!
EWWWWWWWWW.
YOU OKAY?
I'D BE *GASP* FINE IF YOU WEREN'T *GASP* HUGGING ME LIKE YOUR *GASP* TEDDY BEAR OR SOMETHING!
SORRY. JUST SAVING YOUR LIFE.
THAT'S DUMB! WHY WOULD YOU DO THAT?!
BECAUSE... HE'S A DOCTOR?
YOU KNOW, ONE OF THOSE GUYS WITH OATHS AND CODES AND ETHICS STUFF YOU KNOW NOTHING ABOUT?
YEAH, BUT HE'S A DOCTOR I'VE ONLY EVER TRIED TO SELL OUT TO THE ALLIANCE WHO KNOWS HOW MANY TIMES, SO, YOU KNOW, HIM SAVIN' ME IS JUST, UH...
I'M BABBLING. WHY AM I BABBLING?!

"TIMES"?
I THOUGHT THERE WAS JUST THE ONE TIME!
I THINK IN MY DISCOMBOBULATEDNESS, I MIGHT HAVE MISSPOKE...
SHUT UP. ALL OF YOU. THIS ISN'T IMPORTANT RIGHT NOW.
DID YOU SEE THE GHOSTS?
...GHOSTS?
WHEN YOU WERE LOST IN YOUR HEAD, DIDN'T YOU SEE THREE GHOSTS?
NO, I DIDN'T SEE NO THREE GHOSTS! I JUST SAW... UH...
WHAT TZAO-GAO BUSINESS IS IT OF YOURS WHAT I SEE IN MY HEAD?!
MY BAD.
THEY MUST BE COMING LATER.
WHAT ARE YOU TALKING ABOUT, YOU CRAZY WITCH?
LATER?
WHEN LATER?!

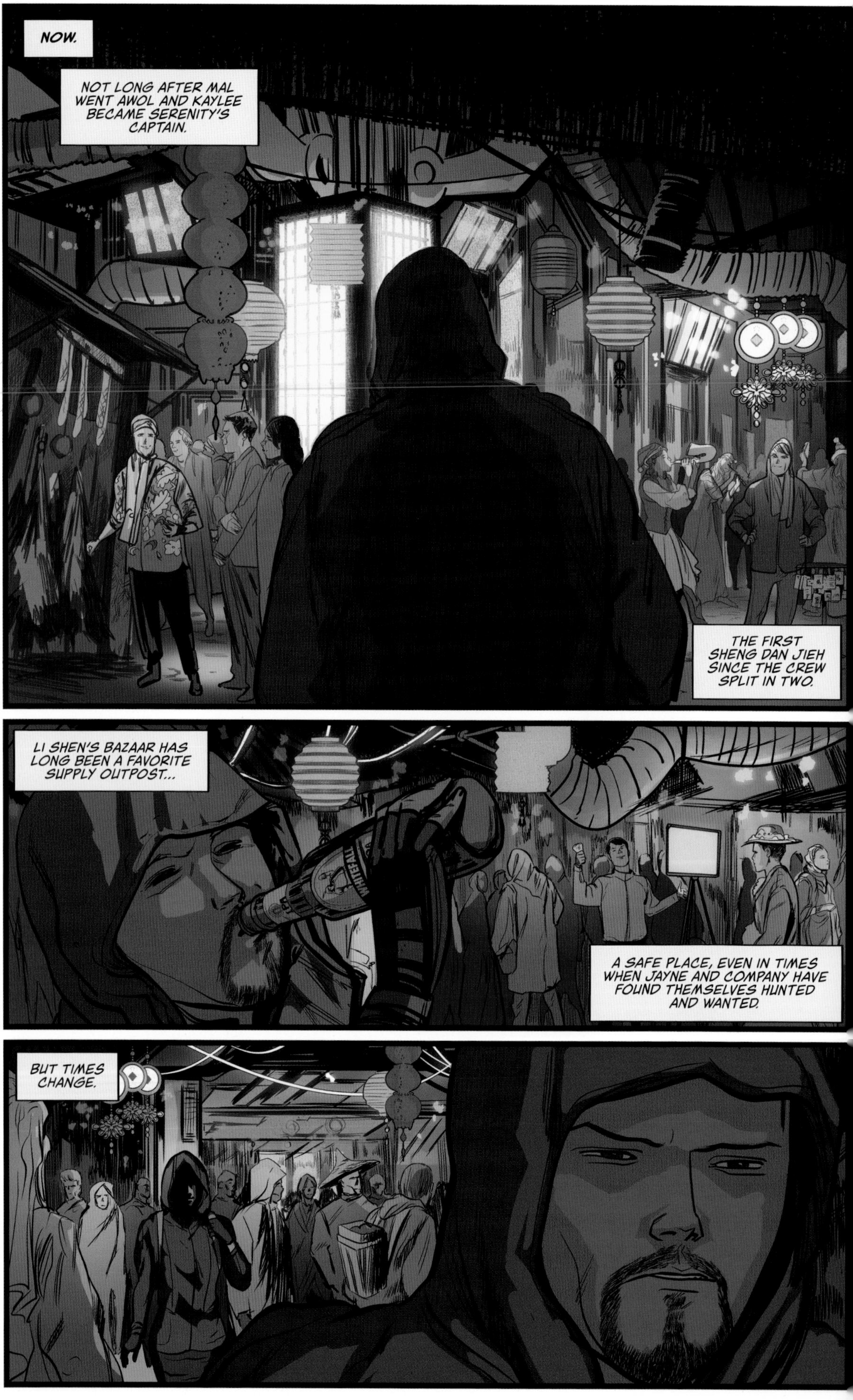
NOW.
NOT LONG AFTER MAL WENT AWOL AND KAYLEE BECAME SERENITY'S CAPTAIN.
THE FIRST SHENG DAN JIEH SINCE THE CREW SPLIT IN TWO.
LI SHEN'S BAZAAR HAS LONG BEEN A FAVORITE SUPPLY OUTPOST...
WHITEFALL
A SAFE PLACE, EVEN IN TIMES WHEN JAYNE AND COMPANY HAVE FOUND THEMSELVES HUNTED AND WANTED.
BUT TIMES CHANGE.

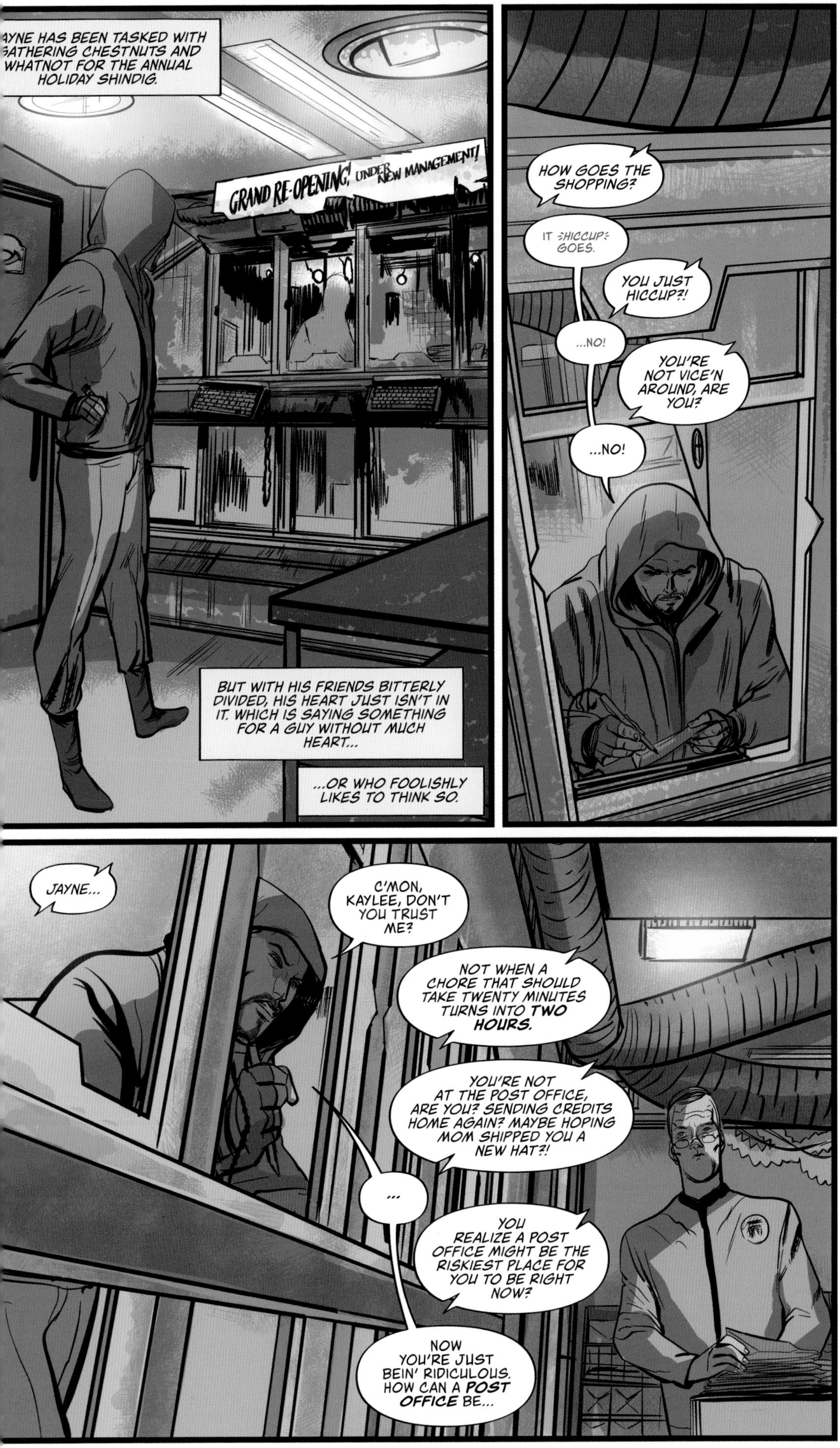
AYNE HAS BEEN TASKED WITH GATHERING CHESTNUTS AND WHATNOT FOR THE ANNUAL HOLIDAY SHINDIG.
GRAND RE-OPENING! UNDER NEW MANAGEMENT!
BUT WITH HIS FRIENDS BITTERLY DIVIDED, HIS HEART JUST ISN'T IN IT. WHICH IS SAYING SOMETHING FOR A GUY WITHOUT MUCH HEART...
...OR WHO FOOLISHLY LIKES TO THINK SO.
HOW GOES THE SHOPPING?
IT =HICCUP= GOES.
YOU JUST HICCUP?!
...NO!
YOU'RE NOT VICE'N AROUND, ARE YOU?
...NO!
JAYNE...
C'MON, KAYLEE, DON'T YOU TRUST ME?
NOT WHEN A CHORE THAT SHOULD TAKE TWENTY MINUTES TURNS INTO **TWO HOURS.**
YOU'RE NOT AT THE POST OFFICE, ARE YOU? SENDING CREDITS HOME AGAIN? MAYBE HOPING MOM SHIPPED YOU A NEW HAT?!
...
YOU REALIZE A POST OFFICE MIGHT BE THE RISKIEST PLACE FOR YOU TO BE RIGHT NOW?
NOW YOU'RE JUST BEIN' RIDICULOUS. HOW CAN A ***POST OFFICE*** BE...

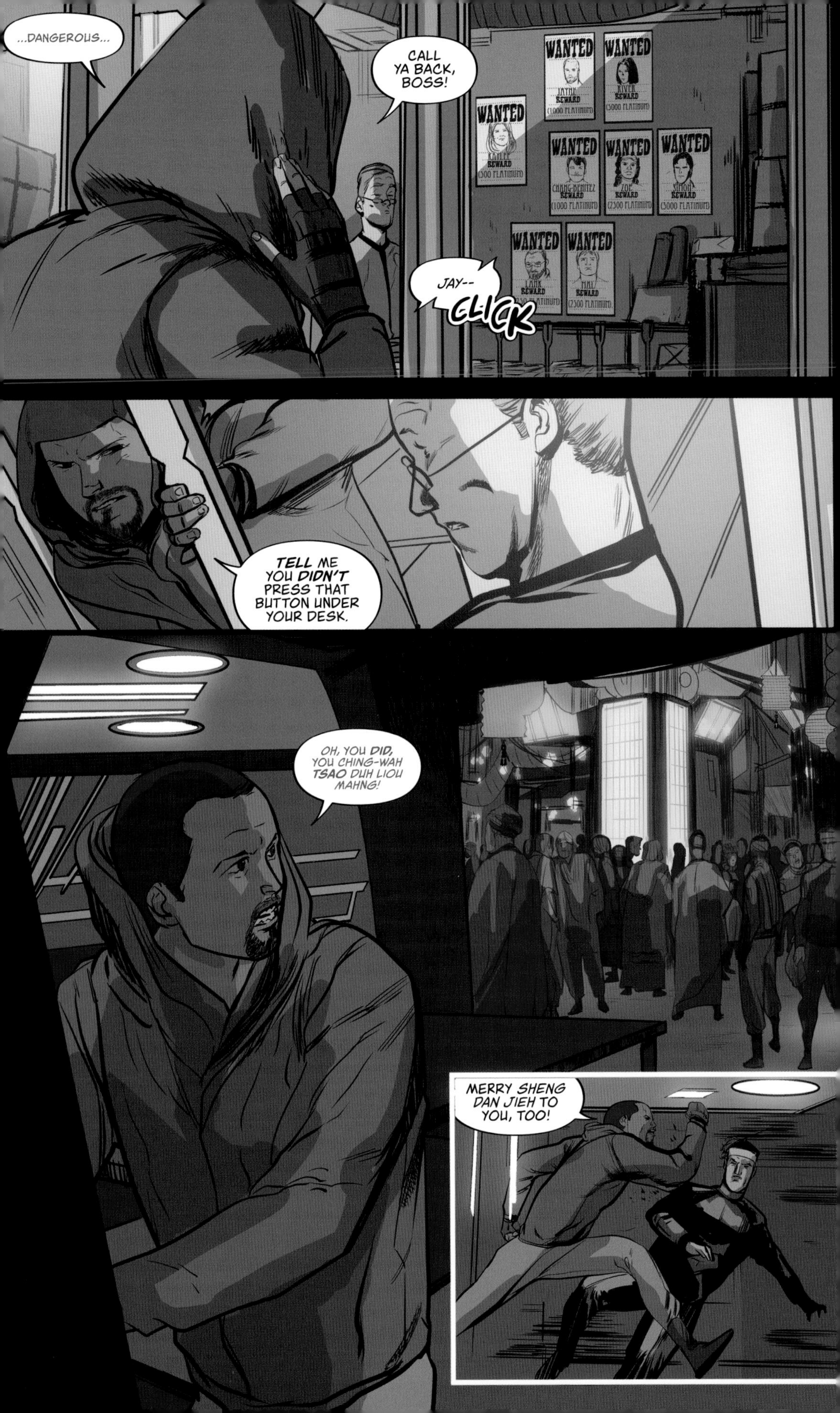

...DANGEROUS...
CALL YA BACK, BOSS!
WANTED JAYNE REWARD (1000 PLATINUM)
WANTED RIVER REWARD (3000 PLATINUM)
WANTED KAYLEE REWARD (500 PLATINUM)
WANTED CHANG-BENITEZ REWARD (1000 PLATINUM)
WANTED ZOE REWARD (2500 PLATINUM)
WANTED SIMON REWARD (3000 PLATINUM)
WANTED LANK REWARD
WANTED MAL REWARD (2500 PLATINUM)
JAY--
CLICK
TELL ME YOU DIDN'T PRESS THAT BUTTON UNDER YOUR DESK.
OH, YOU DID, YOU CHING-WAH TSAO DUH LIOU MAHNG!
MERRY SHENG DAN JIEH TO YOU, TOO!

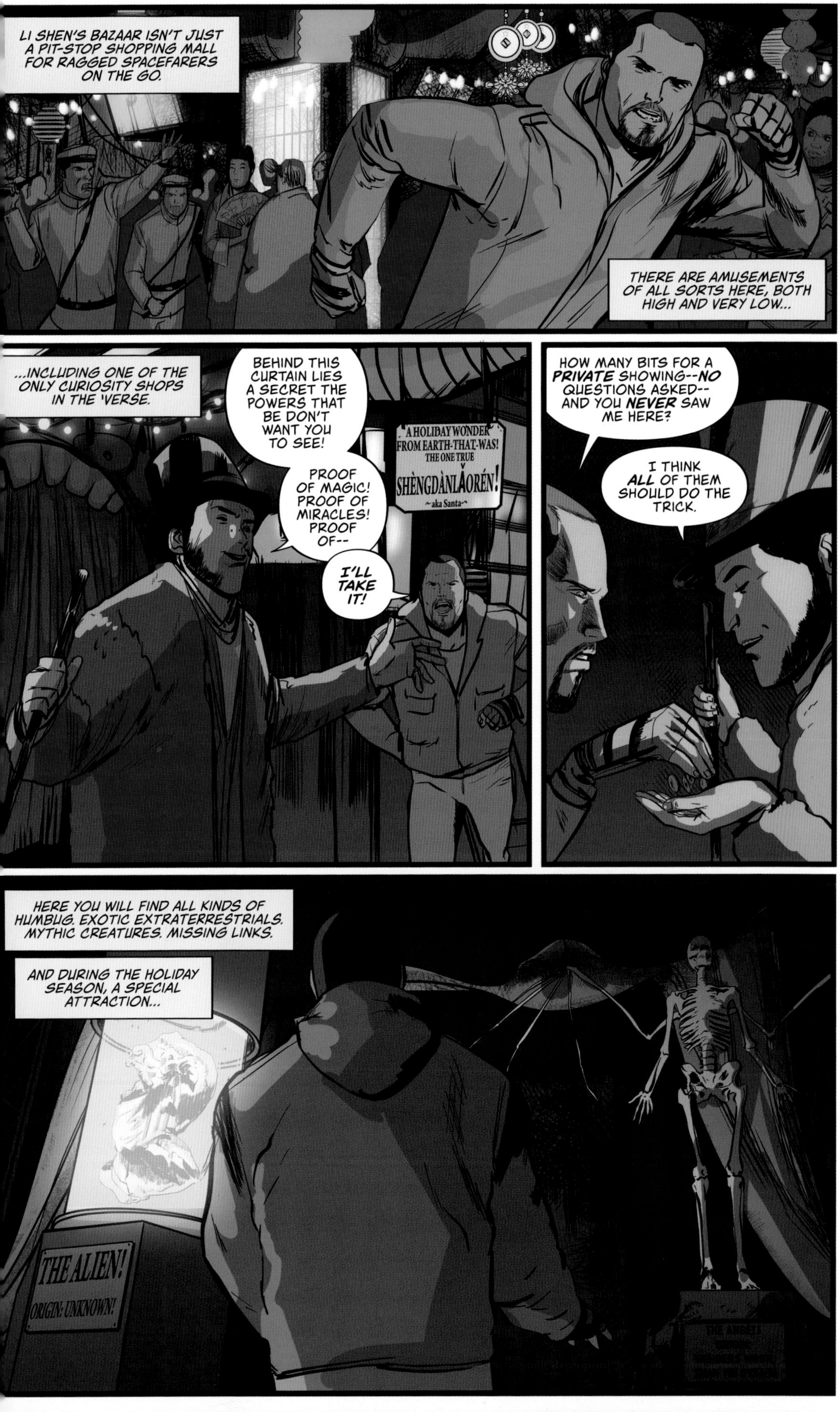
LI SHEN'S BAZAAR ISN'T JUST A PIT-STOP SHOPPING MALL FOR RAGGED SPACEFARERS ON THE GO.
THERE ARE AMUSEMENTS OF ALL SORTS HERE, BOTH HIGH AND VERY LOW...
...INCLUDING ONE OF THE ONLY CURIOSITY SHOPS IN THE 'VERSE.
BEHIND THIS CURTAIN LIES A SECRET THE POWERS THAT BE DON'T WANT YOU TO SEE!
A HOLIDAY WONDER FROM EARTH-THAT-WAS! THE ONE TRUE SHÈNGDÀNLǍORÉN! ~aka Santa~
PROOF OF MAGIC! PROOF OF MIRACLES! PROOF OF--
I'LL TAKE IT!
HOW MANY BITS FOR A *PRIVATE* SHOWING--*NO* QUESTIONS ASKED--AND YOU *NEVER* SAW ME HERE?
I THINK *ALL* OF THEM SHOULD DO THE TRICK.
HERE YOU WILL FIND ALL KINDS OF HUMBUG. EXOTIC EXTRATERRESTRIALS. MYTHIC CREATURES. MISSING LINKS.
AND DURING THE HOLIDAY SEASON, A SPECIAL ATTRACTION...
THE ALIEN! ORIGIN: UNKNOWN!

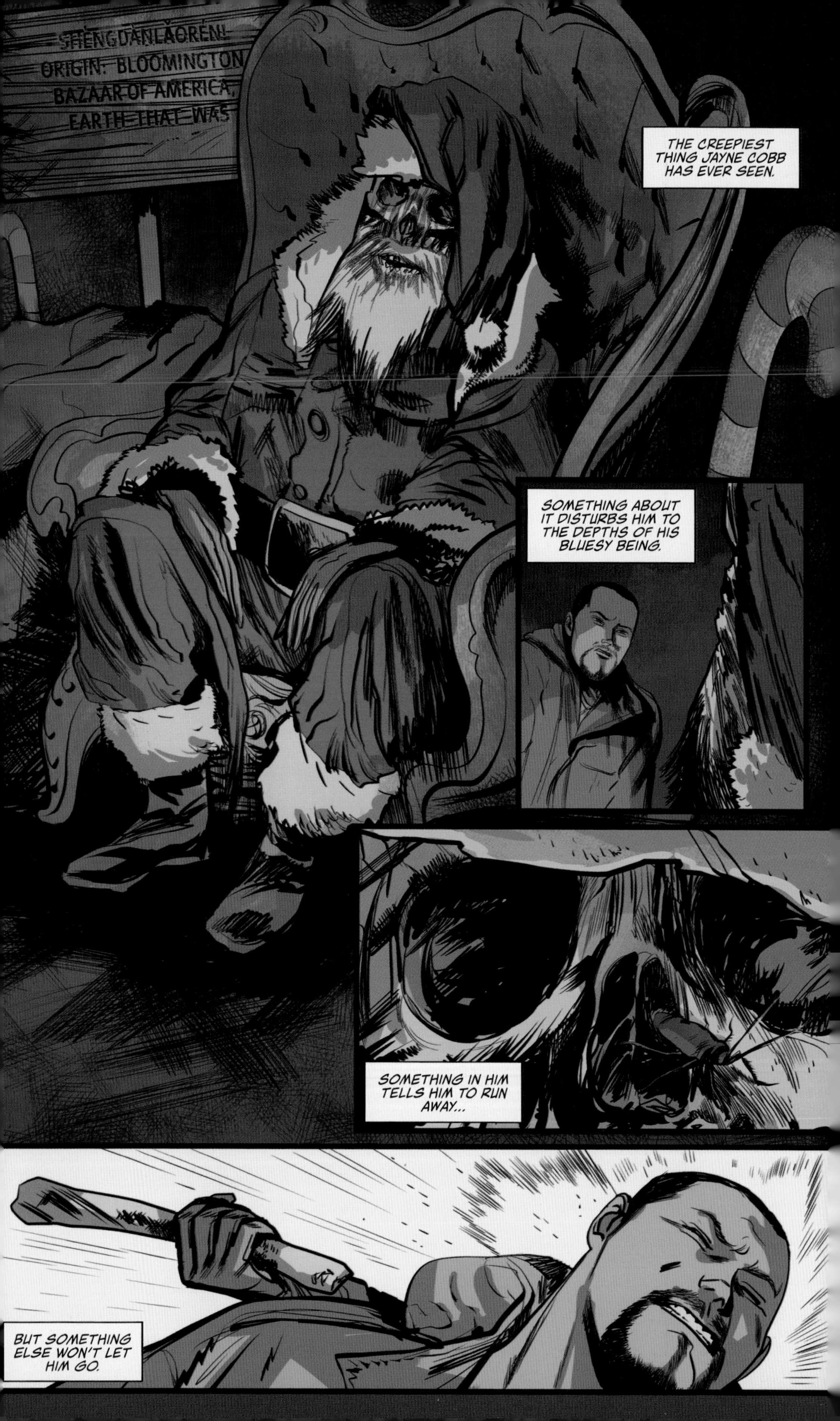
SHENGDANLAOREN!
ORIGIN: BLOOMINGTON
BAZAAR OF AMERICA,
EARTH-THAT-WAS
THE CREEPIEST THING JAYNE COBB HAS EVER SEEN.
SOMETHING ABOUT IT DISTURBS HIM TO THE DEPTHS OF HIS BLUESY BEING.
SOMETHING IN HIM TELLS HIM TO RUN AWAY...
BUT SOMETHING ELSE WON'T LET HIM GO.

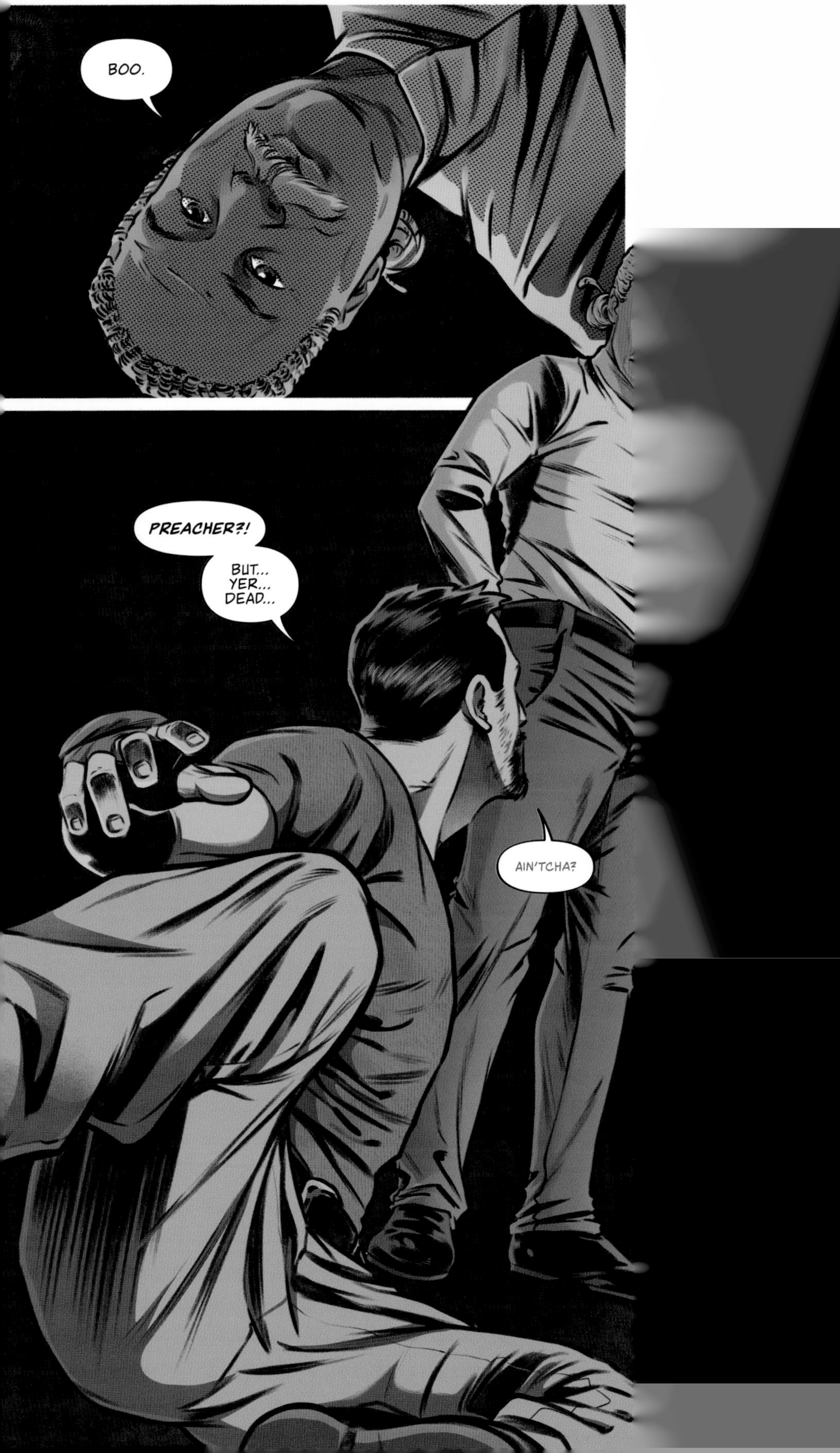
BOO.
PREACHER?!
BUT... YER... DEAD...
AIN'TCHA?

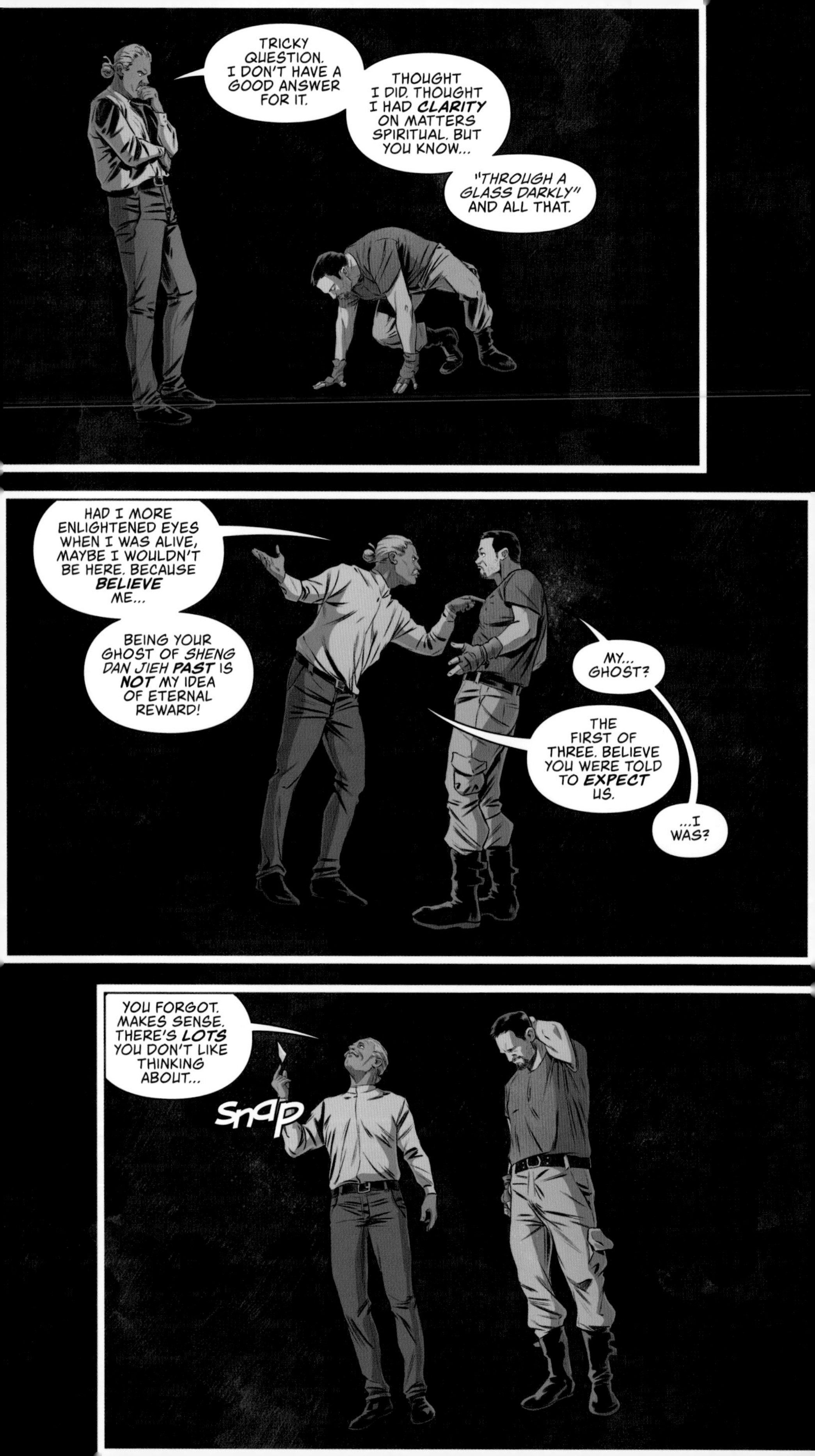
TRICKY QUESTION. I DON'T HAVE A GOOD ANSWER FOR IT.
THOUGHT I DID. THOUGHT I HAD CLARITY ON MATTERS SPIRITUAL. BUT YOU KNOW...
"THROUGH A GLASS DARKLY" AND ALL THAT.
HAD I MORE ENLIGHTENED EYES WHEN I WAS ALIVE, MAYBE I WOULDN'T BE HERE. BECAUSE BELIEVE ME...
BEING YOUR GHOST OF SHENG DAN JIEH PAST IS NOT MY IDEA OF ETERNAL REWARD!
MY... GHOST?
THE FIRST OF THREE. BELIEVE YOU WERE TOLD TO EXPECT US.
...I WAS?
YOU FORGOT. MAKES SENSE. THERE'S LOTS YOU DON'T LIKE THINKING ABOUT...
SNAP

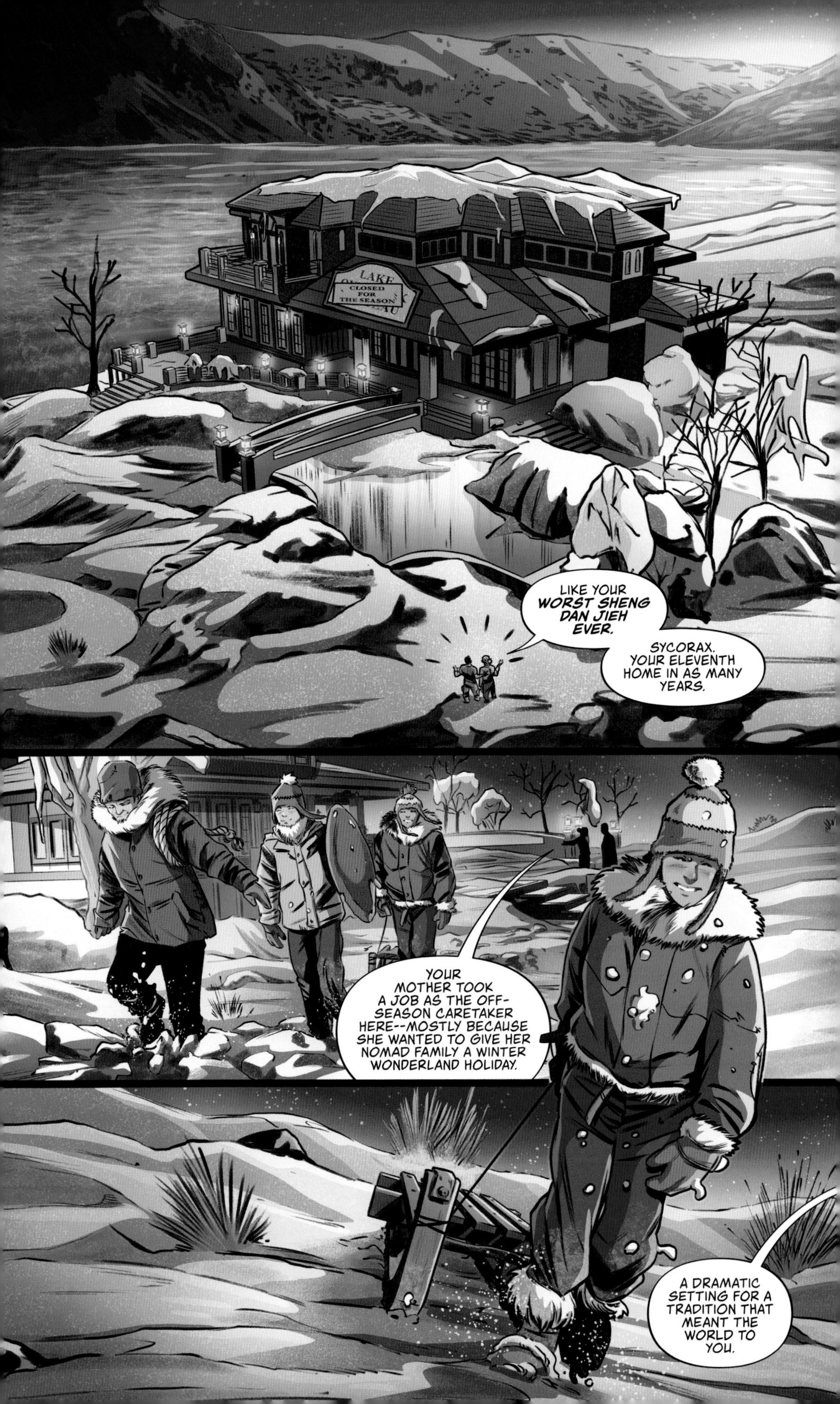

CLOSED FOR THE SEASON
LIKE YOUR WORST SHENG DAN JIEH EVER.
SYCORAX. YOUR ELEVENTH HOME IN AS MANY YEARS.
YOUR MOTHER TOOK A JOB AS THE OFF-SEASON CARETAKER HERE--MOSTLY BECAUSE SHE WANTED TO GIVE HER NOMAD FAMILY A WINTER WONDERLAND HOLIDAY.
A DRAMATIC SETTING FOR A TRADITION THAT MEANT THE WORLD TO YOU.

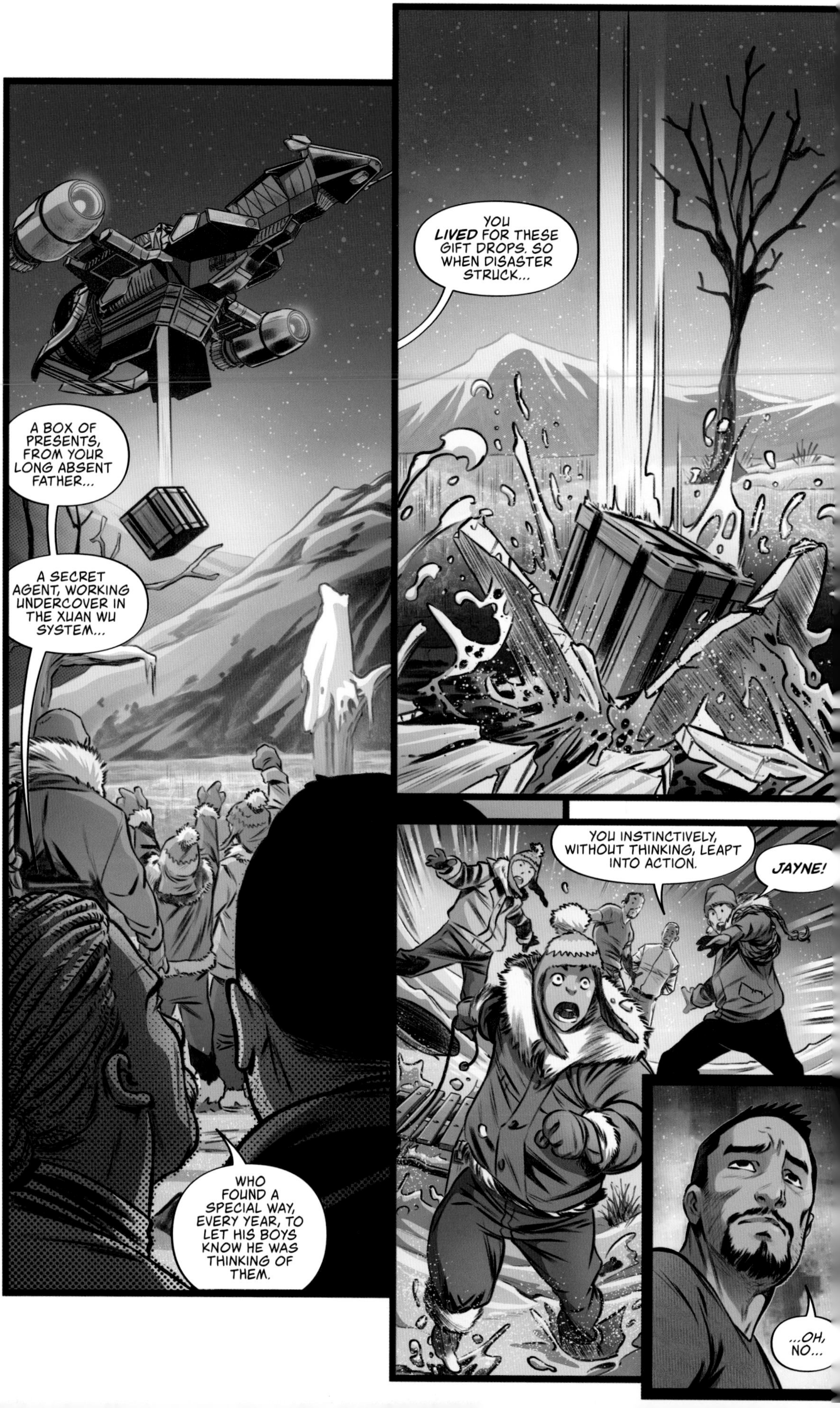
A BOX OF PRESENTS, FROM YOUR LONG ABSENT FATHER...
A SECRET AGENT, WORKING UNDERCOVER IN THE XUAN WU SYSTEM...
WHO FOUND A SPECIAL WAY, EVERY YEAR, TO LET HIS BOYS KNOW HE WAS THINKING OF THEM.
YOU *LIVED* FOR THESE GIFT DROPS. SO WHEN DISASTER STRUCK...
YOU INSTINCTIVELY, WITHOUT THINKING, LEAPT INTO ACTION.
JAYNE!
...OH, NO...

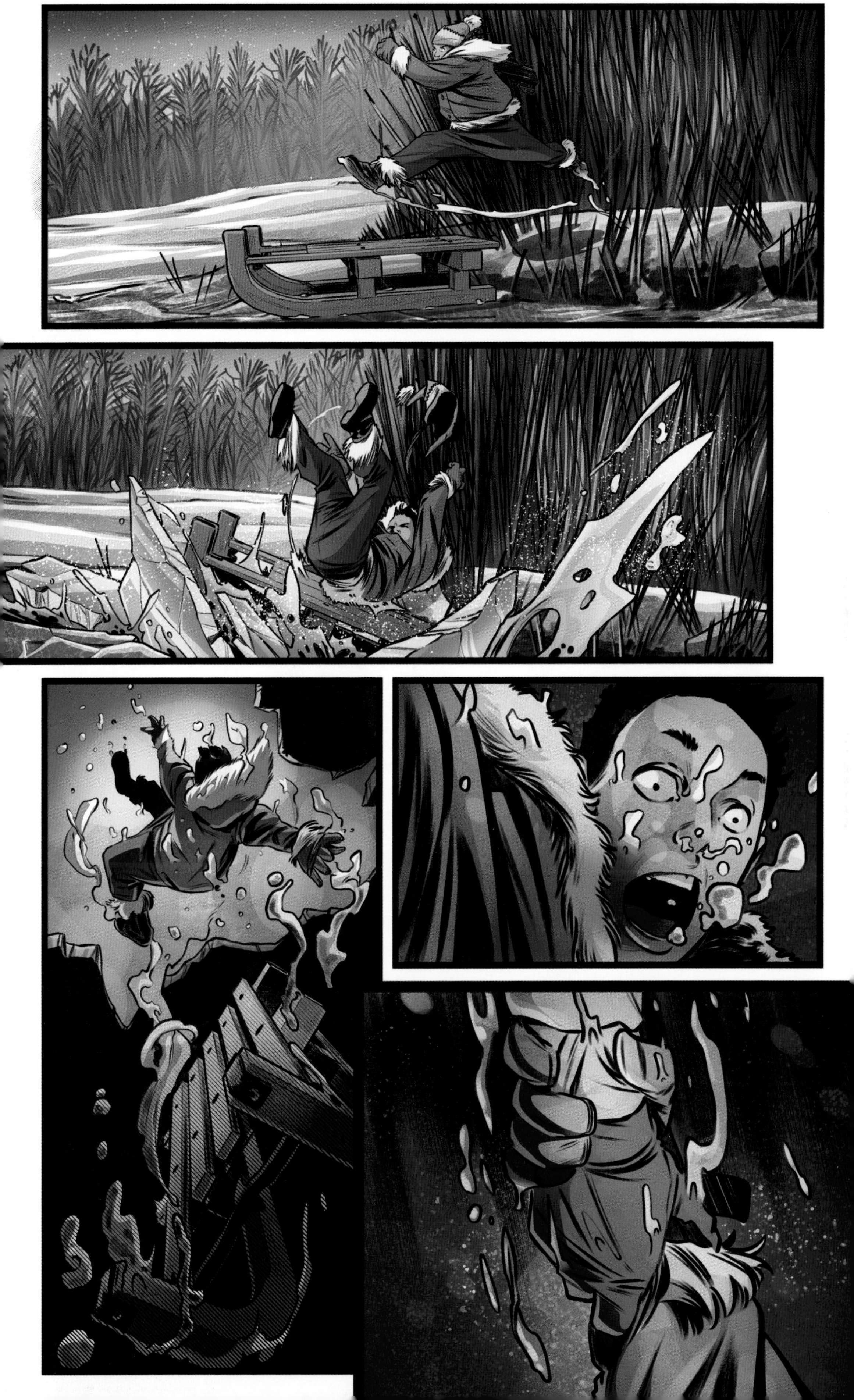

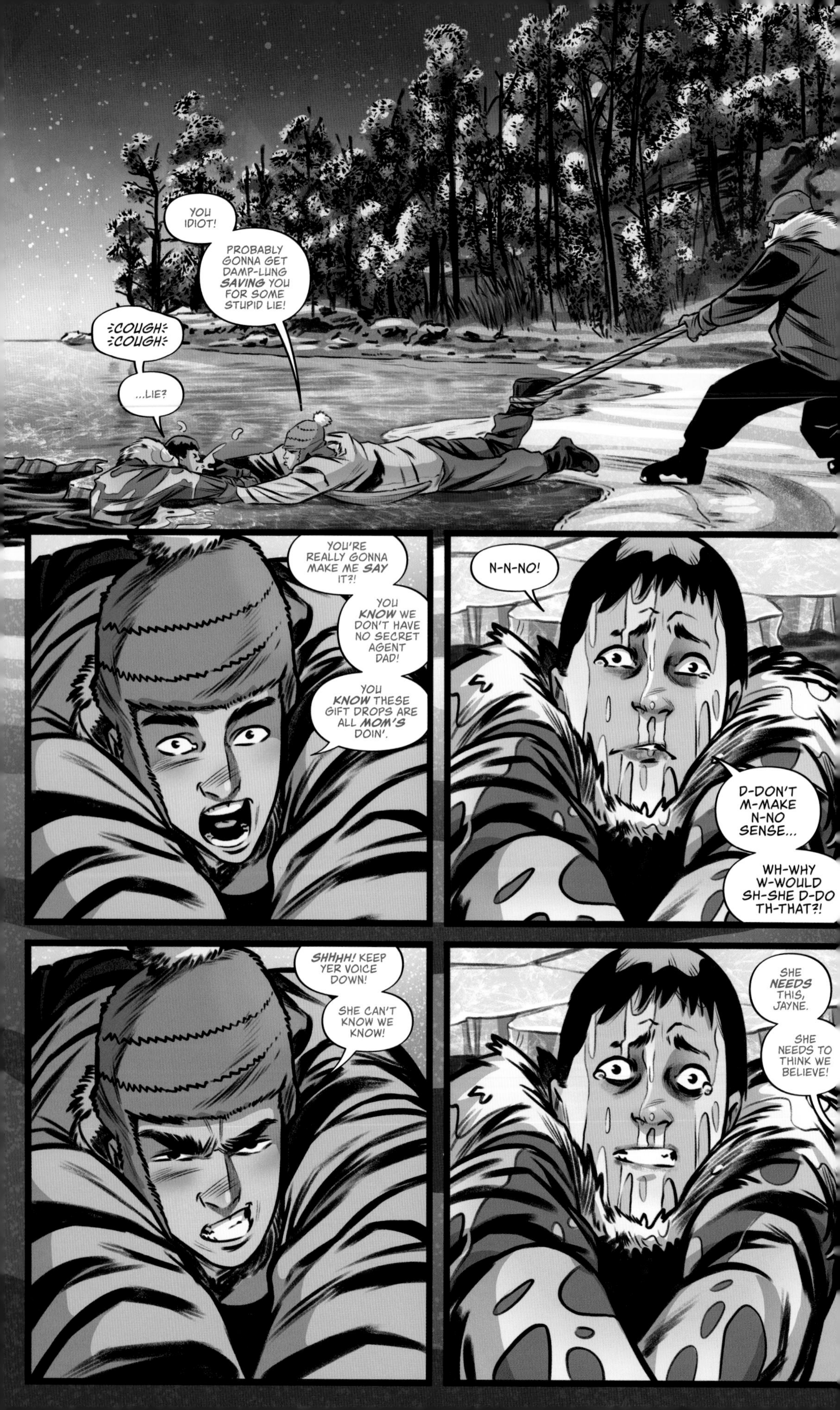
YOU IDIOT!
PROBABLY GONNA GET DAMP-LUNG SAVING YOU FOR SOME STUPID LIE!
COUGH COUGH
...LIE?
YOU'RE REALLY GONNA MAKE ME SAY IT?!
YOU KNOW WE DON'T HAVE NO SECRET AGENT DAD!
YOU KNOW THESE GIFT DROPS ARE ALL MOM'S DOIN'.
N-N-NO!
D-DON'T M-MAKE N-NO SENSE...
WH-WHY W-WOULD SH-SHE D-DO TH-THAT?!
SHHHH! KEEP YER VOICE DOWN!
SHE CAN'T KNOW WE KNOW!
SHE NEEDS THIS, JAYNE.
SHE NEEDS TO THINK WE BELIEVE!

JAYNE! ARE YOU OKAY?
SWEETHEART, I KNOW WHAT THIS MEANS TO YOU, BUT YOU CAN'T GO RUNNING OFF LIKE THAT!
IT'S JUST A BOX OF THINGS! AIN'T WORTH DYING FOR--
NO!
CAN'T BELIEVE YOU'D DO THAT!
CAN'T BELIEVE YOU'D LIE TO ME...
CAN'T... BELIEVE...
...YOU...

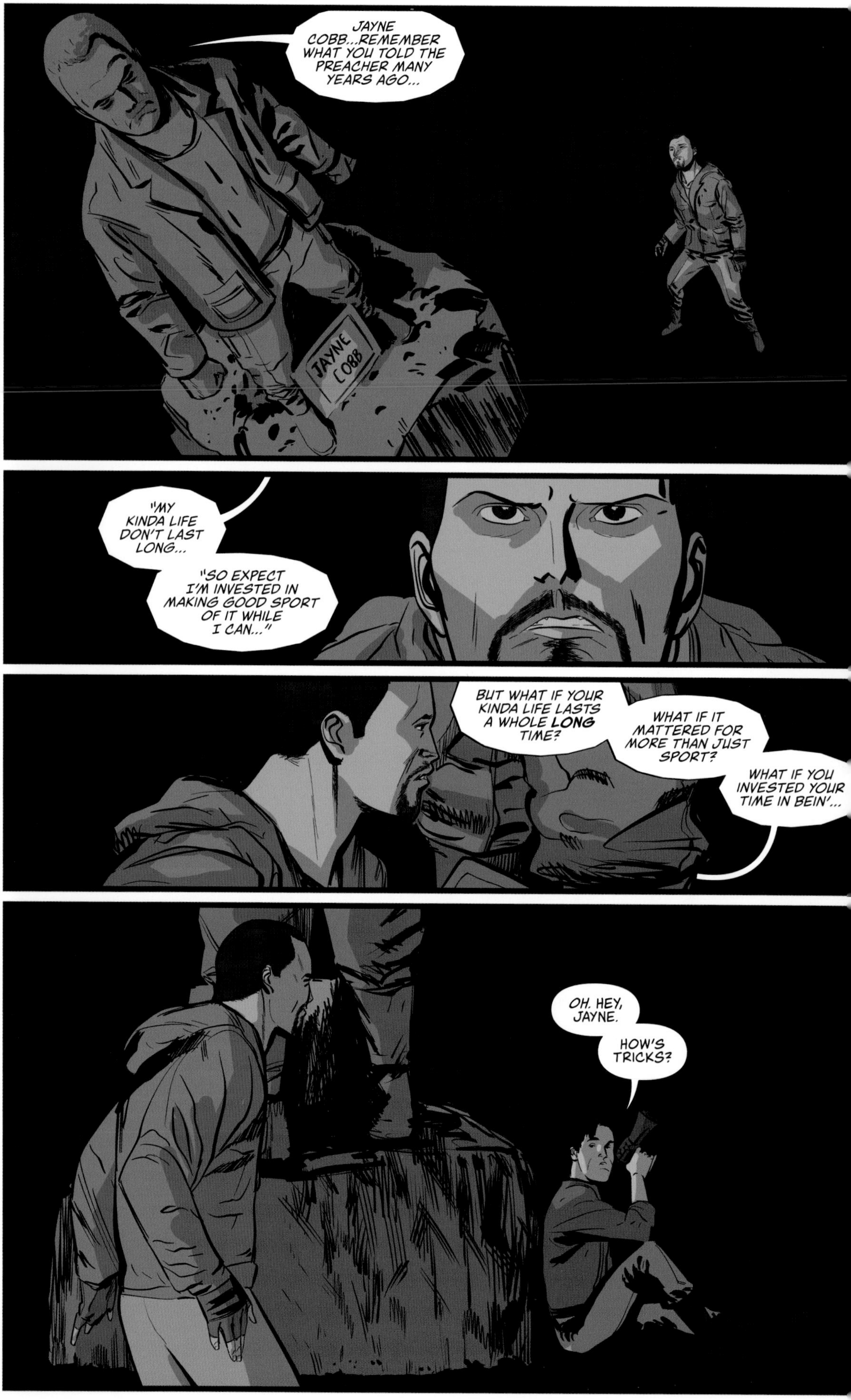
JAYNE COBB...REMEMBER WHAT YOU TOLD THE PREACHER MANY YEARS AGO...
JAYNE COBB
"MY KINDA LIFE DON'T LAST LONG...
"SO EXPECT I'M INVESTED IN MAKING GOOD SPORT OF IT WHILE I CAN..."
BUT WHAT IF YOUR KINDA LIFE LASTS A WHOLE **LONG** TIME?
WHAT IF IT MATTERED FOR MORE THAN JUST SPORT?
WHAT IF YOU INVESTED YOUR TIME IN BEIN'...
OH. HEY, JAYNE.
HOW'S TRICKS?

IN!
CK!

NOPE. AIN'T YER CAPTAIN...

...BUT ALL THE SAME, I HOPE YOU'LL KINDLY RESPECT AN ORDER TO PUT ME THE HELL DOWN.

I'M YOUR SECOND GHOST. RECKON I GOT PICKED 'CUZ I'M PRESENTLY GHOSTIN' YOU AND SUCH.

SORRY ABOUT THAT BUSINESS IN THE PAST. WHAT A PAINFUL MEMORY!

NO WONDER YOU WANTED TO GET OUT OF TELLIN' US YOUR WORST CHRISTMAS YEARS BACK.

SECOND: *NOT* MY WORST *SHENG DAN JIEH!* FAR FROM IT! THE *WORST* WAS WHEN MY TURTLE *VERA*--

KNOW WHAT? DON'T CARE. NOT MY DEPARTMENT.

MY JURISDICTION'S THE *HERE AND NOW...*

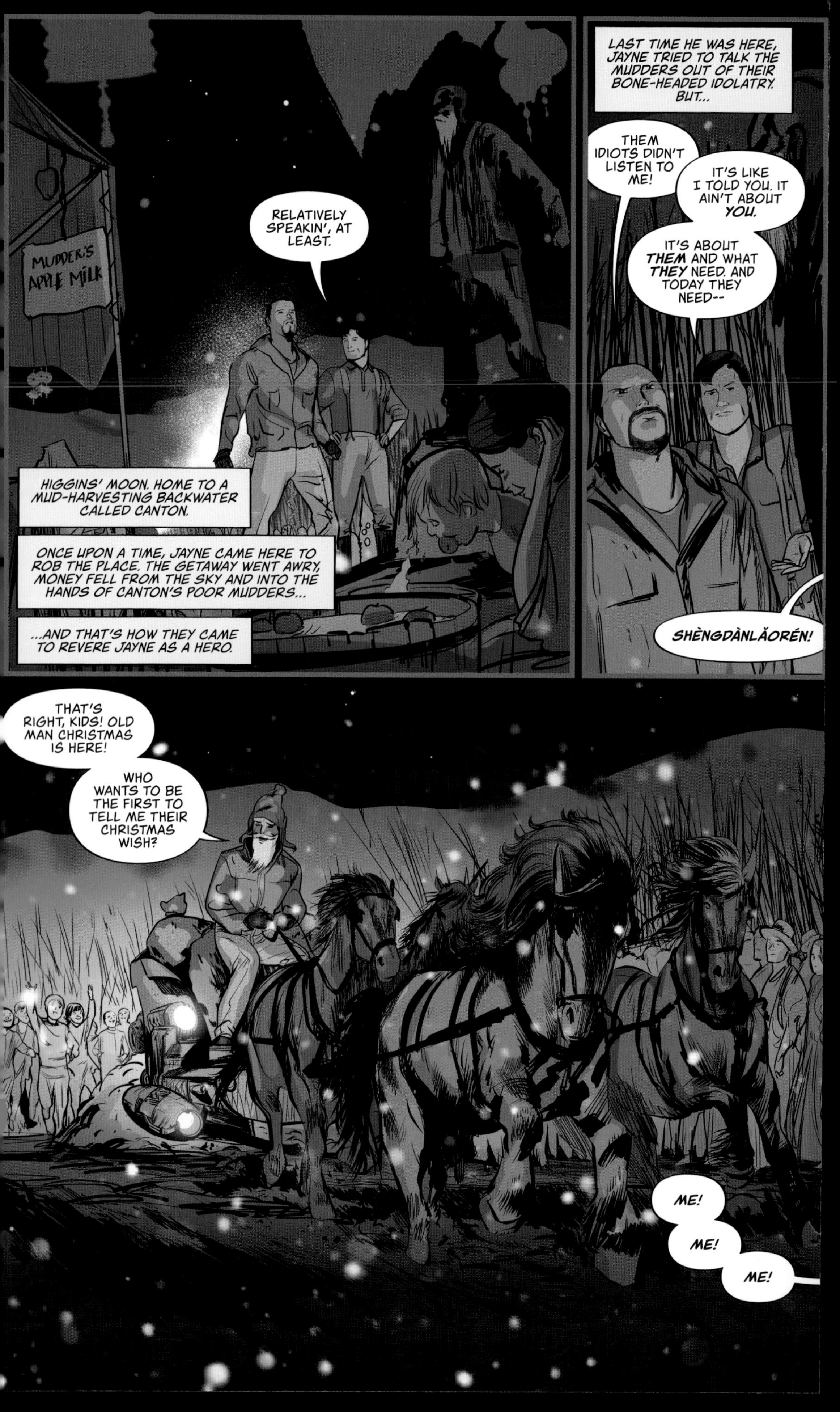
RELATIVELY SPEAKIN', AT LEAST.
MUDDER'S APPLE MILK
HIGGINS' MOON. HOME TO A MUD-HARVESTING BACKWATER CALLED CANTON.
ONCE UPON A TIME, JAYNE CAME HERE TO ROB THE PLACE. THE GETAWAY WENT AWRY, MONEY FELL FROM THE SKY AND INTO THE HANDS OF CANTON'S POOR MUDDERS...
...AND THAT'S HOW THEY CAME TO REVERE JAYNE AS A HERO.
LAST TIME HE WAS HERE, JAYNE TRIED TO TALK THE MUDDERS OUT OF THEIR BONE-HEADED IDOLATRY. BUT...
THEM IDIOTS DIDN'T LISTEN TO ME!
IT'S LIKE I TOLD YOU. IT AIN'T ABOUT ***YOU.***
IT'S ABOUT ***THEM*** AND WHAT ***THEY*** NEED. AND TODAY THEY NEED--
SHÈNGDÀNLǍORÉN!
THAT'S RIGHT, KIDS! OLD MAN CHRISTMAS IS HERE!
WHO WANTS TO BE THE FIRST TO TELL ME THEIR CHRISTMAS WISH?
ME!
ME!
ME!

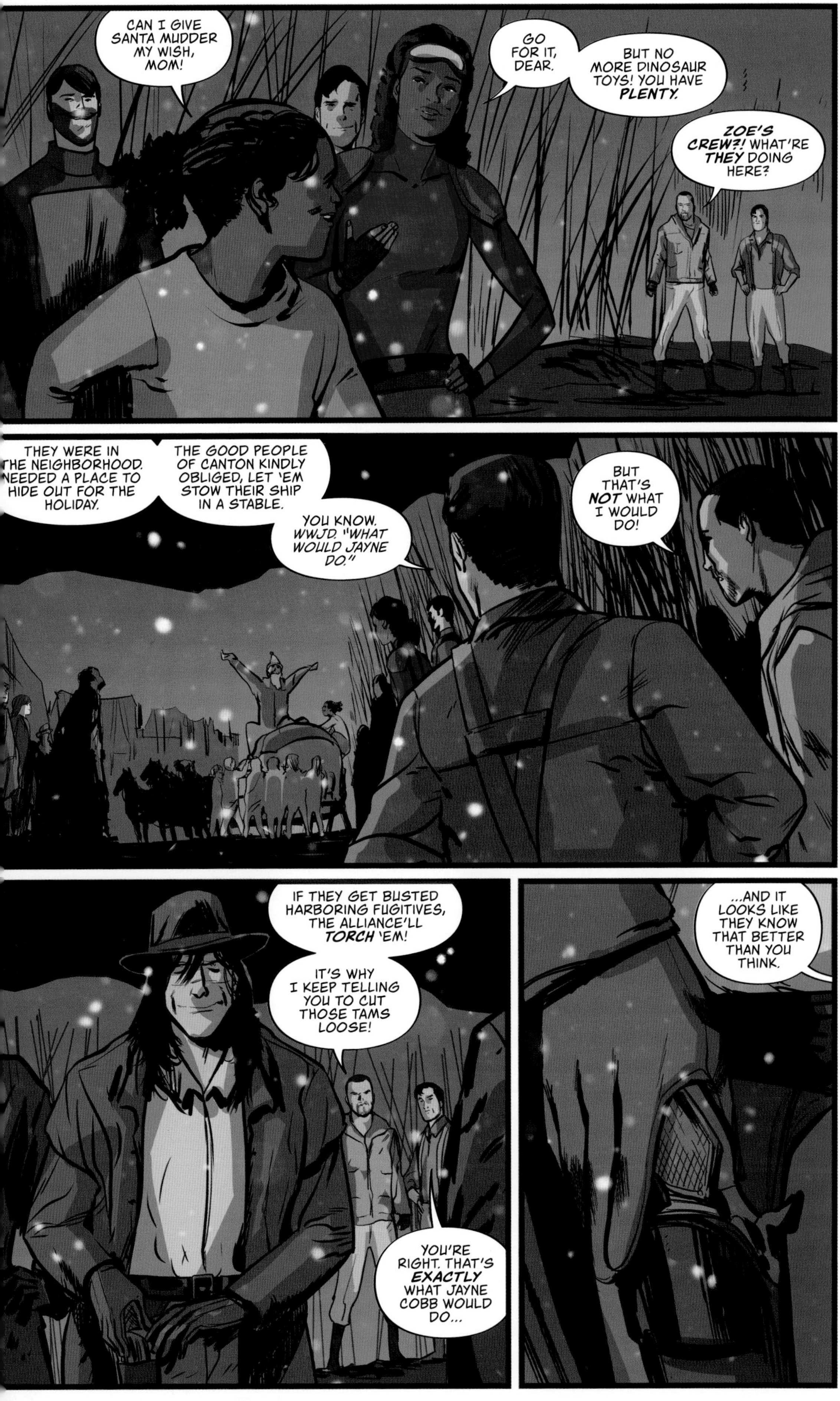
CAN I GIVE SANTA MUDDER MY WISH, MOM!
GO FOR IT, DEAR.
BUT NO MORE DINOSAUR TOYS! YOU HAVE PLENTY.
ZOE'S CREW?! WHAT'RE THEY DOING HERE?
THEY WERE IN THE NEIGHBORHOOD. NEEDED A PLACE TO HIDE OUT FOR THE HOLIDAY.
THE GOOD PEOPLE OF CANTON KINDLY OBLIGED, LET 'EM STOW THEIR SHIP IN A STABLE.
YOU KNOW. WWJD. "WHAT WOULD JAYNE DO."
BUT THAT'S NOT WHAT I WOULD DO!
IF THEY GET BUSTED HARBORING FUGITIVES, THE ALLIANCE'LL TORCH 'EM!
IT'S WHY I KEEP TELLING YOU TO CUT THOSE TAMS LOOSE!
YOU'RE RIGHT. THAT'S EXACTLY WHAT JAYNE COBB WOULD DO...
...AND IT LOOKS LIKE THEY KNOW THAT BETTER THAN YOU THINK.

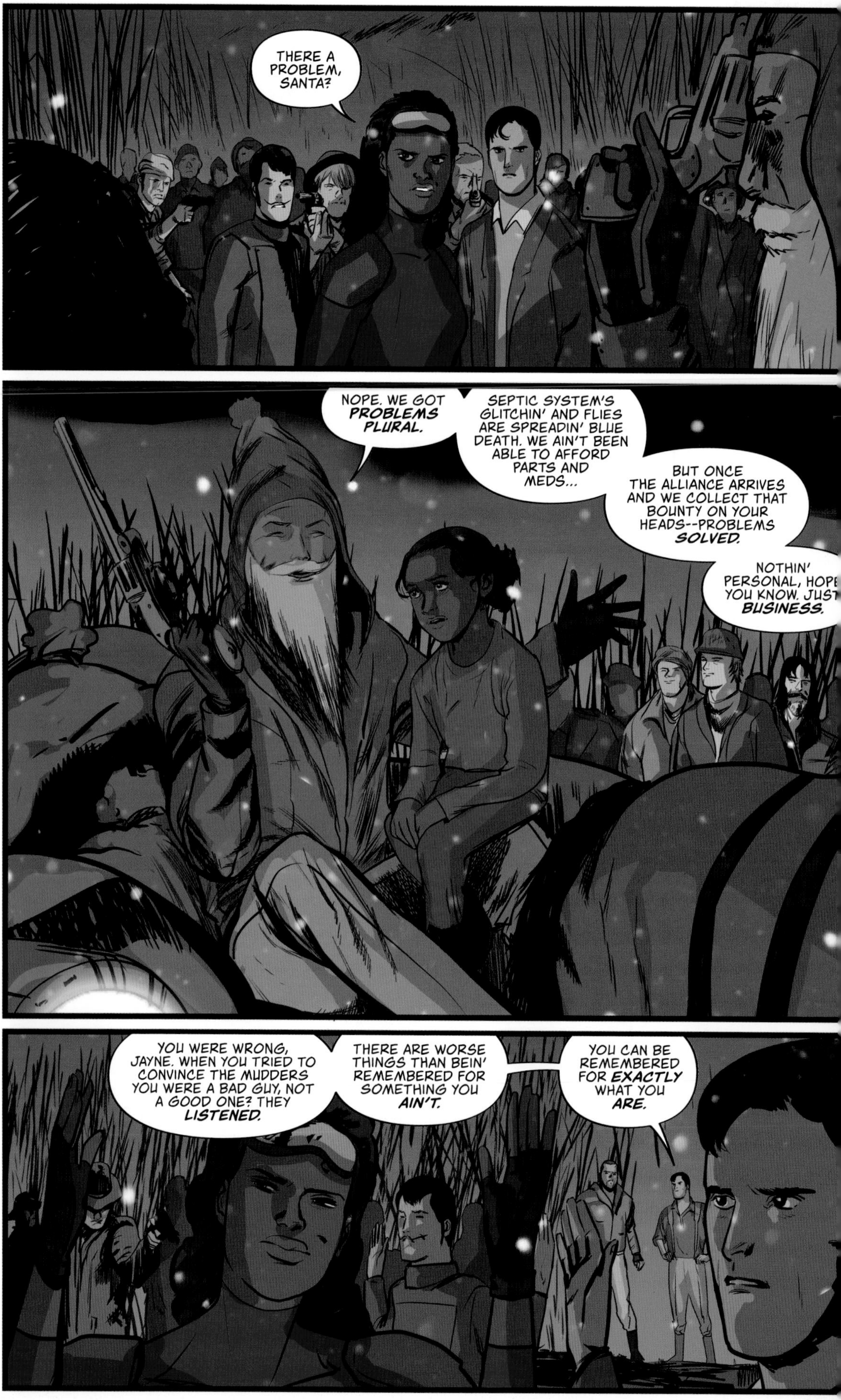
THERE A PROBLEM, SANTA?
NOPE. WE GOT **PROBLEMS PLURAL.**
SEPTIC SYSTEM'S GLITCHIN' AND FLIES ARE SPREADIN' BLUE DEATH. WE AIN'T BEEN ABLE TO AFFORD PARTS AND MEDS...
BUT ONCE THE ALLIANCE ARRIVES AND WE COLLECT THAT BOUNTY ON YOUR HEADS--PROBLEMS **SOLVED.**
NOTHIN' PERSONAL, HOPE YOU KNOW. JUST **BUSINESS.**
YOU WERE WRONG, JAYNE. WHEN YOU TRIED TO CONVINCE THE MUDDERS YOU WERE A BAD GUY, NOT A GOOD ONE? THEY **LISTENED.**
THERE ARE WORSE THINGS THAN BEIN' REMEMBERED FOR SOMETHING YOU **AIN'T.**
YOU CAN BE REMEMBERED FOR **EXACTLY** WHAT YOU **ARE.**

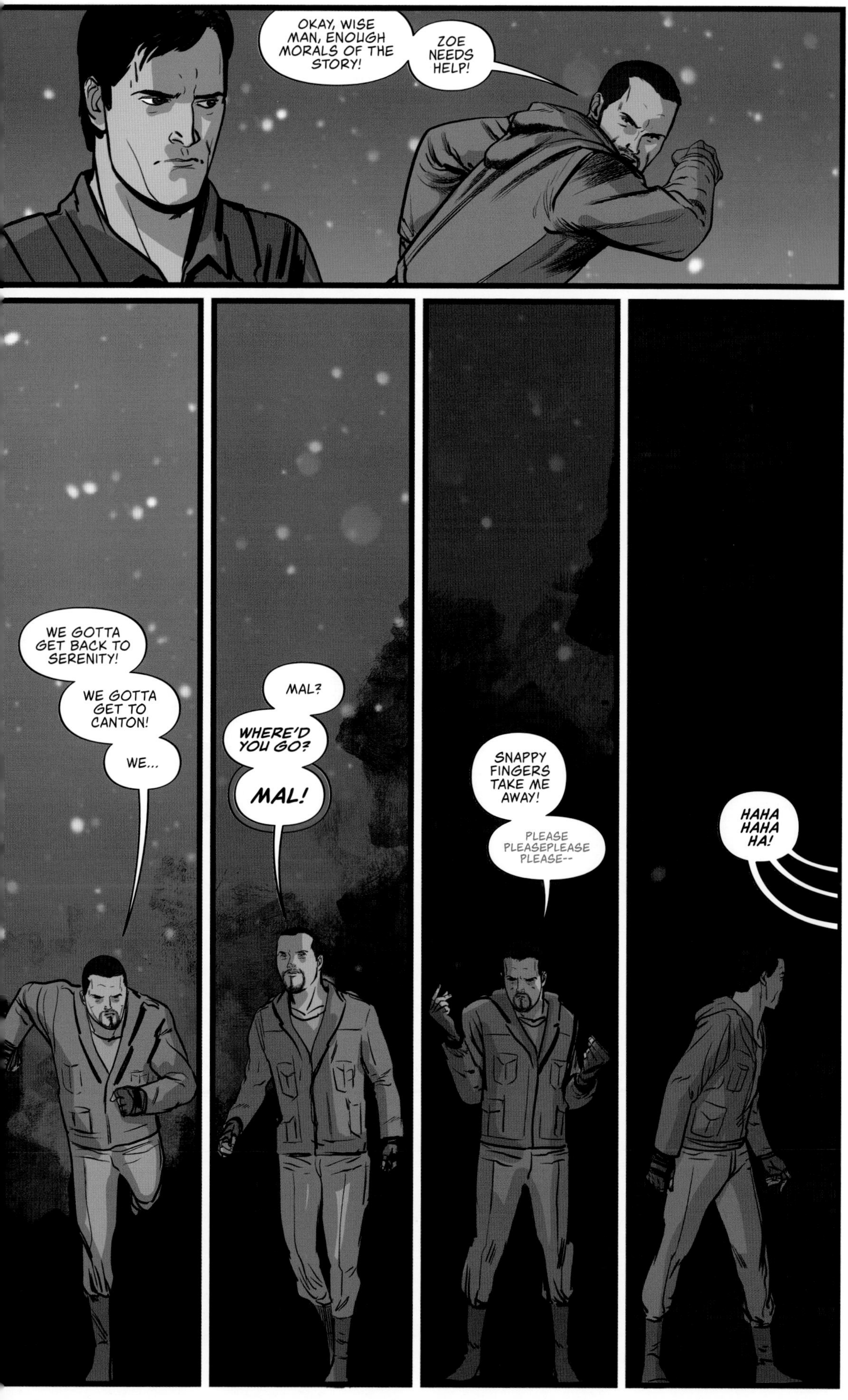
OKAY, WISE MAN, ENOUGH MORALS OF THE STORY!
ZOE NEEDS HELP!
WE GOTTA GET BACK TO SERENITY!
WE GOTTA GET TO CANTON!
WE...
MAL?
WHERE'D YOU GO?
MAL!
SNAPPY FINGERS TAKE ME AWAY!
PLEASE PLEASEPLEASE PLEASE--
HAHA HAHA HA!

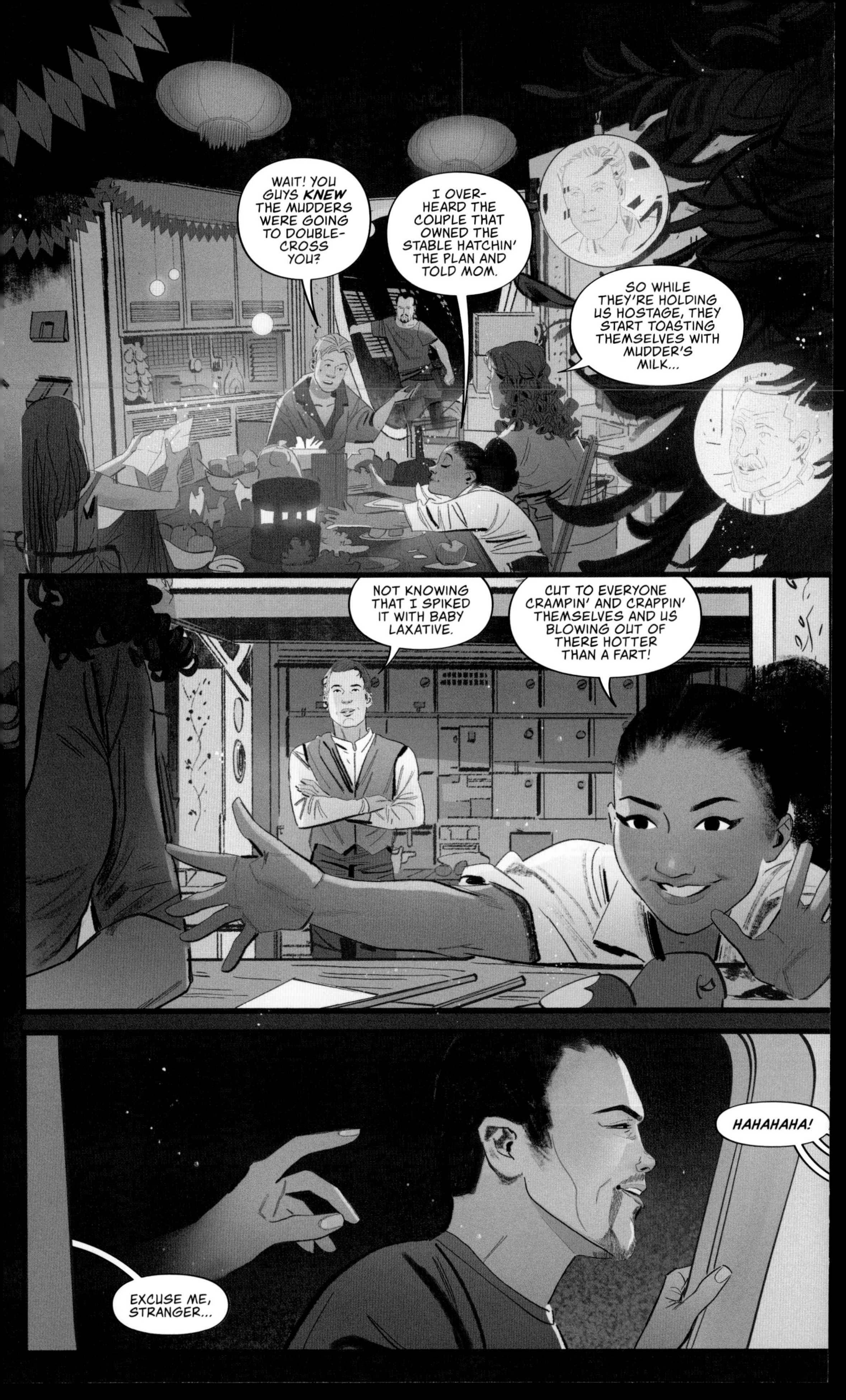
WAIT! YOU GUYS KNEW THE MUDDERS WERE GOING TO DOUBLE-CROSS YOU?
I OVER-HEARD THE COUPLE THAT OWNED THE STABLE HATCHIN' THE PLAN AND TOLD MOM.
SO WHILE THEY'RE HOLDING US HOSTAGE, THEY START TOASTING THEMSELVES WITH MUDDER'S MILK...
NOT KNOWING THAT I SPIKED IT WITH BABY LAXATIVE.
CUT TO EVERYONE CRAMPIN' AND CRAPPIN' THEMSELVES AND US BLOWING OUT OF THERE HOTTER THAN A FART!
HAHAHAHA!
EXCUSE ME, STRANGER...

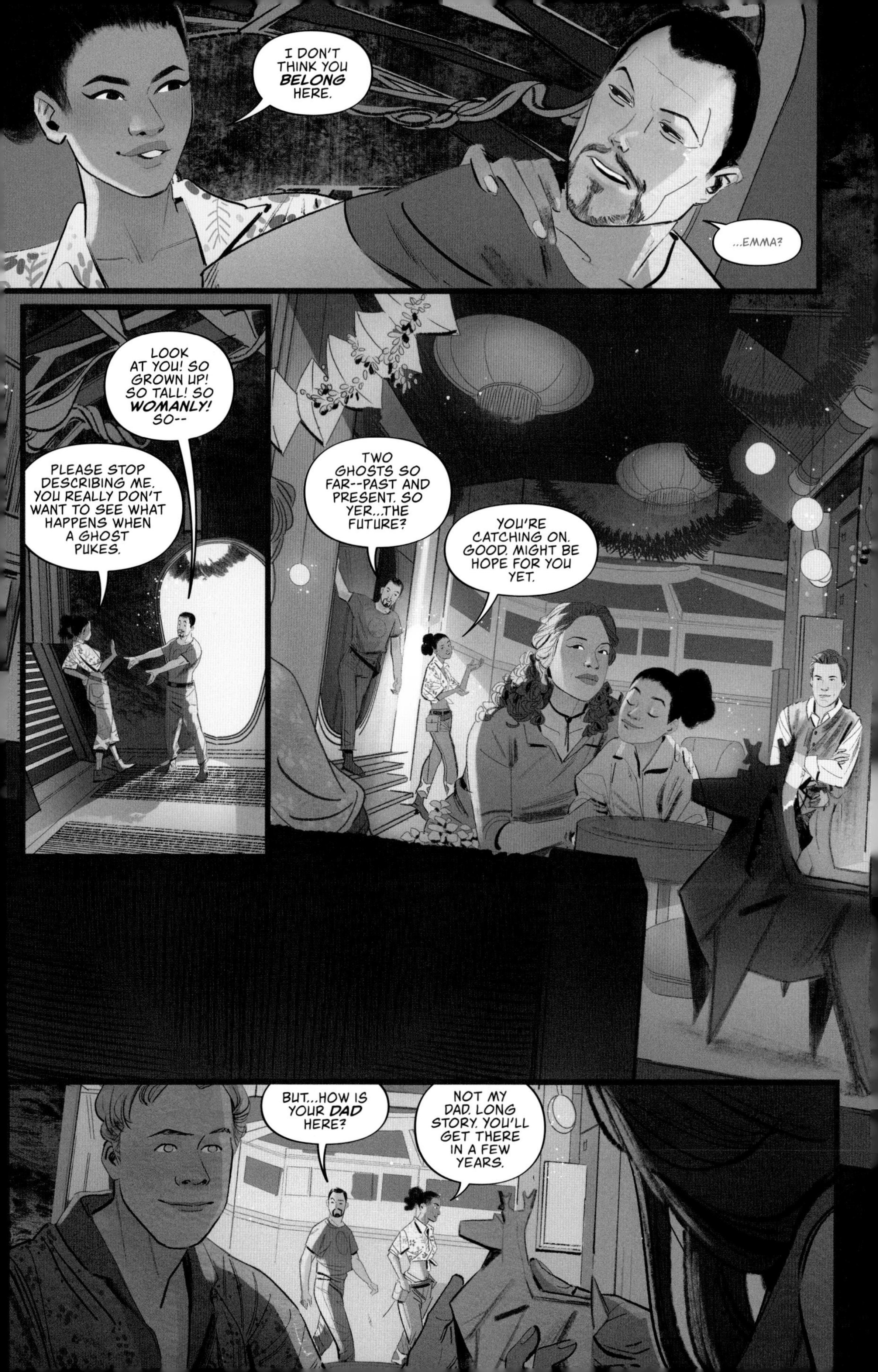

I DON'T THINK YOU **BELONG** HERE.
...EMMA?
LOOK AT YOU! SO GROWN UP! SO TALL! SO **WOMANLY!** SO--
PLEASE STOP DESCRIBING ME. YOU REALLY DON'T WANT TO SEE WHAT HAPPENS WHEN A GHOST PUKES.
TWO GHOSTS SO FAR--PAST AND PRESENT. SO YER...THE FUTURE?
YOU'RE CATCHING ON. GOOD. MIGHT BE HOPE FOR YOU YET.
BUT...HOW IS YOUR **DAD** HERE?
NOT MY DAD. LONG STORY. YOU'LL GET THERE IN A FEW YEARS.

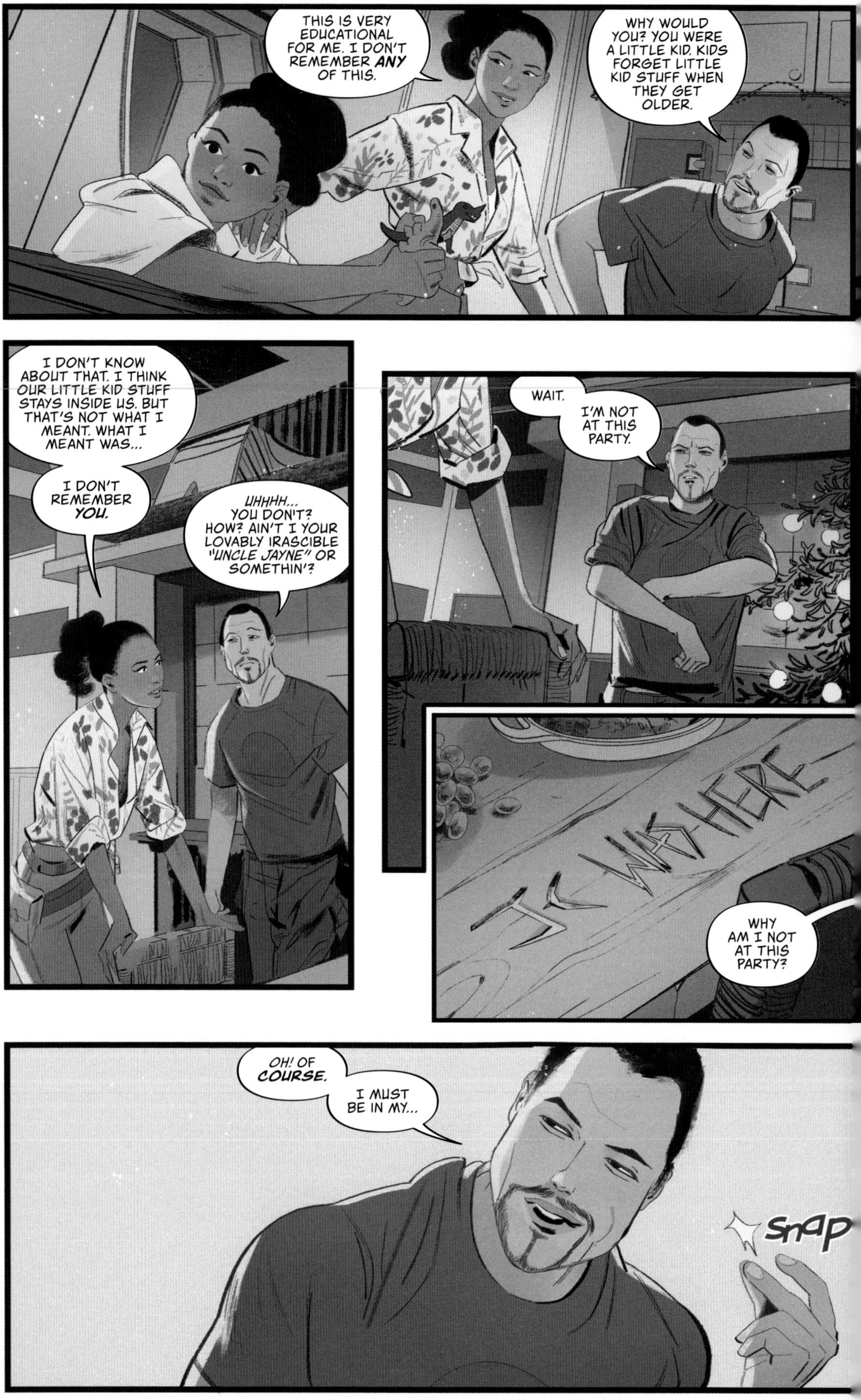
THIS IS VERY EDUCATIONAL FOR ME. I DON'T REMEMBER **ANY** OF THIS.
WHY WOULD YOU? YOU WERE A LITTLE KID. KIDS FORGET LITTLE KID STUFF WHEN THEY GET OLDER.
I DON'T KNOW ABOUT THAT. I THINK OUR LITTLE KID STUFF STAYS INSIDE US. BUT THAT'S NOT WHAT I MEANT. WHAT I MEANT WAS...
I DON'T REMEMBER ***YOU.***
UHHHH... YOU DON'T? HOW? AIN'T I YOUR LOVABLY IRASCIBLE *"UNCLE JAYNE"* OR SOMETHIN'?
WAIT.
I'M NOT AT THIS PARTY.
WAS HERE
WHY AM I NOT AT THIS PARTY?
OH! OF ***COURSE.***
I MUST BE IN MY...
SNAP

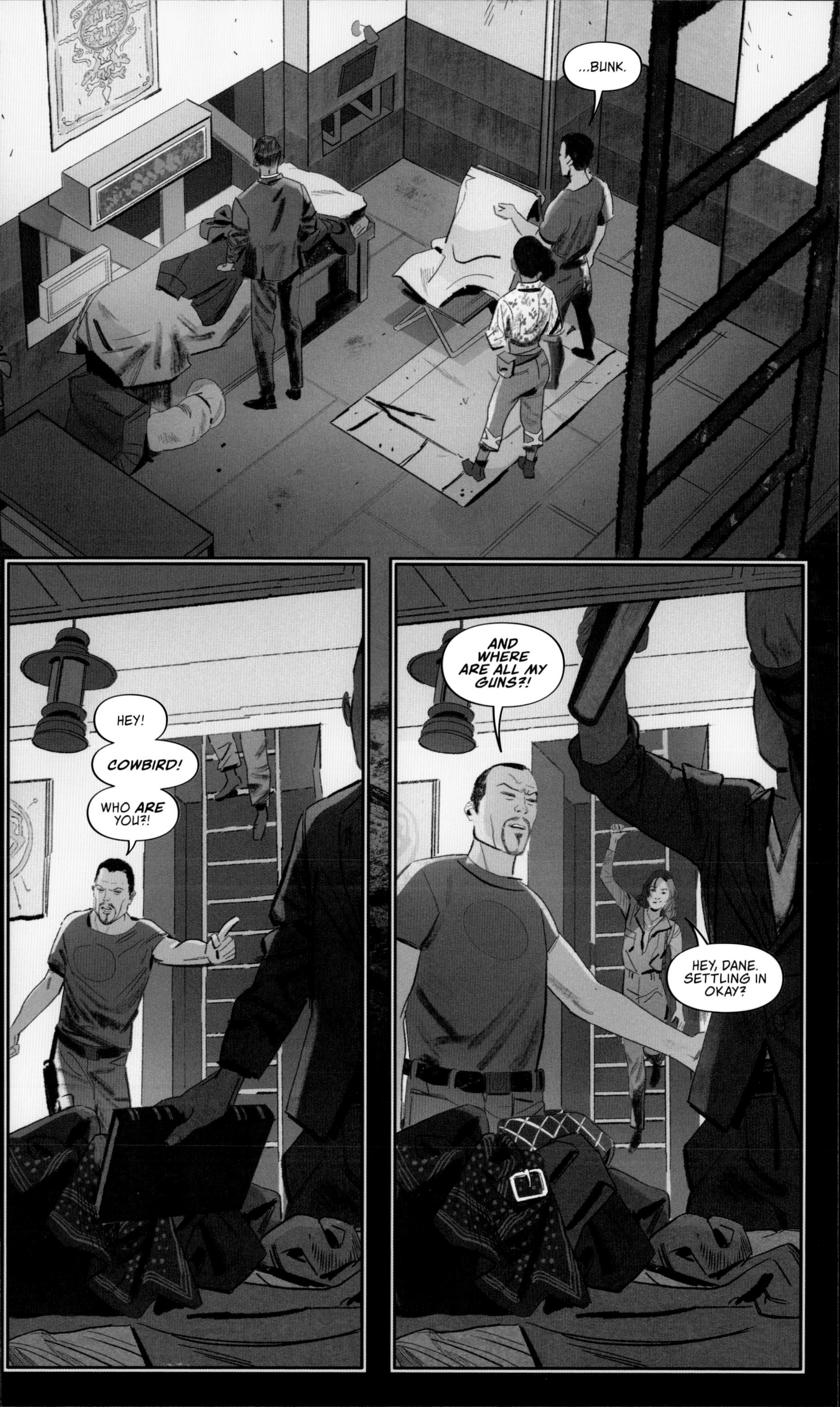
...BUNK.
HEY!
COWBIRD!
WHO ARE YOU?!
AND WHERE ARE ALL MY GUNS?!
HEY, DANE. SETTLING IN OKAY?

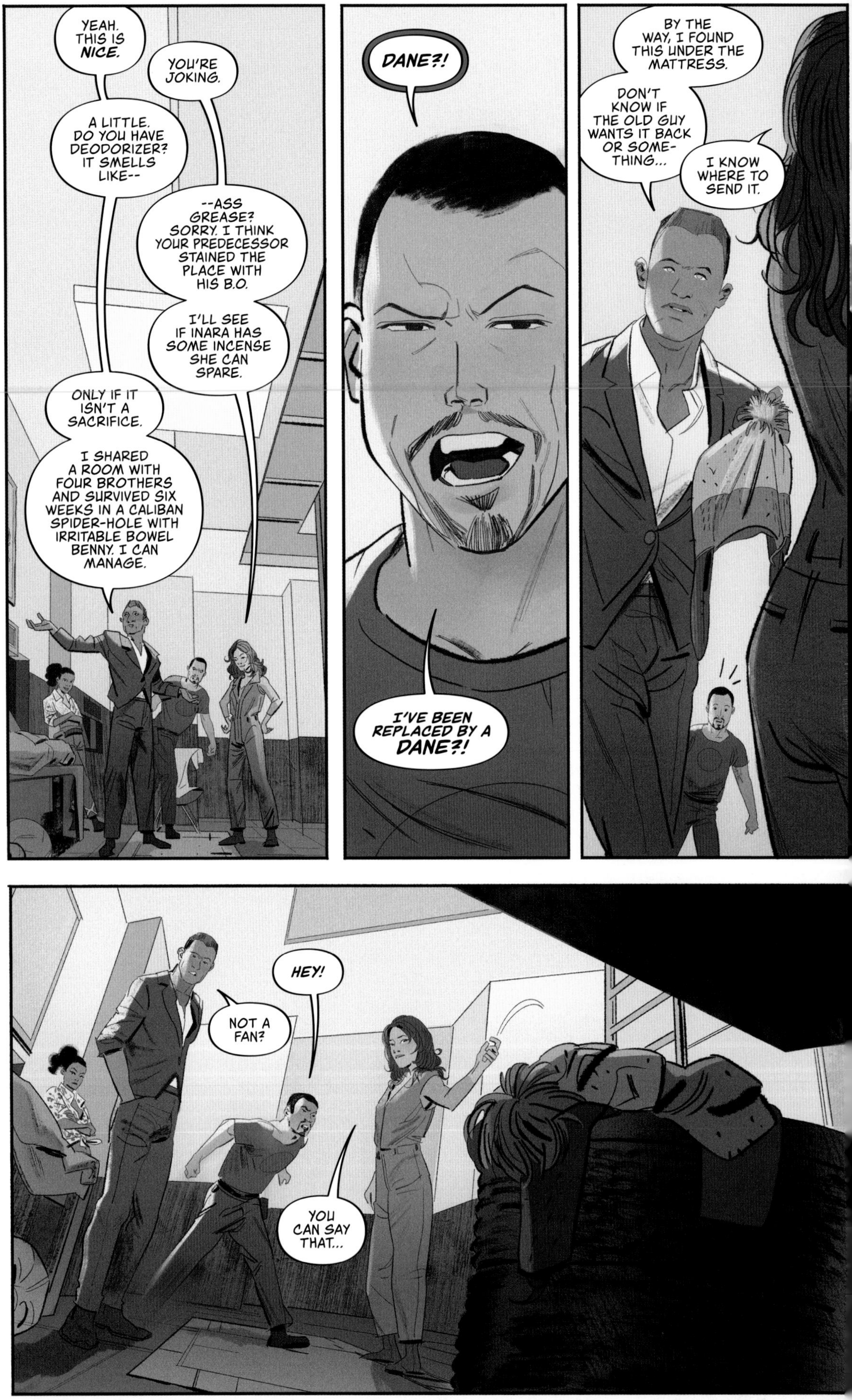
YEAH. THIS IS *NICE.*
YOU'RE JOKING.
A LITTLE. DO YOU HAVE DEODORIZER? IT SMELLS LIKE--
--ASS GREASE? SORRY. I THINK YOUR PREDECESSOR STAINED THE PLACE WITH HIS B.O.
I'LL SEE IF INARA HAS SOME INCENSE SHE CAN SPARE.
ONLY IF IT ISN'T A SACRIFICE.
I SHARED A ROOM WITH FOUR BROTHERS AND SURVIVED SIX WEEKS IN A CALIBAN SPIDER-HOLE WITH IRRITABLE BOWEL BENNY. I CAN MANAGE.
DANE?!
I'VE BEEN REPLACED BY A DANE?!
BY THE WAY, I FOUND THIS UNDER THE MATTRESS.
DON'T KNOW IF THE OLD GUY WANTS IT BACK OR SOME-THING...
I KNOW WHERE TO SEND IT.
HEY!
NOT A FAN?
YOU CAN SAY THAT...

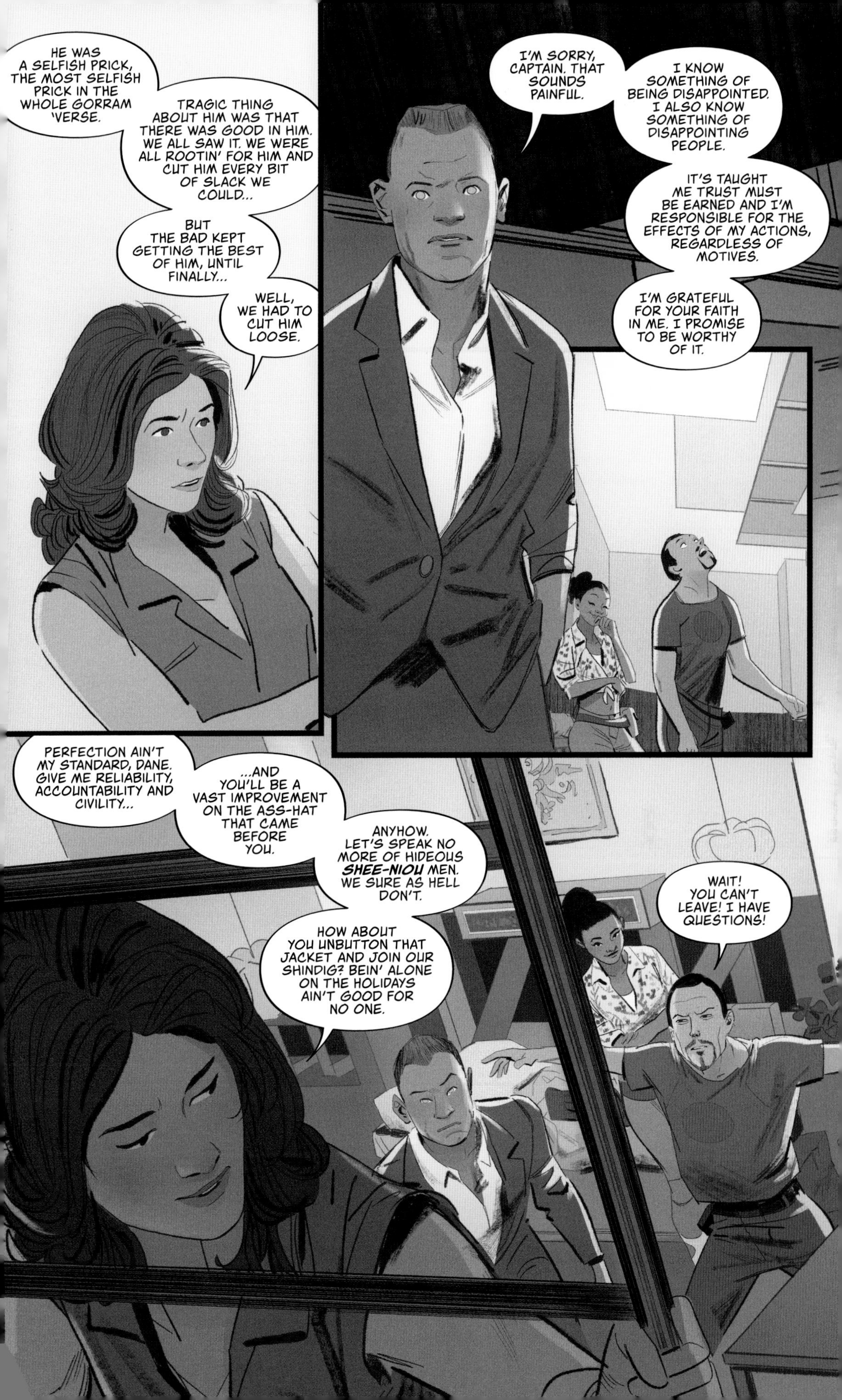
HE WAS A SELFISH PRICK, THE MOST SELFISH PRICK IN THE WHOLE GORRAM 'VERSE.
TRAGIC THING ABOUT HIM WAS THAT THERE WAS GOOD IN HIM. WE ALL SAW IT. WE WERE ALL ROOTIN' FOR HIM AND CUT HIM EVERY BIT OF SLACK WE COULD...
BUT THE BAD KEPT GETTING THE BEST OF HIM, UNTIL FINALLY...
WELL, WE HAD TO CUT HIM LOOSE.
I'M SORRY, CAPTAIN. THAT SOUNDS PAINFUL.
I KNOW SOMETHING OF BEING DISAPPOINTED. I ALSO KNOW SOMETHING OF DISAPPOINTING PEOPLE.
IT'S TAUGHT ME TRUST MUST BE EARNED AND I'M RESPONSIBLE FOR THE EFFECTS OF MY ACTIONS, REGARDLESS OF MOTIVES.
I'M GRATEFUL FOR YOUR FAITH IN ME. I PROMISE TO BE WORTHY OF IT.
PERFECTION AIN'T MY STANDARD, DANE. GIVE ME RELIABILITY, ACCOUNTABILITY AND CIVILITY...
...AND YOU'LL BE A VAST IMPROVEMENT ON THE ASS-HAT THAT CAME BEFORE YOU.
ANYHOW. LET'S SPEAK NO MORE OF HIDEOUS SHEE-NIOU MEN. WE SURE AS HELL DON'T.
HOW ABOUT YOU UNBUTTON THAT JACKET AND JOIN OUR SHINDIG? BEIN' ALONE ON THE HOLIDAYS AIN'T GOOD FOR NO ONE.
WAIT! YOU CAN'T LEAVE! I HAVE QUESTIONS!

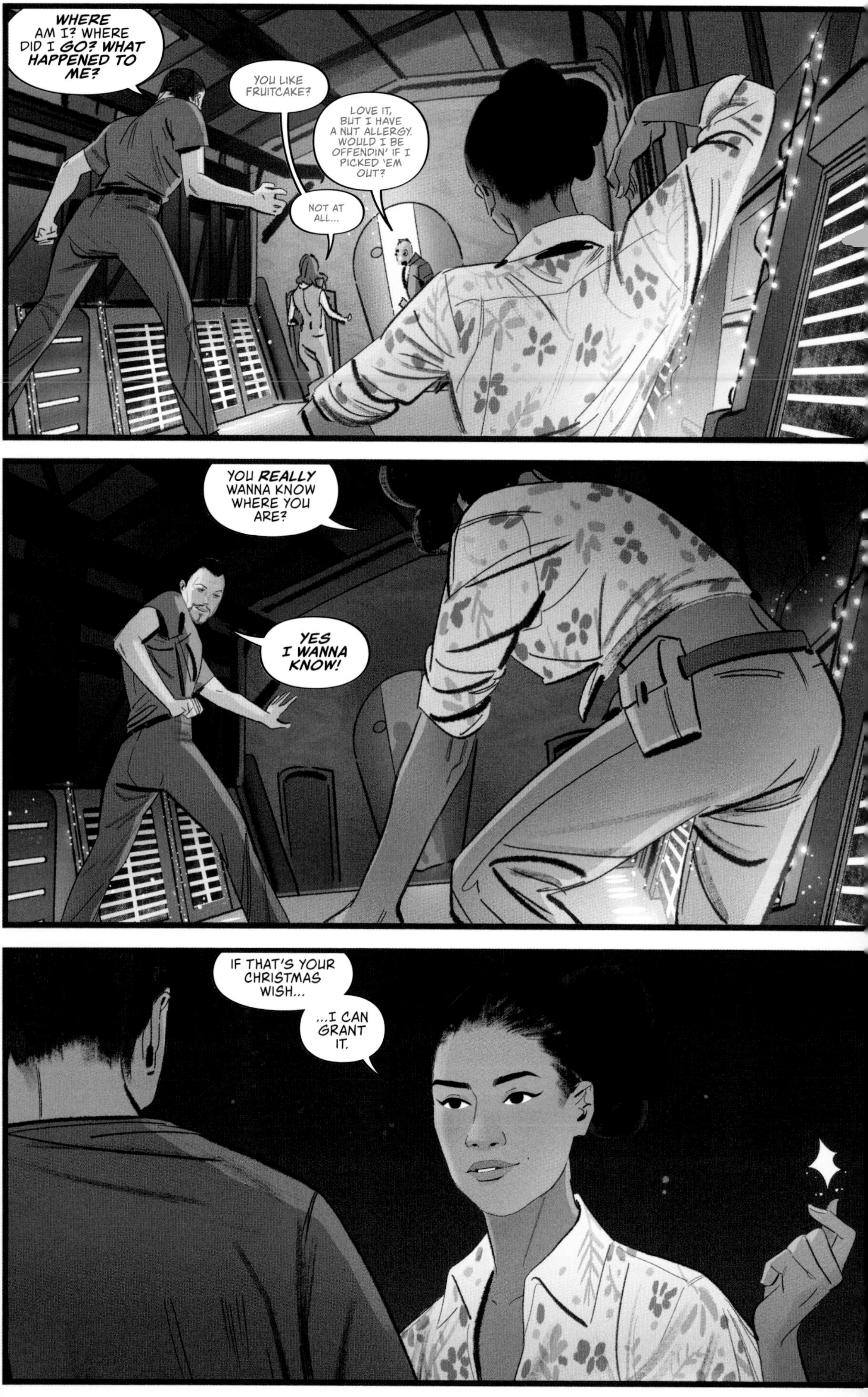
WHERE AM I? WHERE DID I GO? WHAT HAPPENED TO ME?
YOU LIKE FRUITCAKE?
LOVE IT, BUT I HAVE A NUT ALLERGY. WOULD I BE OFFENDIN' IF I PICKED 'EM OUT?
NOT AT ALL...
YOU REALLY WANNA KNOW WHERE YOU ARE?
YES I WANNA KNOW!
IF THAT'S YOUR CHRISTMAS WISH...
...I CAN GRANT IT.

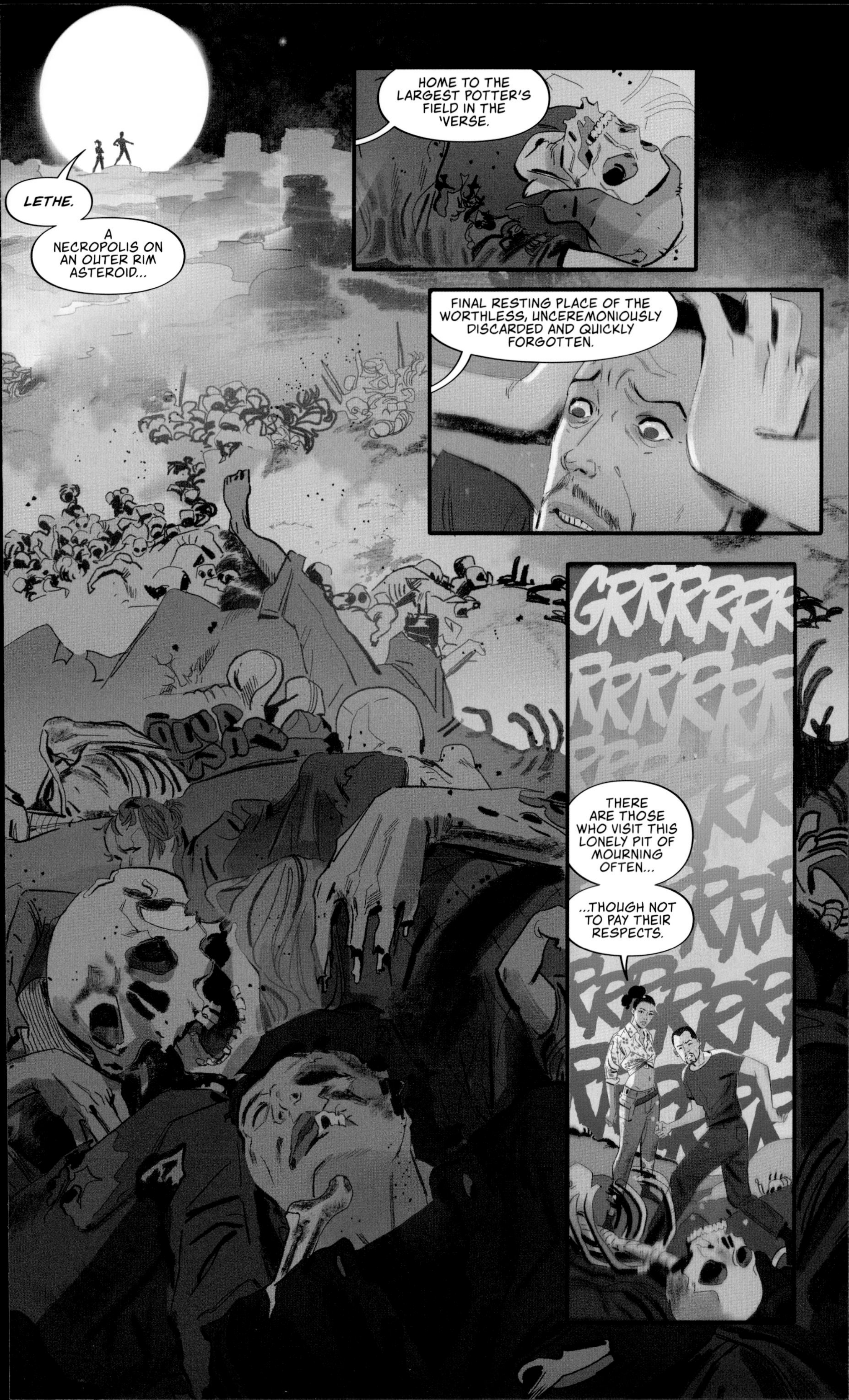
LETHE.
A NECROPOLIS ON AN OUTER RIM ASTEROID...
HOME TO THE LARGEST POTTER'S FIELD IN THE 'VERSE.
FINAL RESTING PLACE OF THE WORTHLESS, UNCEREMONIOUSLY DISCARDED AND QUICKLY FORGOTTEN.
GRRRRRR
THERE ARE THOSE WHO VISIT THIS LONELY PIT OF MOURNING OFTEN...
...THOUGH NOT TO PAY THEIR RESPECTS.

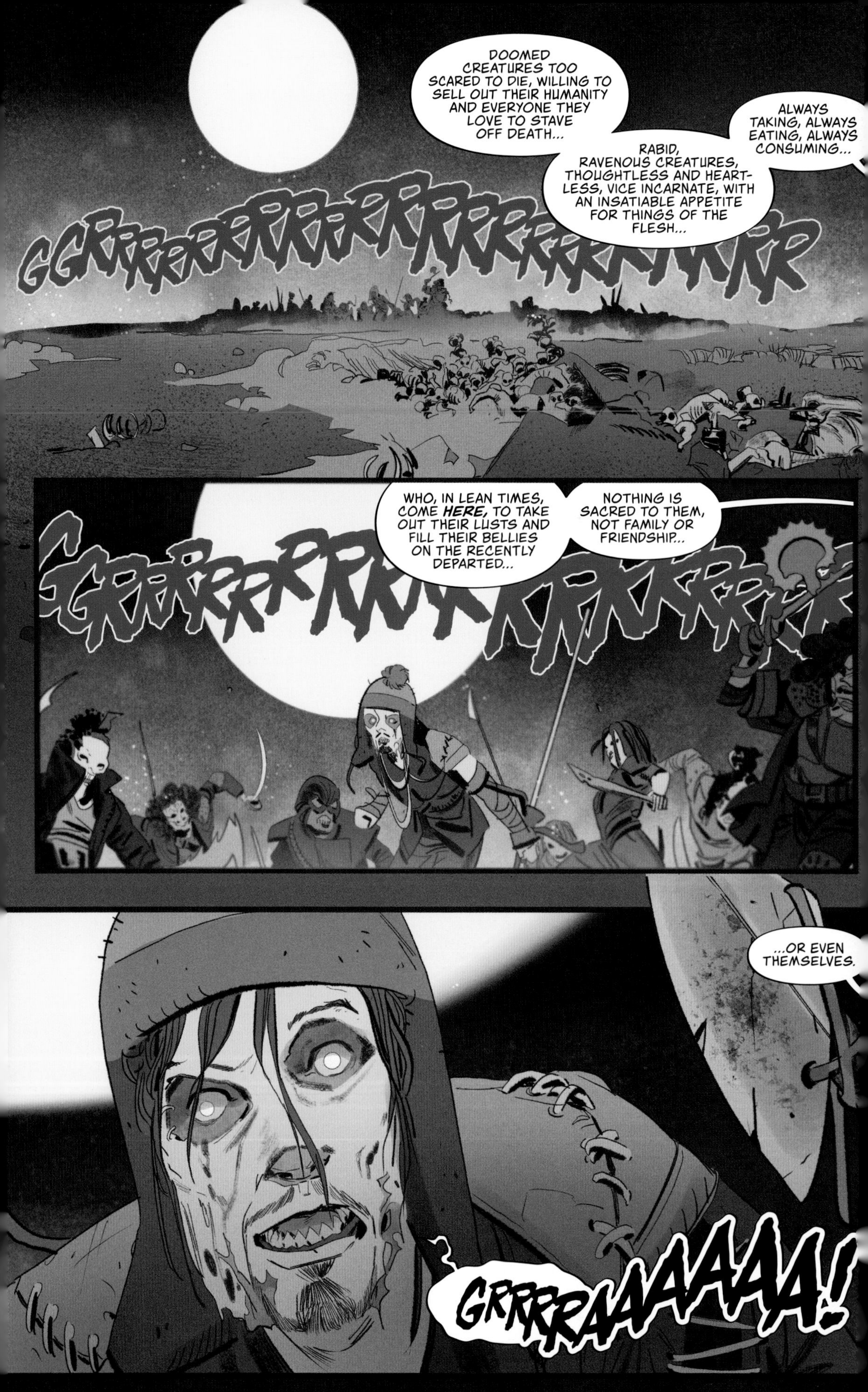
DOOMED CREATURES TOO SCARED TO DIE, WILLING TO SELL OUT THEIR HUMANITY AND EVERYONE THEY LOVE TO STAVE OFF DEATH...
RABID, RAVENOUS CREATURES, THOUGHTLESS AND HEART-LESS, VICE INCARNATE, WITH AN INSATIABLE APPETITE FOR THINGS OF THE FLESH...
ALWAYS TAKING, ALWAYS EATING, ALWAYS CONSUMING...
GGRRRRRRRRRRRRRRRRRRRRRRRRRRR
WHO, IN LEAN TIMES, COME HERE, TO TAKE OUT THEIR LUSTS AND FILL THEIR BELLIES ON THE RECENTLY DEPARTED...
NOTHING IS SACRED TO THEM, NOT FAMILY OR FRIENDSHIP...
GRRRRRRRRRRRRRRRR
...OR EVEN THEMSELVES.
GRRRRAAAAAAA!

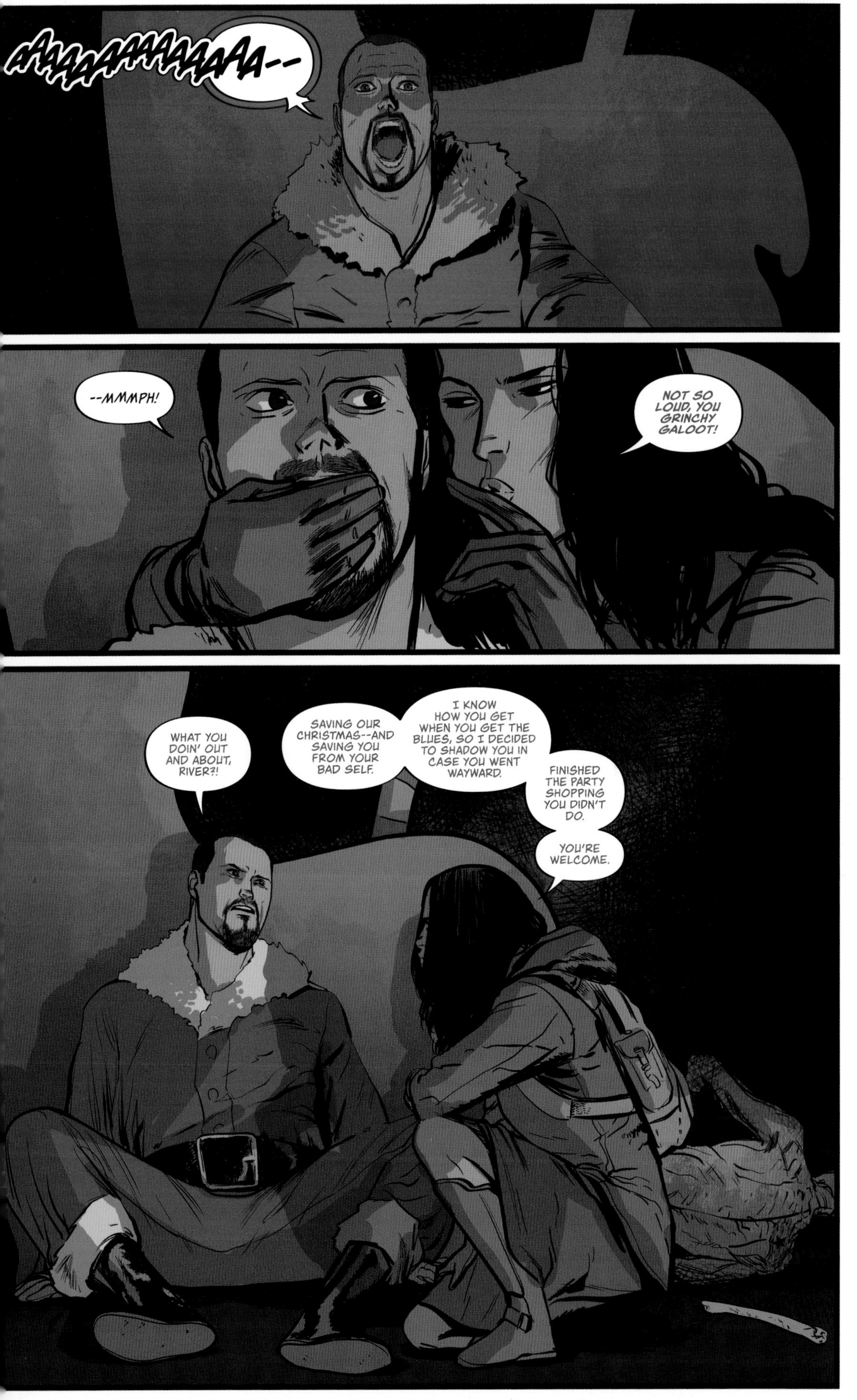
AAAAAAAAAAAAA--
--MMMPH!
NOT SO LOUD, YOU GRINCHY GALOOT!
WHAT YOU DOIN' OUT AND ABOUT, RIVER?!
SAVING OUR CHRISTMAS--AND SAVING YOU FROM YOUR BAD SELF.
I KNOW HOW YOU GET WHEN YOU GET THE BLUES, SO I DECIDED TO SHADOW YOU IN CASE YOU WENT WAYWARD.
FINISHED THE PARTY SHOPPING YOU DIDN'T DO.
YOU'RE WELCOME.

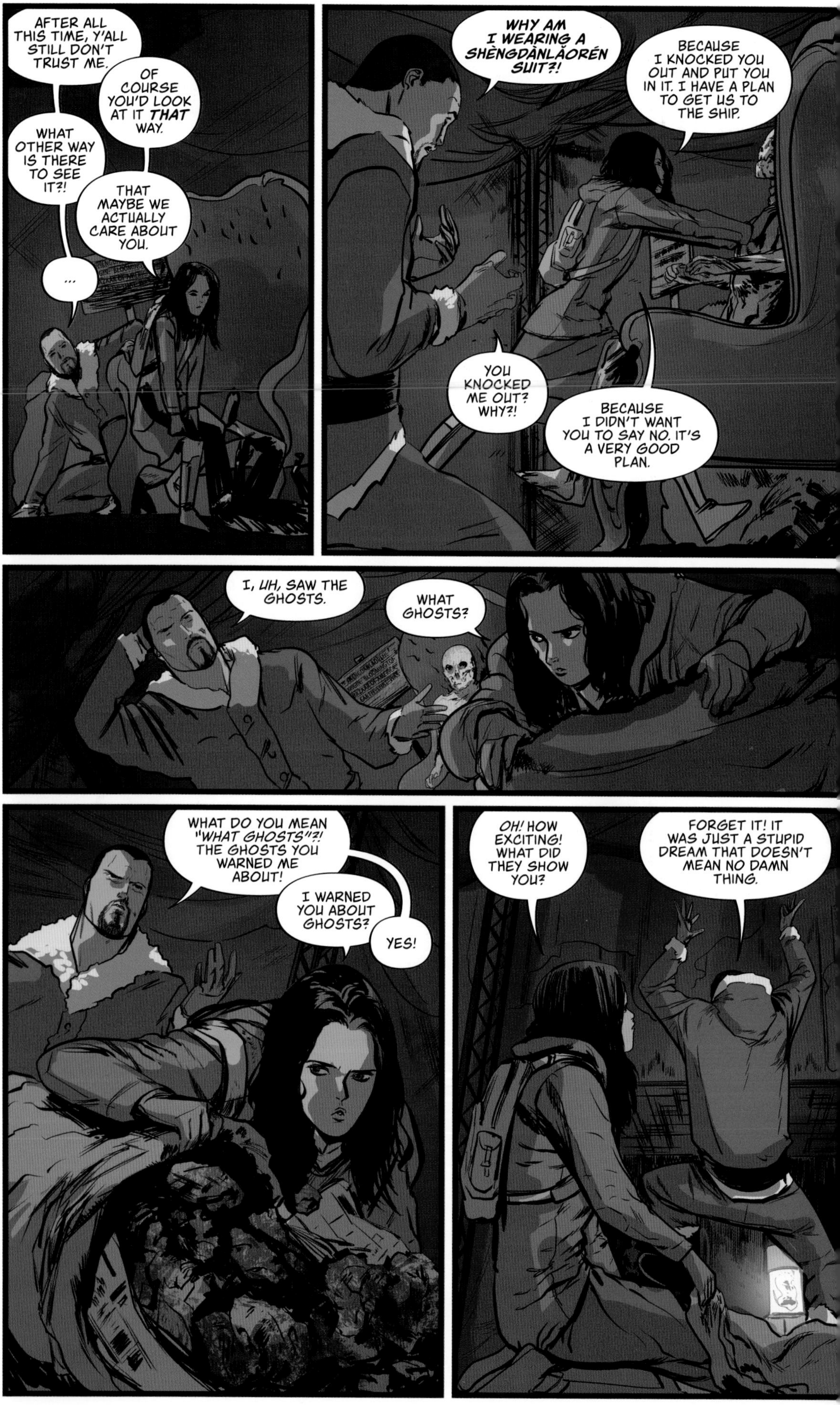
AFTER ALL THIS TIME, Y'ALL STILL DON'T TRUST ME.
OF COURSE YOU'D LOOK AT IT *THAT* WAY.
WHAT OTHER WAY IS THERE TO SEE IT?!
THAT MAYBE WE ACTUALLY CARE ABOUT YOU.
...
WHY AM I WEARING A SHÈNGDÀNLǍORÉN SUIT?!
BECAUSE I KNOCKED YOU OUT AND PUT YOU IN IT. I HAVE A PLAN TO GET US TO THE SHIP.
YOU KNOCKED ME OUT? WHY?!
BECAUSE I DIDN'T WANT YOU TO SAY NO. IT'S A VERY GOOD PLAN.
I, *UH*, SAW THE GHOSTS.
WHAT GHOSTS?
WHAT DO YOU MEAN "*WHAT GHOSTS*"?! THE GHOSTS YOU WARNED ME ABOUT!
I WARNED YOU ABOUT GHOSTS?
YES!
OH! HOW EXCITING! WHAT DID THEY SHOW YOU?
FORGET IT! IT WAS JUST A STUPID DREAM THAT DOESN'T MEAN NO DAMN THING.

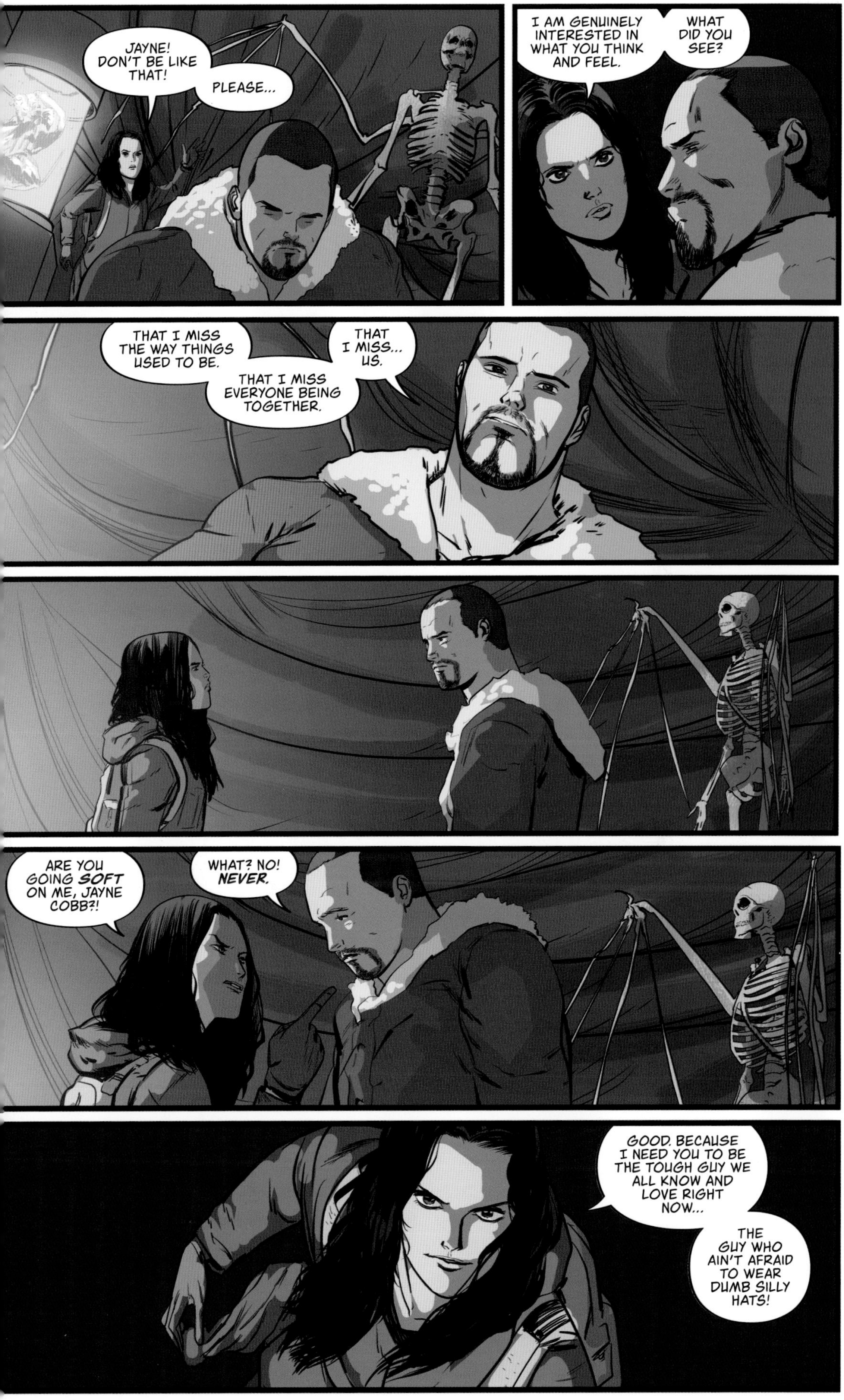
JAYNE! DON'T BE LIKE THAT!
PLEASE...
I AM GENUINELY INTERESTED IN WHAT YOU THINK AND FEEL.
WHAT DID YOU SEE?
THAT I MISS THE WAY THINGS USED TO BE.
THAT I MISS EVERYONE BEING TOGETHER.
THAT I MISS... US.
ARE YOU GOING SOFT ON ME, JAYNE COBB?!
WHAT? NO! NEVER.
GOOD. BECAUSE I NEED YOU TO BE THE TOUGH GUY WE ALL KNOW AND LOVE RIGHT NOW...
THE GUY WHO AIN'T AFRAID TO WEAR DUMB SILLY HATS!

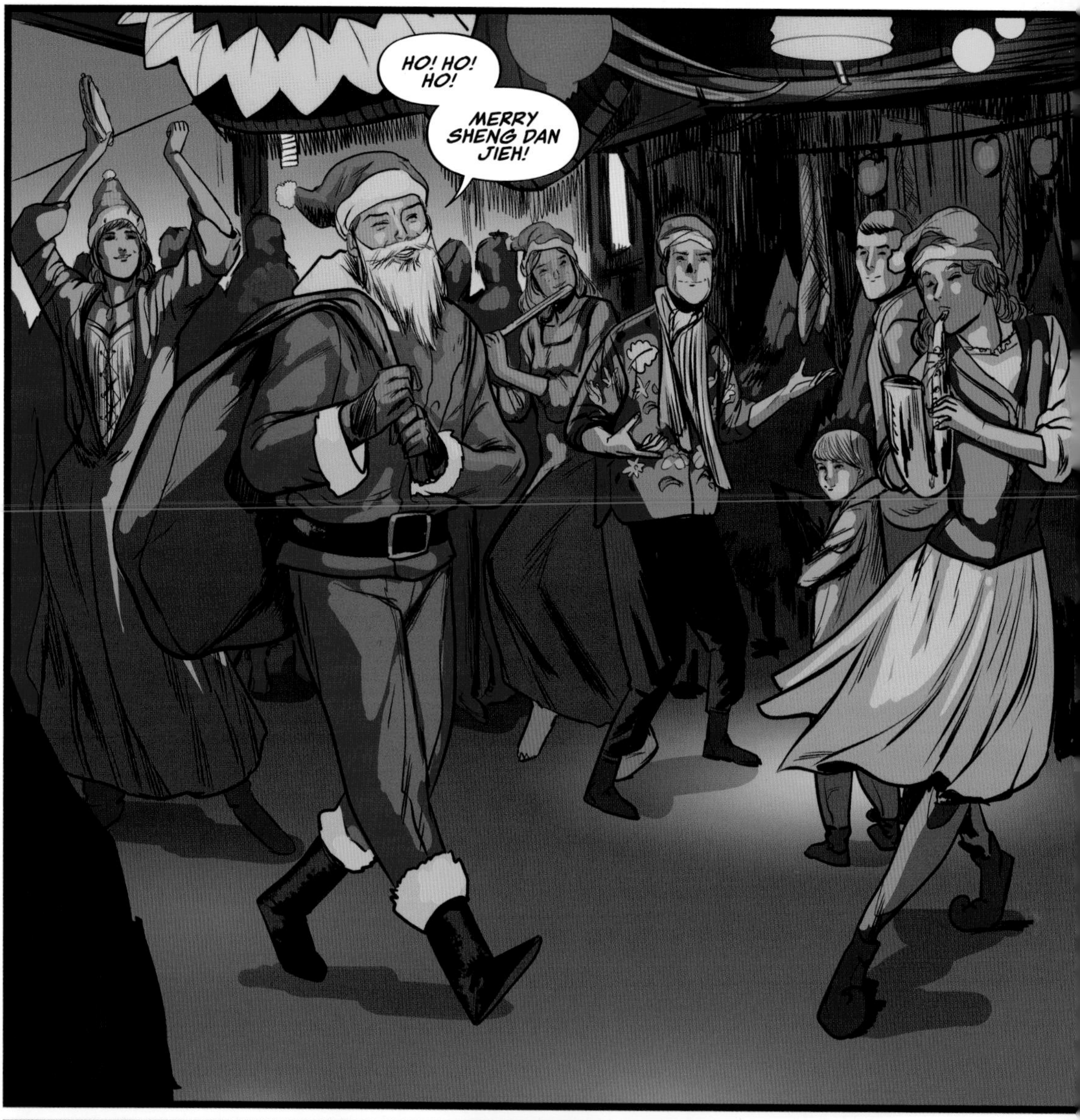
HO! HO! HO!
MERRY SHENG DAN JIEH!

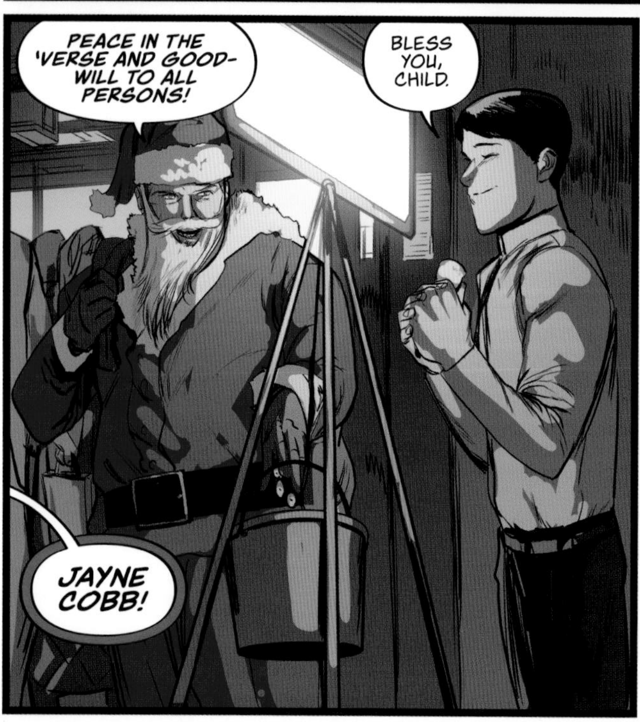
PEACE IN THE 'VERSE AND GOOD-WILL TO ALL PERSONS!
BLESS YOU, CHILD.
JAYNE COBB!

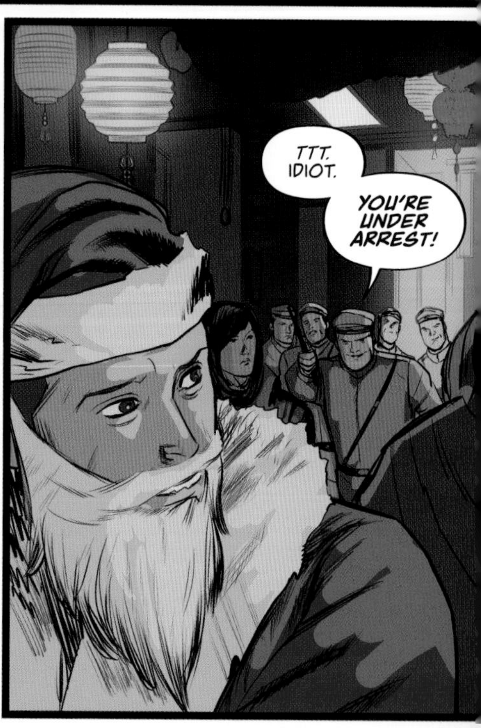
TTT. IDIOT.
YOU'RE UNDER ARREST!

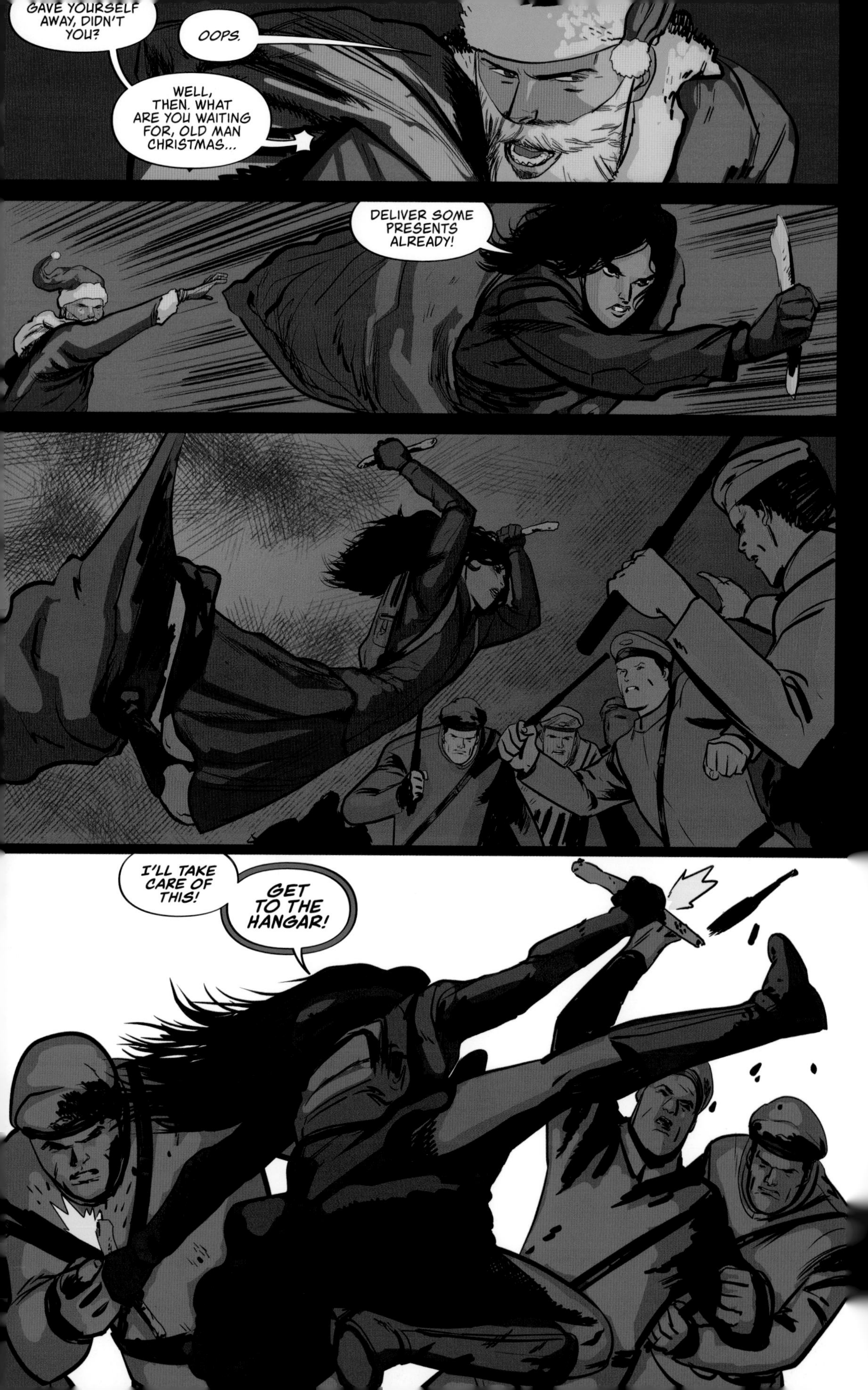
GAVE YOURSELF AWAY, DIDN'T YOU?
OOPS.
WELL, THEN. WHAT ARE YOU WAITING FOR, OLD MAN CHRISTMAS...
DELIVER SOME PRESENTS ALREADY!
I'LL TAKE CARE OF THIS!
GET TO THE HANGAR!

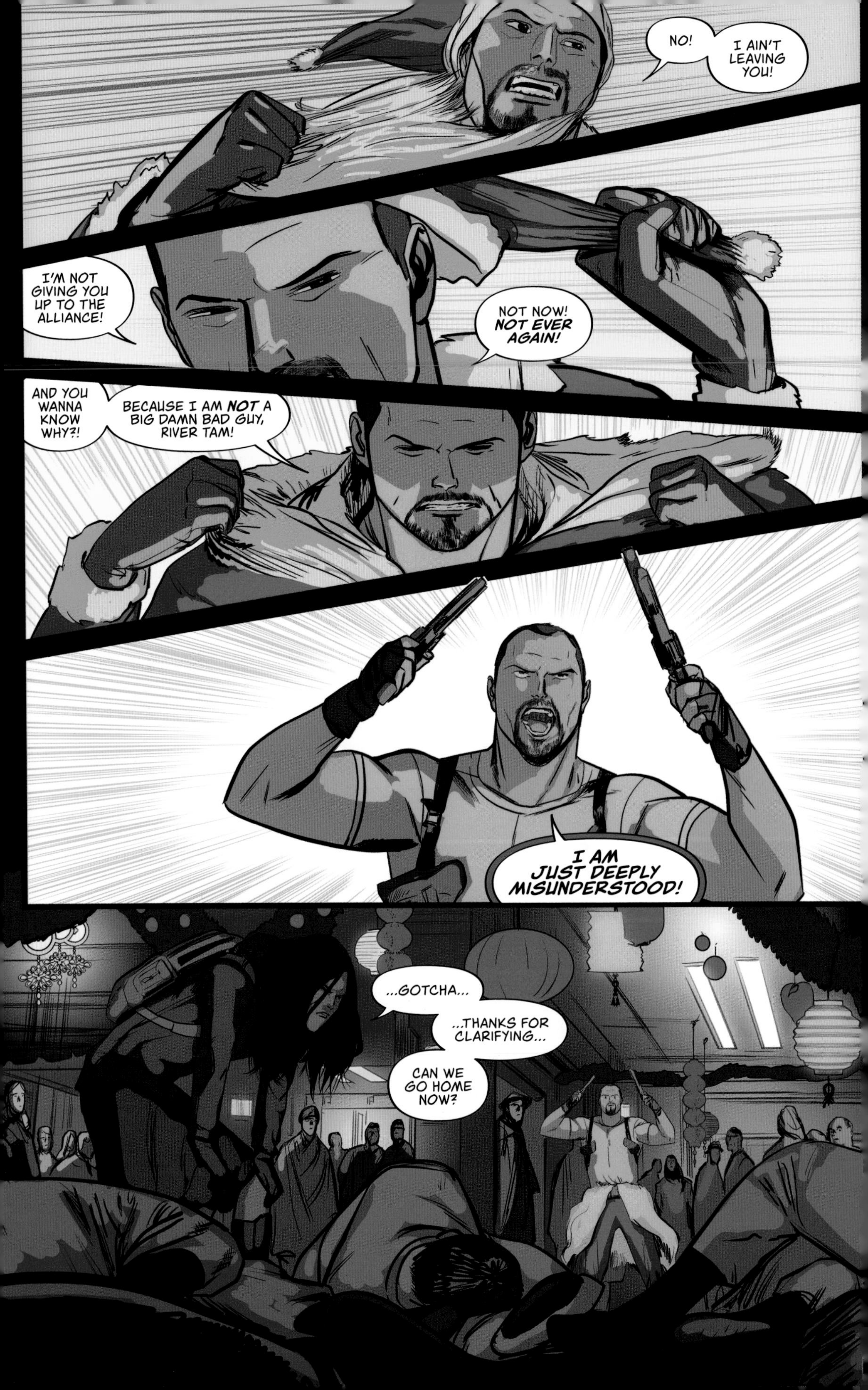
NO!
I AIN'T LEAVING YOU!
I'M NOT GIVING YOU UP TO THE ALLIANCE!
NOT NOW! NOT EVER AGAIN!
AND YOU WANNA KNOW WHY?!
BECAUSE I AM NOT A BIG DAMN BAD GUY, RIVER TAM!
I AM JUST DEEPLY MISUNDERSTOOD!
...GOTCHA...
...THANKS FOR CLARIFYING...
CAN WE GO HOME NOW?

LATER.

AFTER PUTTING LI SHEN'S BAZAAR BEHIND THEM AND FINDING SOME SPACE TO DRIFT...

MMMM. THIS FRUITCAKE IS SURPRISINGLY EXCELLENT!

"SURPRISINGLY"? WHY ARE YOU SURPRISED THAT MY BAKING IS SURPRISINGLY EXCELLENT?

BECAUSE IT'S FRUITCAKE, AND FRUITCAKE IS, YOU KNOW, FRUITCAKE?

POINT TAKEN.

THE CHESTNUTS ARE RATHER *CHOICE*, GOOD SHOPPIN', JAYNE! I WAS *WORRIED* THERE FOR A BIT...

ACTUALLY, I--

OH, *GOD*, DO I *HAVE* TO HEAR THIS STORY *AGAIN*?!

PICKY McNUTJOB HERE KEPT *BRAGGING* ON HIMSELF WHILE WE WERE MAKING DINNER...

HOW HE WOULDN'T SETTLE FOR ANY OLD BAG OF NUTS, HOW HE KEPT FORAGING UNTIL HE FOUND ONLY THE *FINEST* NUTS IN THE LOWER LEVEL OF THE SPACE BAZAAR...

THAT SO, *HUH*?

RECKON IT IS. ONLY MY BEST EFFORTS ON THE HOLIDAYS. MY GIFT TO YOU ALL.

END

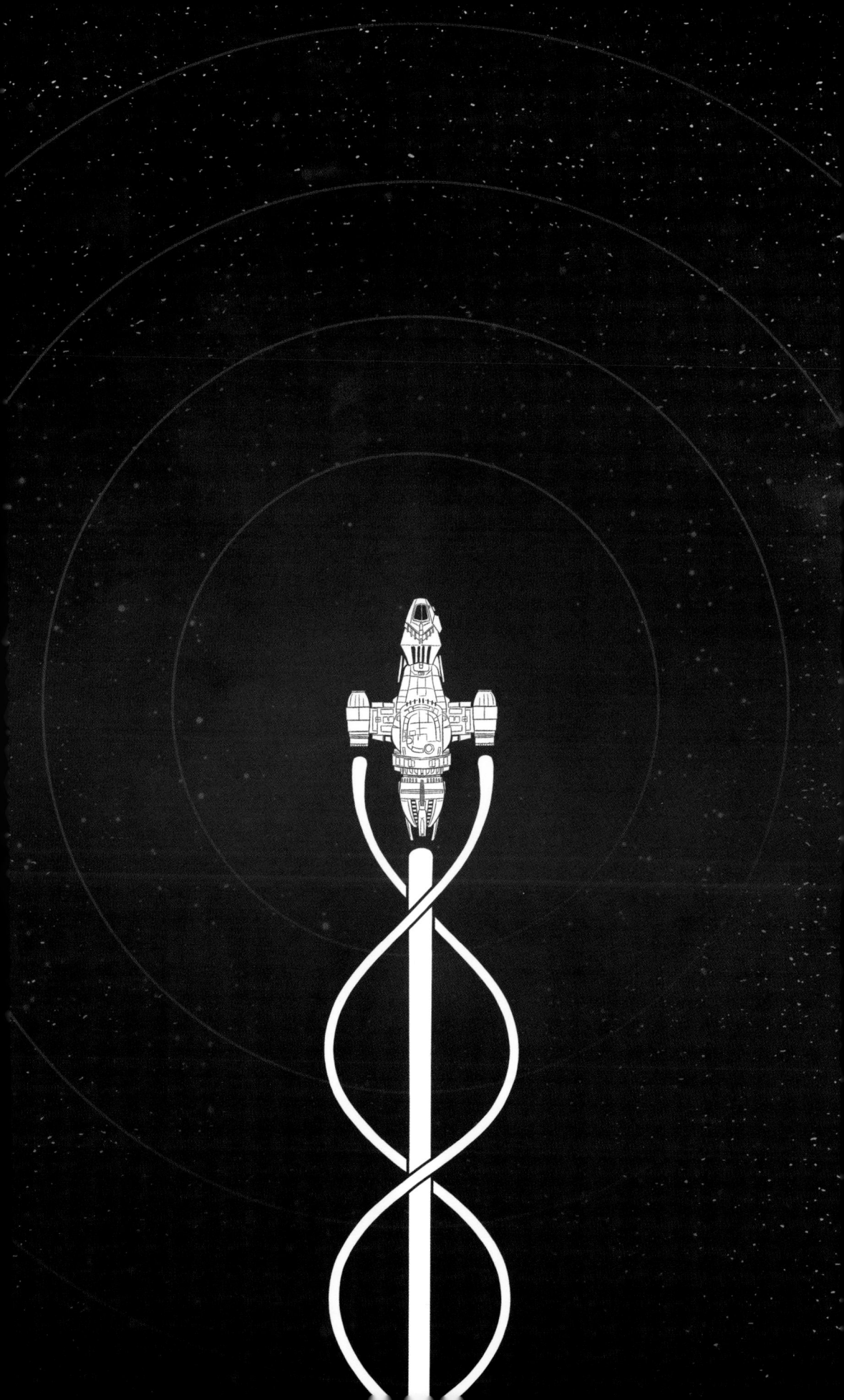

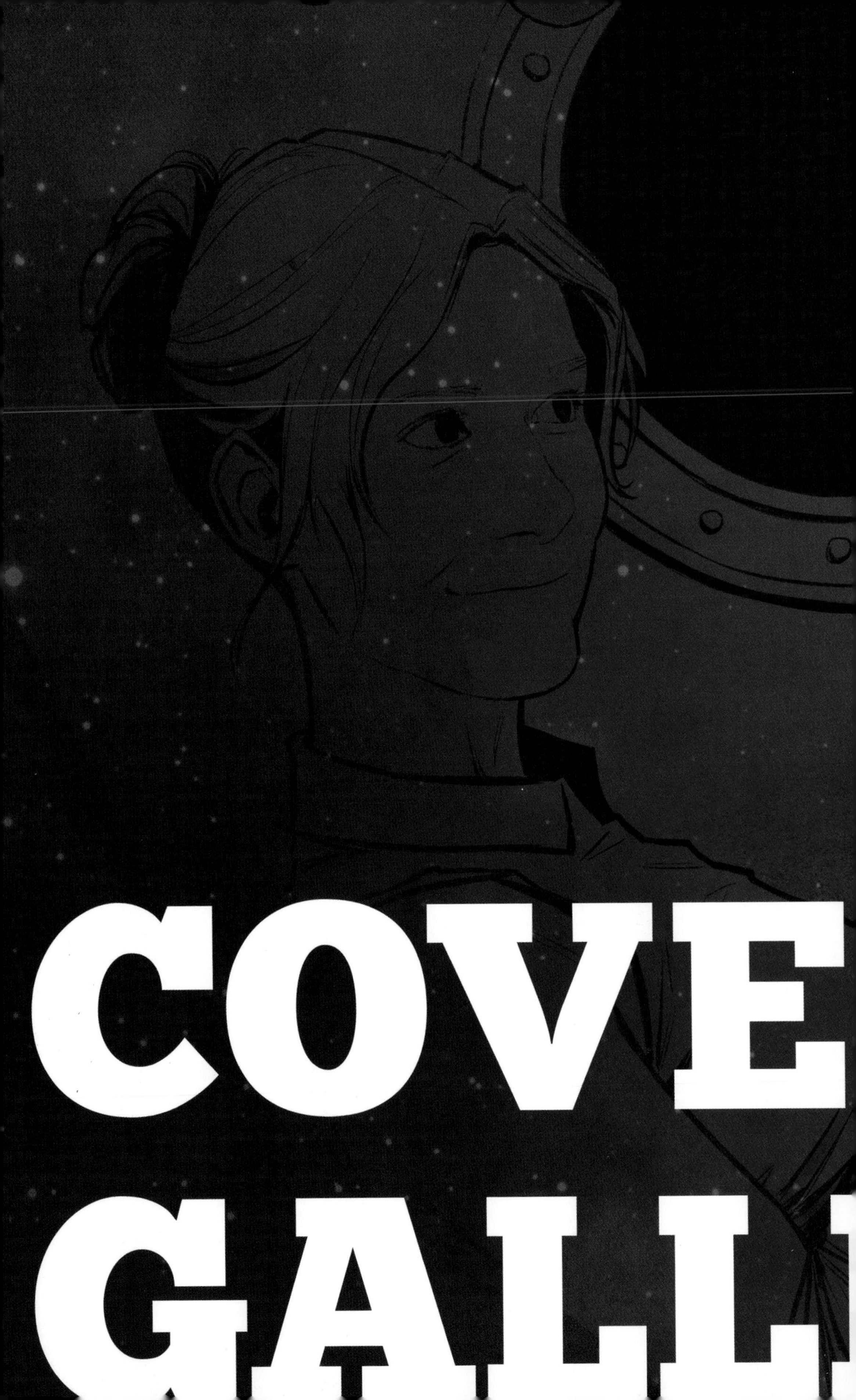
COVE
GALL

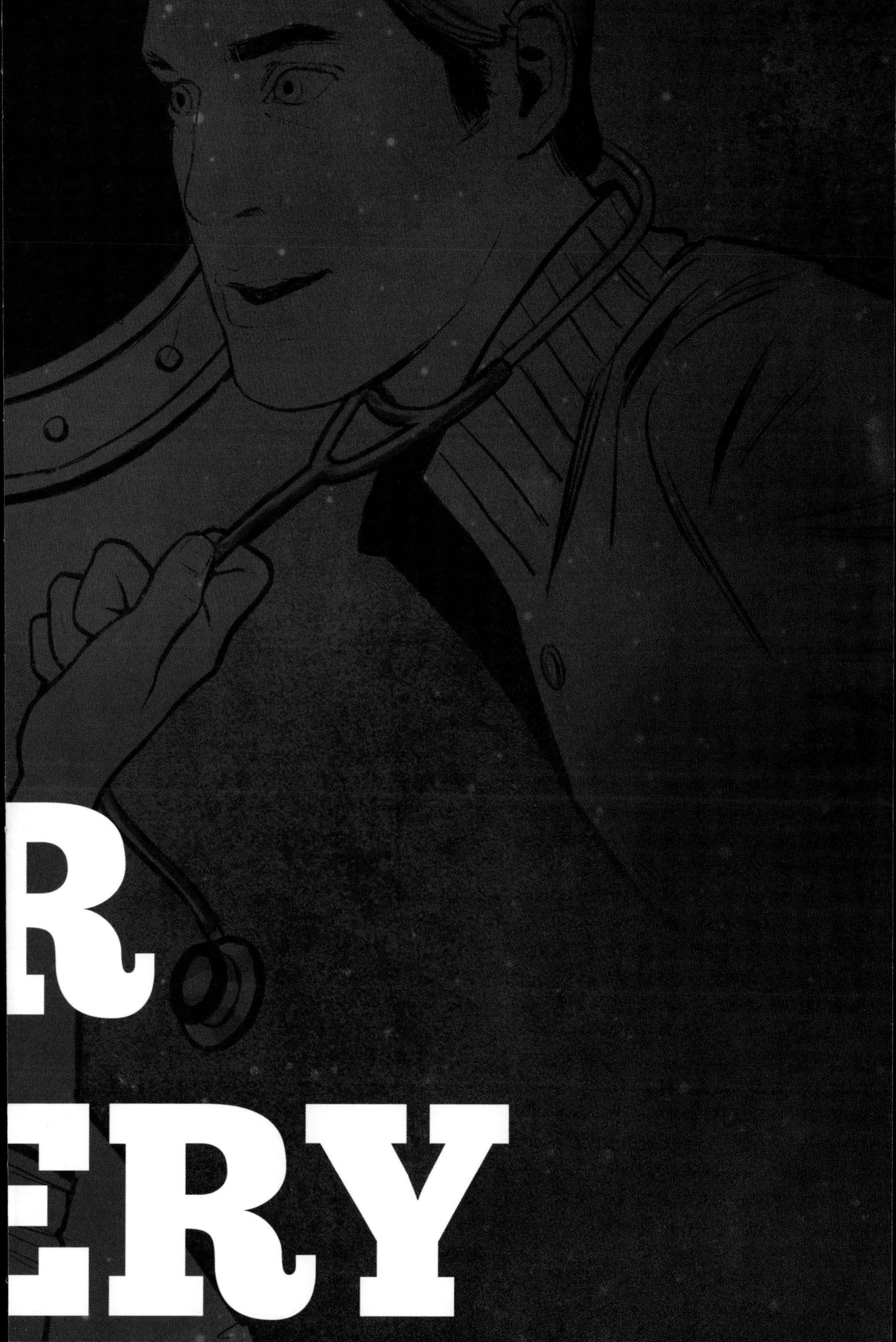
R
ERY

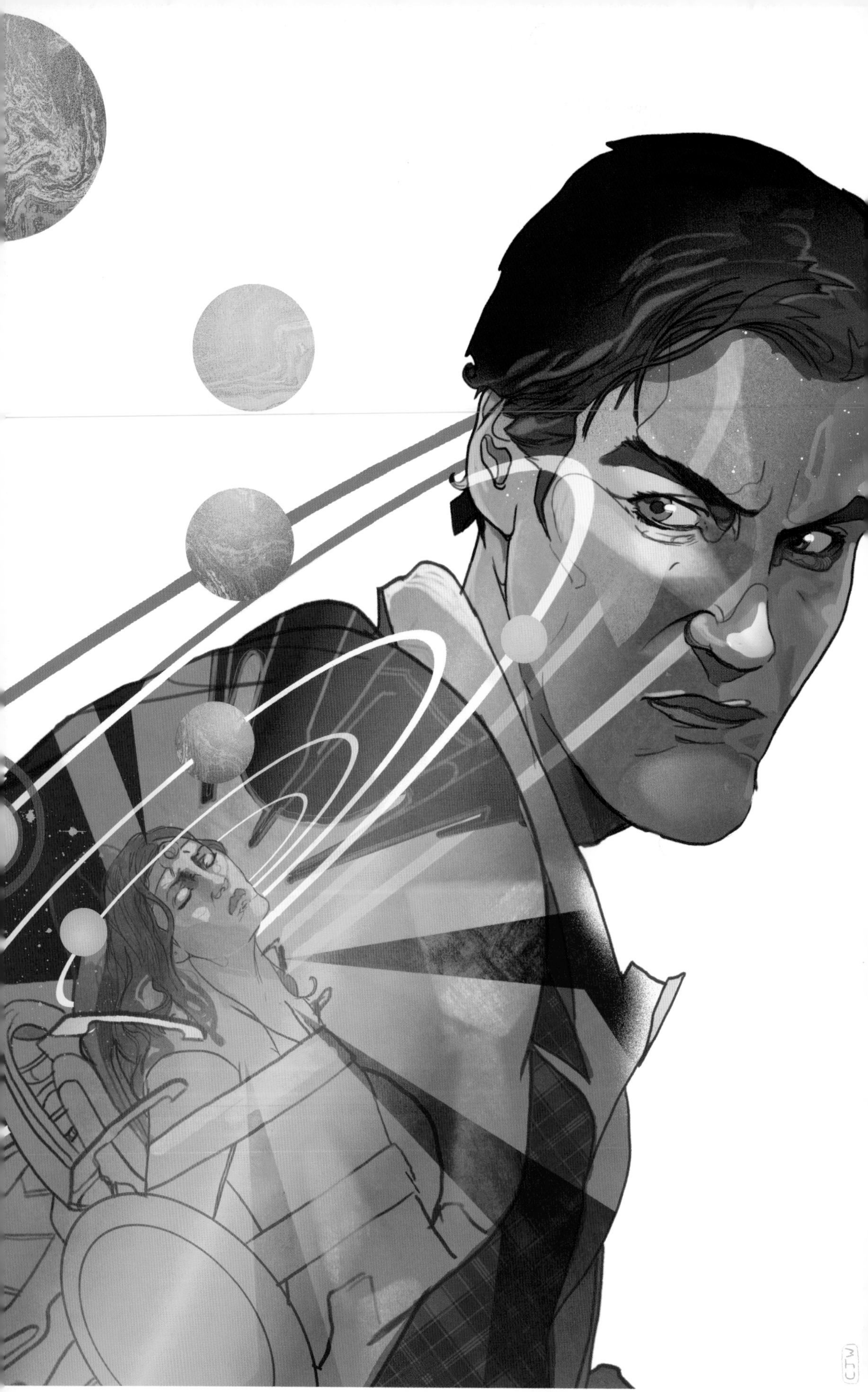
CTW

Firefly River Run #1 Main Cover by **Christian Ward**

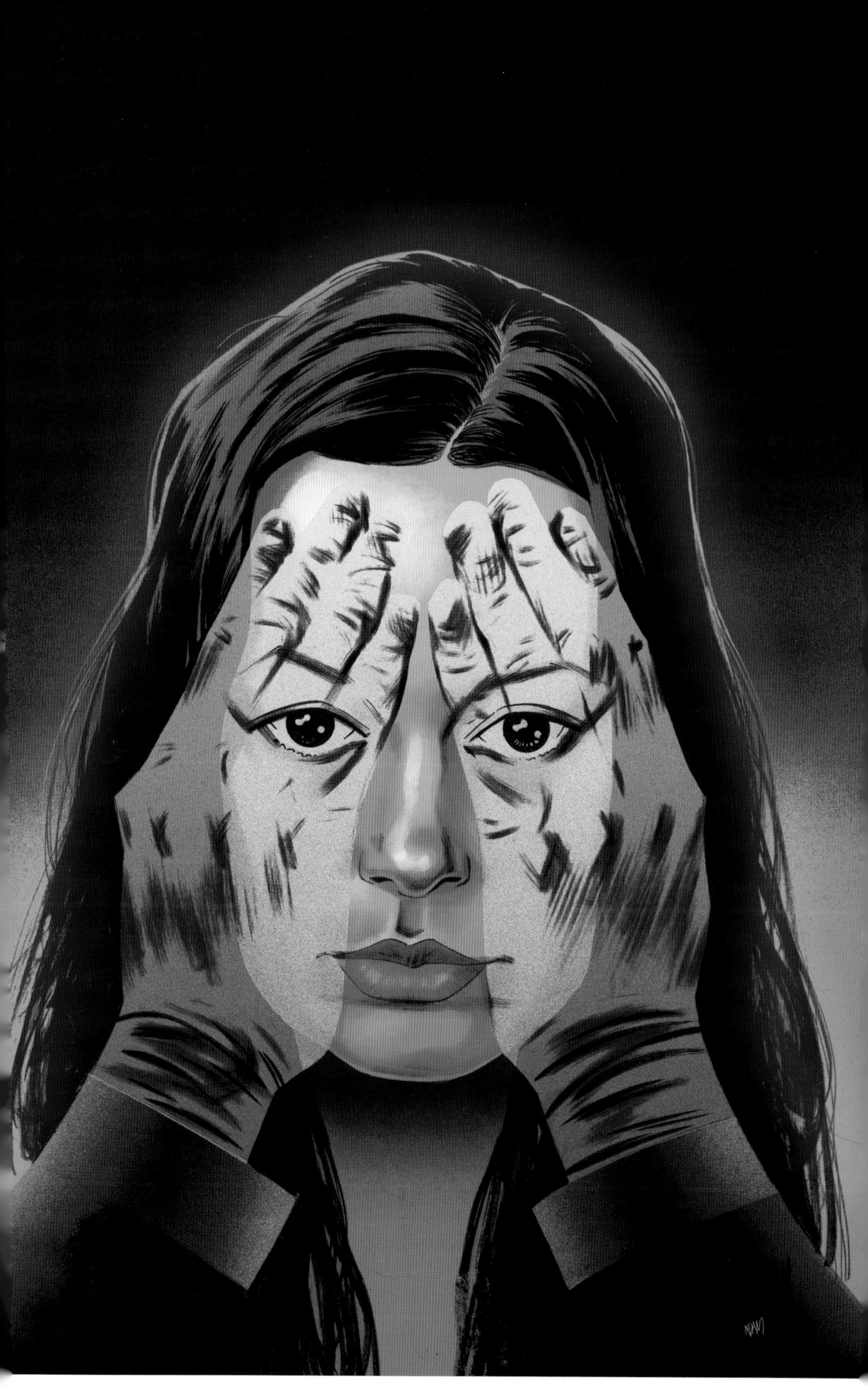

Firefly River Run #1 Variant Cover by **Adam Gorham**

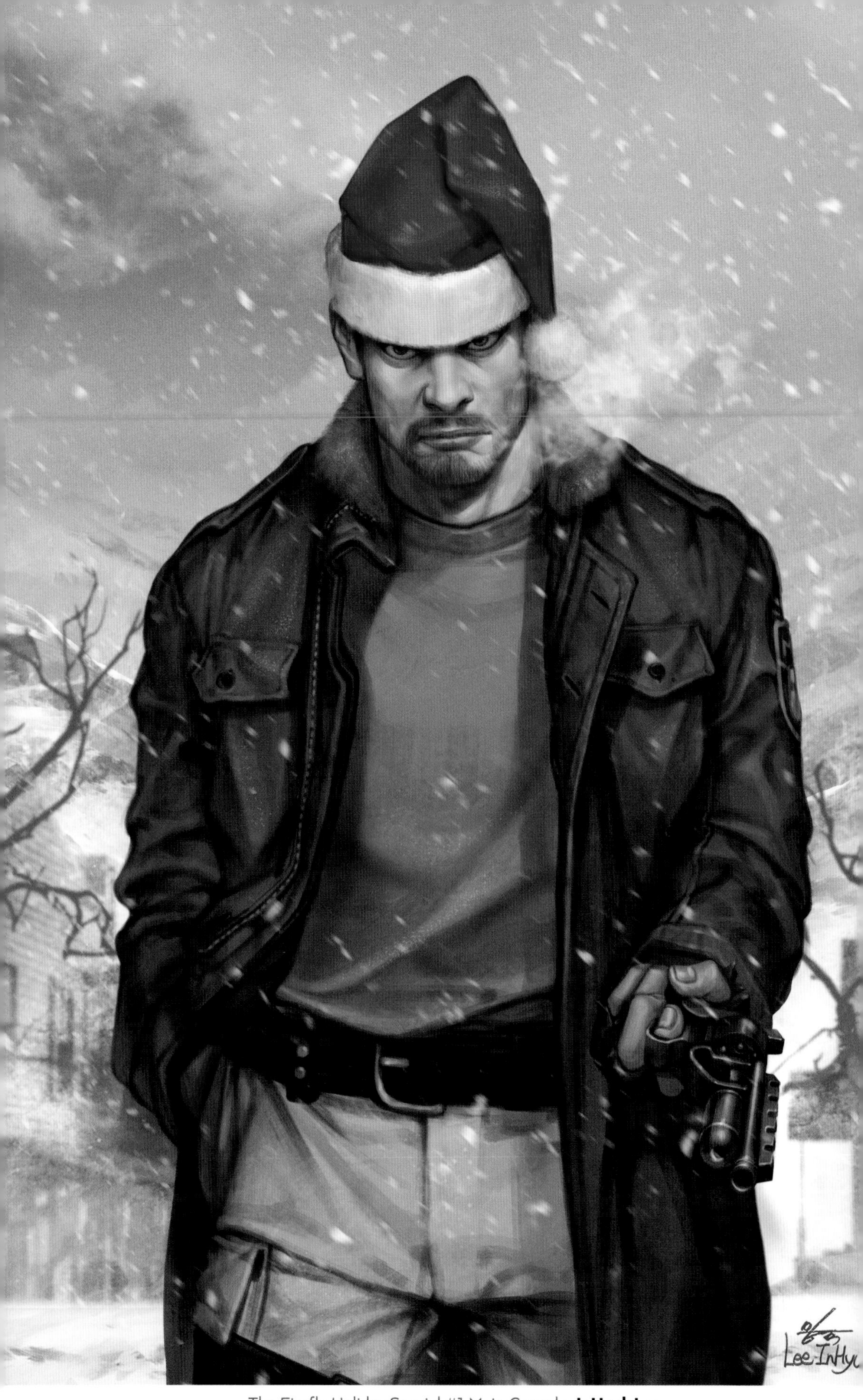
Lee InHyuk

The Firefly Holiday Special #1 Main Cover by **InHyuk Lee**

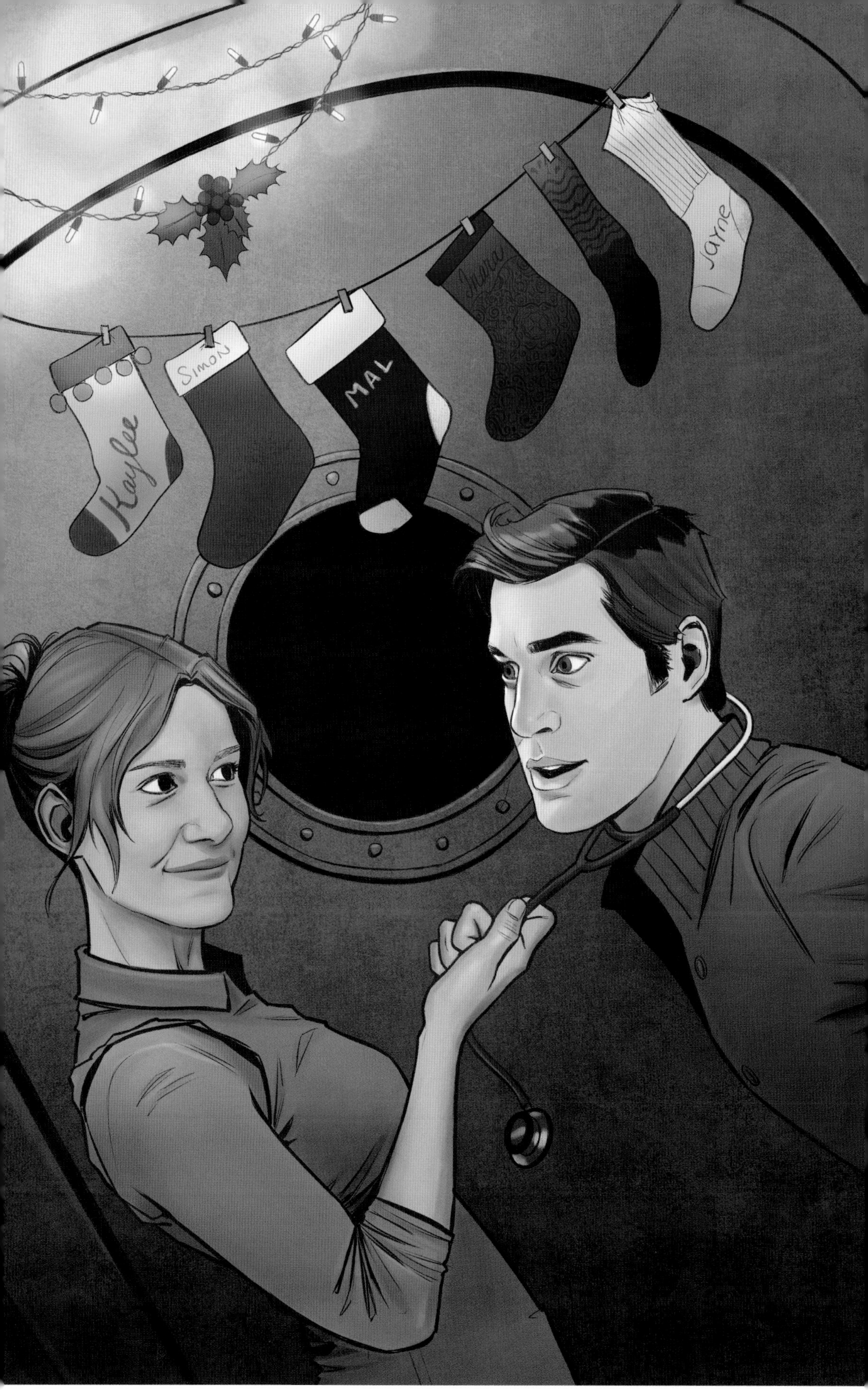
Kaylee
SIMON
MAL
Jayne

The Firefly Holiday Special #1 Variant Cover by **Caitlin Yarsky**

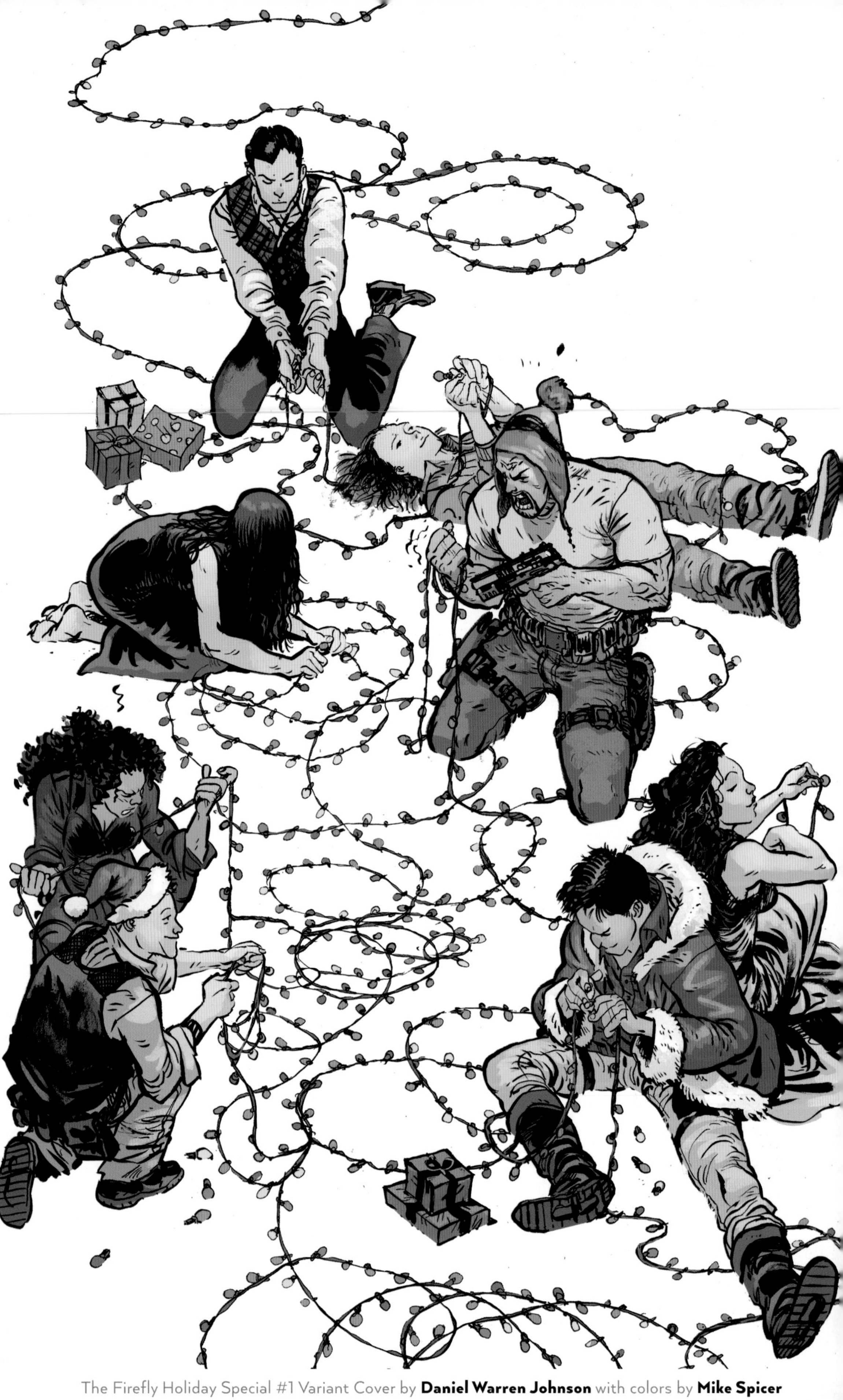

The Firefly Holiday Special #1 Variant Cover by **Daniel Warren Johnson** with colors by **Mike Spicer**

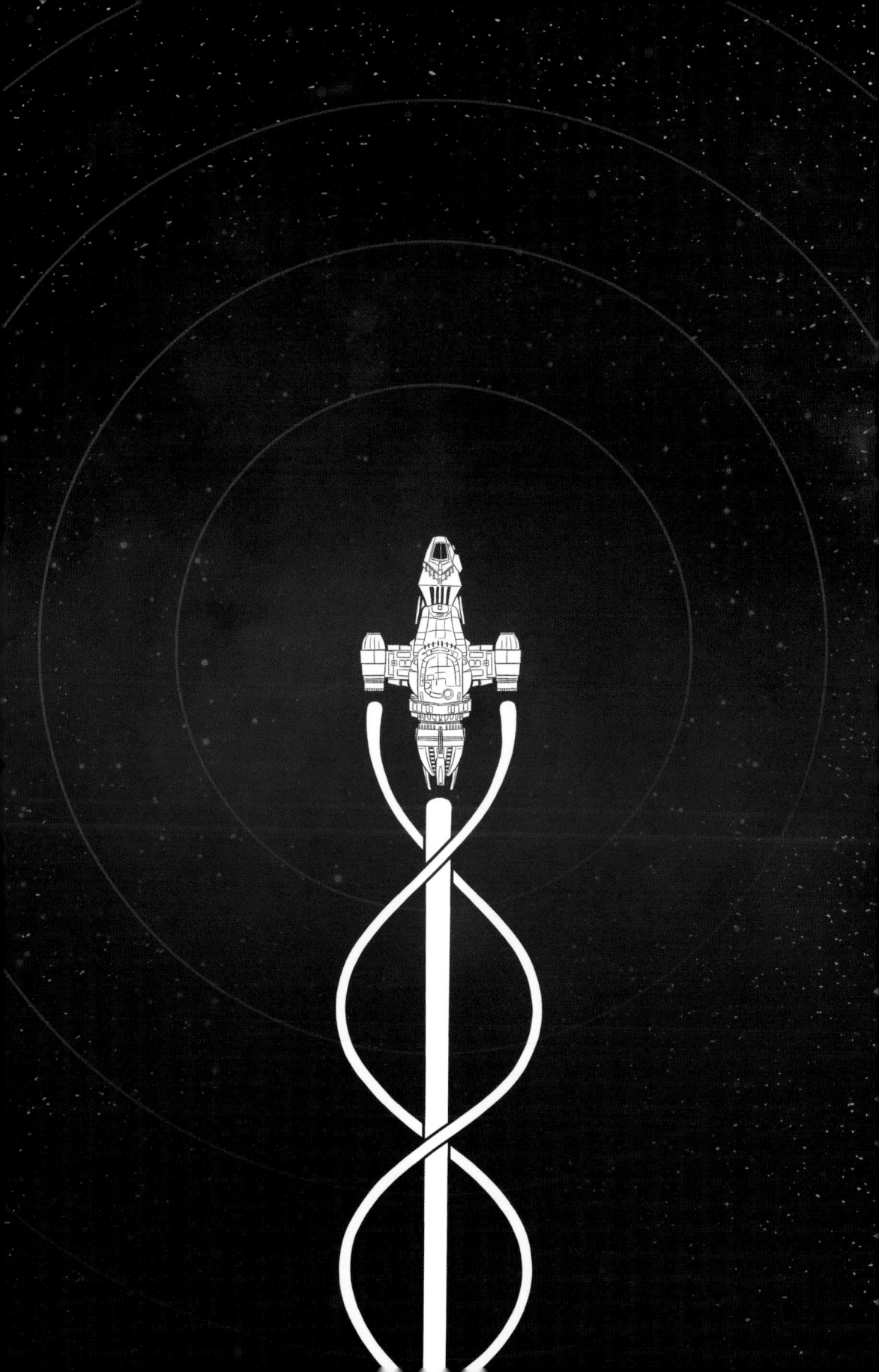

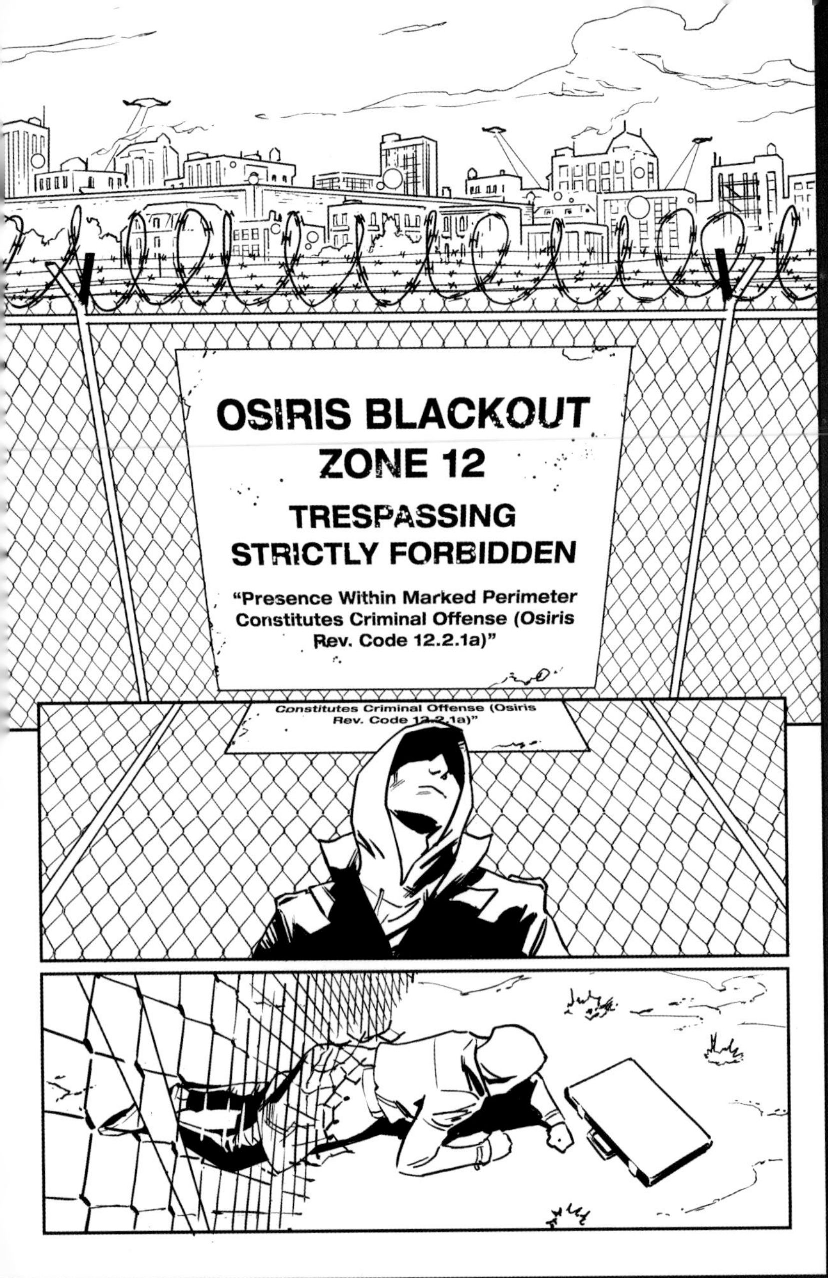
OSIRIS BLACKOUT
ZONE 12
TRESPASSING
STRICTLY FORBIDDEN
"Presence Within Marked Perimeter
Constitutes Criminal Offense (Osiris
Rev. Code 12.2.1a)"

PAGE: FIREFLY RIVER RUN #1, PAGE 3

Angle on a TALL FENCE topped with RAZOR WIRE. Beyond it, we can see some short BUILDINGS. S patrol with SPOTLIGHTS pointed toward the ground. This is a BLACKOUT ZONE—areas within sed off because criminal monitoring tech doesn't work. Picture a few city blocks fortified , government-controlled area in the city.

gs on the fence that says:
ZONE 12
CTLY FORBIDDEN
Marked Perimeter Constitutes Criminal Offense (Osiris Rev. Code 12.2.1a)"

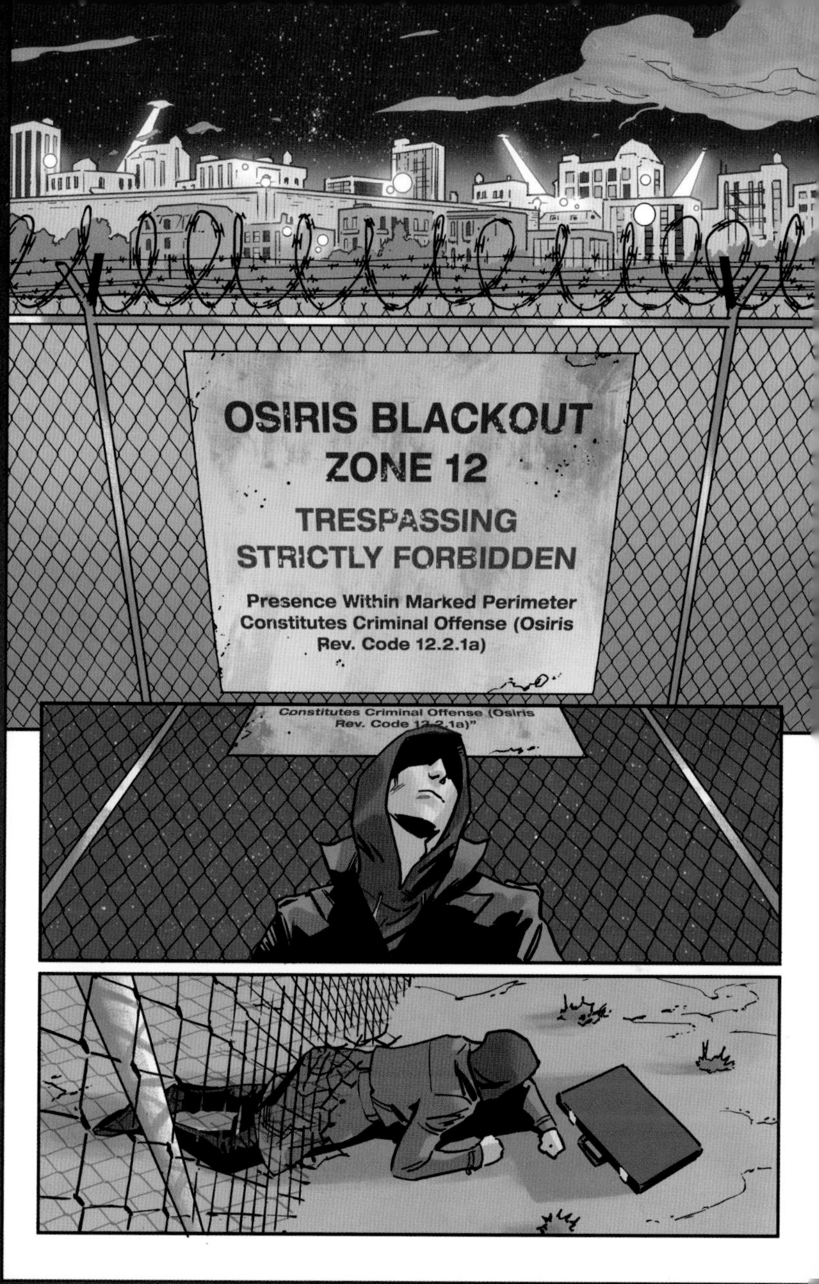

OSIRIS BLACKOUT ZONE 12
TRESPASSING STRICTLY FORBIDDEN
Presence Within Marked Perimeter Constitutes Criminal Offense (Osiris Rev. Code 12.2.1a)
Constitutes Criminal Offense (Osiris Rev. Code 12.2.1a)"

PANEL 2: Simon leans against this sign outside the zone, head on swivel to ensure he's not ALL-BLACK. A LONG BLACK COAT over a BLACK HOODIE with the hood pulled up over his head. Eve disguise, he still manages to be well-dressed. His face is partly hidden in shadow. If we ca panel, he holds a BLACK HARDSHELL CASE about the size of a small briefcase.

SIMON (quietly, to himself): Not sure what's worse, Simon. That your list of question continues to grow…

PANEL 3: Simon crawls through a CUT OUT in the fence into the Blackout Zone. Now we ca HARDSHELL CASE he's carrying.

SIMON (quietly, to himself):…or that this one doesn't crack the top five.

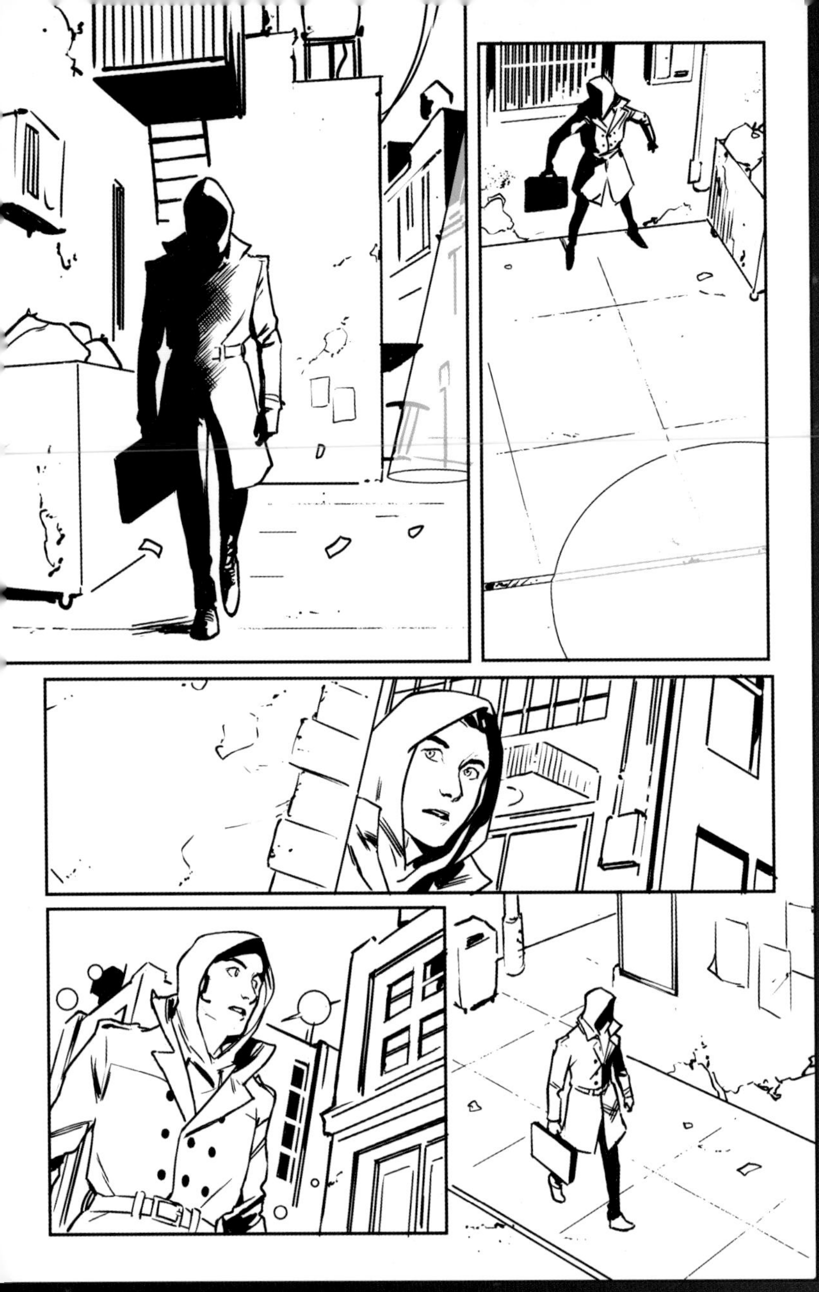

PAGE: FIREFLY RIVER RUN #1, PAGE 4

wn and face concealed by the shadow of his hood, Simon walks between buildings carrying the
on't see it, but he's wearing a COMM EARPIECE. Behind him, one of the overhead SPOTLIGHTS
ts. He's safely beyond the splash of the light.

rom his earpiece): Doc, that must be quite the list. They don't call it a "blackout zone"
e away the tourists.
rom earpiece): Or maybe they do. Never thought about it much.

resses himself against the wall of a building to avoid an OVERHEAD SPOTLIGHT sweeping past.

It's because criminal monitoring devices don't work inside the perimeter.

PANEL 3: Simon peeks around the corner to see if the coast is clear.

    SIMON: Which I assume is why you wanted to meet here instead of somewhere…*safer*.

PANEL 4: Angle on Simon, walking down the dark street. He holds a hand up to his ear and we he's wearing.

    SIMON: Which way do I go?

PANEL 5: Simon starts to turn right at the corner.

    COMM: Swing a right at the next corner.

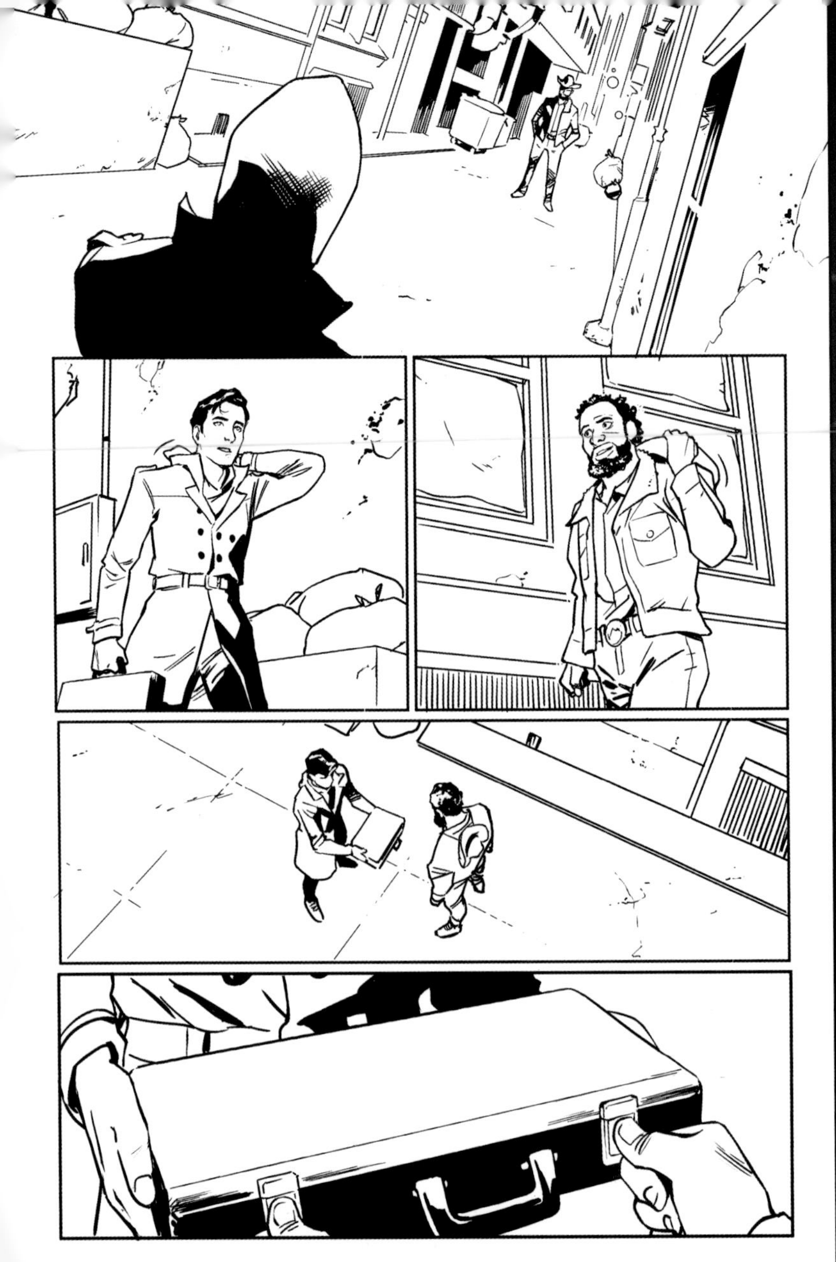

PAGE: FIREFLY RIVER RUN #1, PAGE 5

enters an ALLEY and walks toward a MAN in a COWBOY HAT. African-American, 40's. Grizzled. stubble. When we get closer look at him, we'll see a SCAR across one cheek.

Howdy, Doc.

You must be "The Cowboy"? The one I'm supposed to meet?

What gave it away?

n Simon, pulling his hood off as he approaches the Cowboy.

One doesn't see many *cowboy hats* on Osiris.

n the Cowboy, tipping his hat back. We get a better view of his face and that scar.

You know what they say. The man can leave the Rim Planets, but the Rim Planets never eave the man.

COWBOY: Besides, I figured you should be able to pick me out of a crowd.

PANEL 4: Wide angle on the two of them standing face-to-face. Simon holds out the CASE to holds it horizontally so the top can open. Leave lots of empty space around them to emphasiz This will make sure Simon's sarcastic line lands.

SIMON: I can see why that would be important.
SIMON: It's all here. You have my word. I'd prefer not to wait around while you take a

PANEL 5: Angle on the case. It's closed. The Cowboy's hands reach into frame to unfasten th

SFX of the latches: *click! click!*
COWBOY: And I'd prefer not to end the day gettin' swindled.

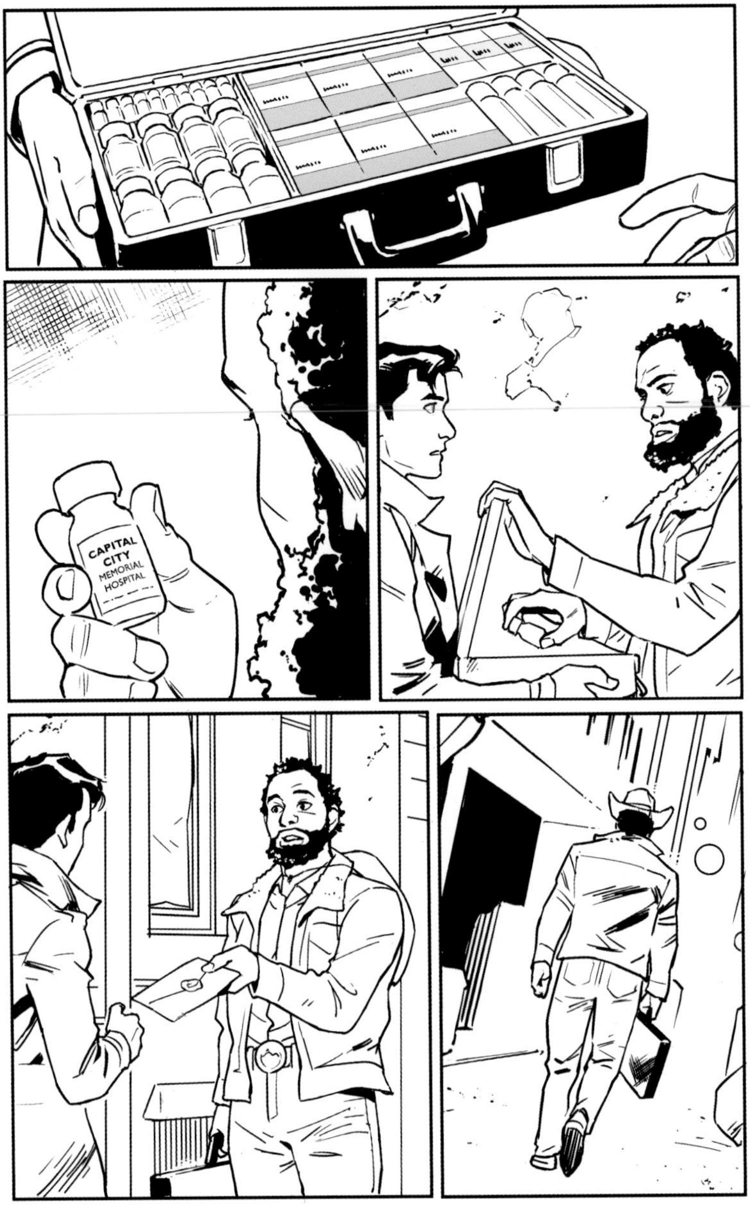
CAPITAL CITY MEMORIAL HOSPITAL

ᴾAGE: FIREFLY RIVER RUN #1, PAGE 6

ₗgle on the OPEN CASE. It's filled with VIALS OF MEDICATION.

(OP): Well, then.

ᵥboy holds up a VIAL in front of his face. We can see the largest words on the label, with ggles (we don't need to see what the medication actually is).

CAPITAL CITY HOSPITAL

The penalty for trespassin' in a blackout zone's nothin' compared to Capital City's top stealin' meds from an Alliance hospital.

on the two of them. The COWBOY puts the vial back in the case and starts to close it.

This information about your sister must be mighty important--

It is.

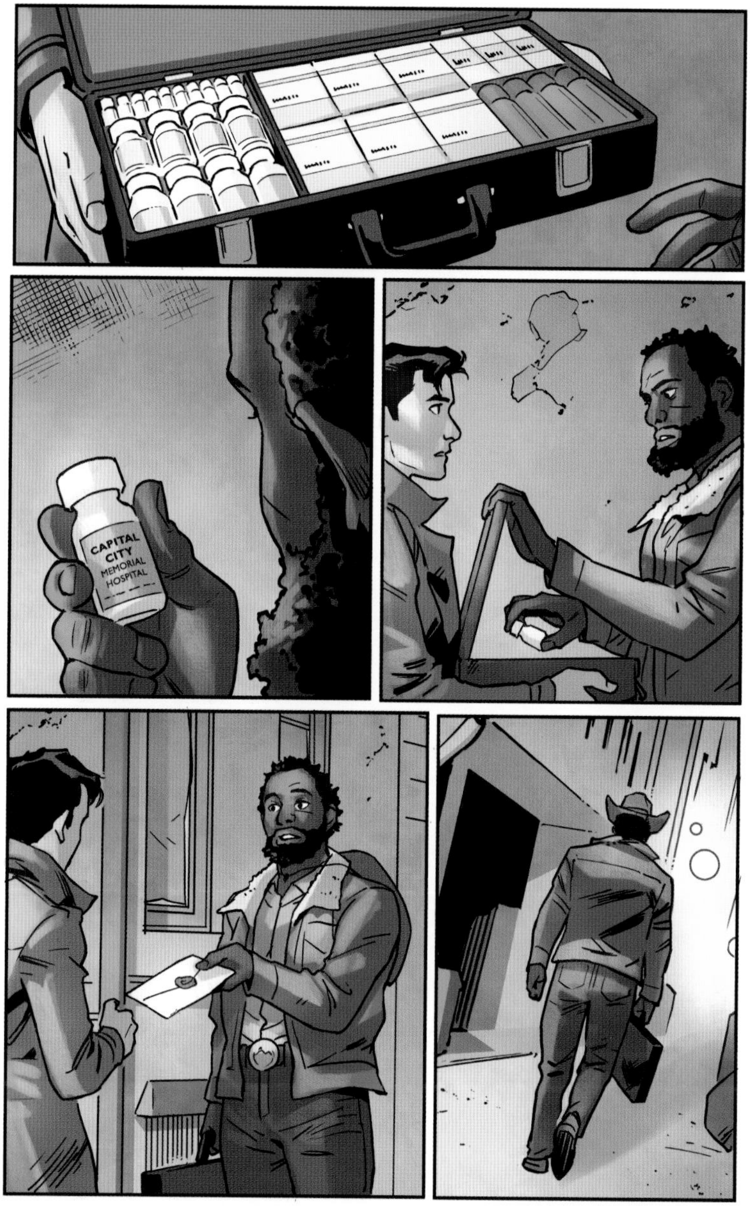
CAPITAL CITY MEMORIAL HOSPITAL

PANEL 4: The Cowboy takes the case and offers Simon a SEALED ENVELOPE.

COWBOY: Deal's a deal.
COWBOY: Don't read it until I'm disappeared. Lots of eyes 'round here.

PANEL 5: The Cowboy walks away carrying the case, fading into the shadows.

COWBOY: Can't be having them slidin' back in *my* direction.

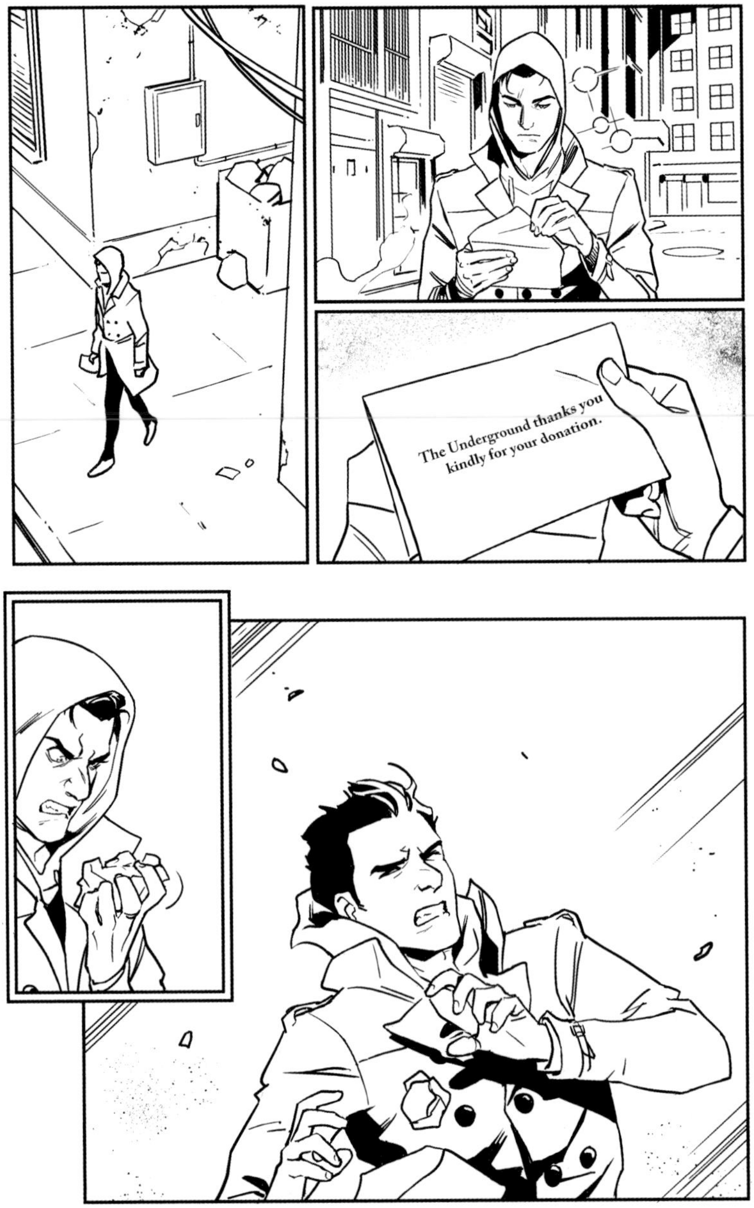
The Underground thanks you kindly for your donation.

ᴾAGE: FIREFLY RIVER RUN #1, PAGE 7

ʳalks out of the darkened alley.

.'s alone in the street, he opens the envelope.

.own on the LETTER Simon is holding. There's only one sentence written on it:

The Underground thanks you kindly for your donation.

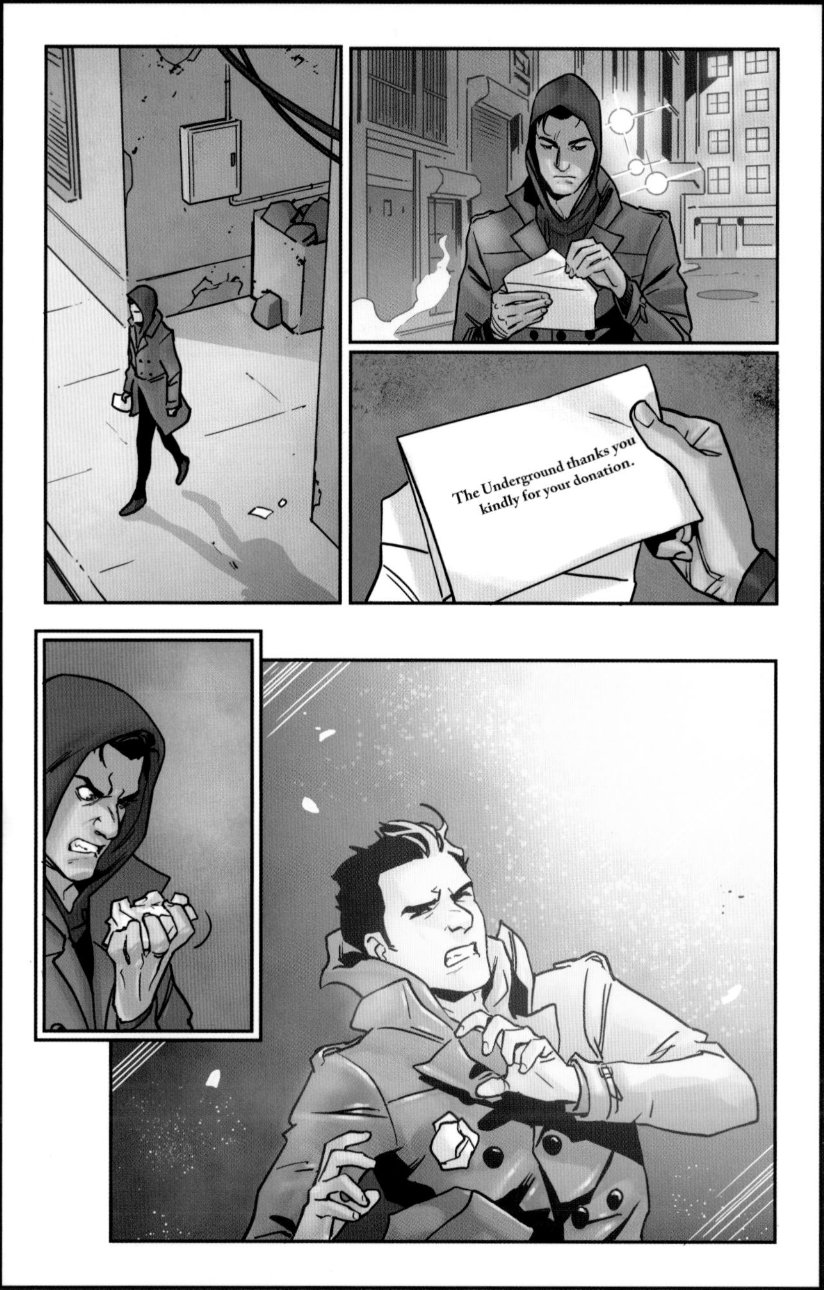
The Underground thanks you kindly for your donation.

PANEL 4: Simon crumples up the letter. Angry.

SIMON (to himself): *Damn it.*

PANEL 5: Close on Simon as he looks up over his head. His face is FULLY ILLUMINATED by the SPOTLIGHT from one of the PATROL SHIPS overhead.

PATROL SHIP COMM (OP, from the overhead ship): *HALT!*
SIMON (to himself): You were wrong about that list of questionable choices, Simon.

DISCOVER
VISIONARY CREATORS

KIERON GILLEN DAN MORA
TAMRA BONVILLAIN
ONCE & FUTURE
VOLUME ONE
THE KING IS UNDEAD

JAMES TYNION IV
WERTHER DELL'EDERA
MIQUEL MUERTO
SOMETHING is KILLING the CHILDREN
VOLUME ONE
SCOTT SNYDER

Brian Azzarello · Maria Llovet
FAITHLESS

GRANT MORRISON DAN MORA
Klaus
How Santa Claus Began

SIMON SPURRIER × MATÍAS BERGARA
CODA
VOLUME ONE
"This one is really special!" —JEFF LEMIRE

matt kindt tyler jenkins
GRASS KINGS
volume one

BOOM! STUDIOS™

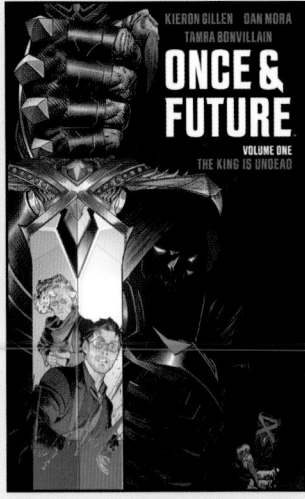

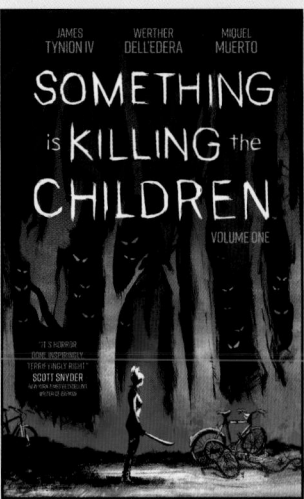

AVAILABLE AT YOUR LOCAL COMICS SHOP AND BOOKSTORE

To find a comics shop in your area, visit www.comicshoplocator.com

WWW.**BOOM-STUDIOS**.COM

Once & Future
Kieron Gillen, Dan Mora
Volume 1
ISBN: 978-1-68415-491-3 | $16.99 US

Something is Killing the Children
James Tynion IV, Werther Dell'Edera
Volume 1
ISBN: 978-1-68415-558-3 | $14.99 US

Faithless
Brian Azzarello, Maria Llovet
ISBN: 978-1-68415-432-6 | $17.99 US

Klaus
Grant Morrison, Dan Mora
Klaus: How Santa Claus Began SC
ISBN: 978-1-68415-393-0 | $15.99 US
Klaus: The New Adventures of Santa Claus HC
ISBN: 978-1-68415-666-5 | $17.99 US

Coda
Simon Spurrier, Matias Bergara
Volume 1
ISBN: 978-1-68415-321-3 | $14.99 US
Volume 2
ISBN: 978-1-68415-369-5 | $14.99 US
Volume 3
ISBN: 978-1-68415-429-6 | $14.99 US

Grass Kings
Matt Kindt, Tyler Jenkins
Volume 1
ISBN: 978-1-64144-362-3 | $17.99 US
Volume 2
ISBN: 978-1-64144-557-3 | $17.99 US
Volume 3
ISBN: 978-1-64144-650-1 | $17.99 US

Bone Parish
Cullen Bunn, Jonas Scharf
Volume 1
ISBN: 978-1-64144-337-1 | $14.99 US
Volume 2
ISBN: 978-1-64144-542-9 | $14.99 US
Volume 3
ISBN: 978-1-64144-543-6 | $14.99 US

Ronin Island
Greg Pak, Giannis Milonogiannis
Volume 1
ISBN: 978-1-64144-576-4 | $14.99 US
Volume 2
ISBN: 978-1-64144-723-2 | $14.99 US
Volume 3
ISBN: 978-1-64668-035-1 | $14.99 US

Victor LaValle's Destroyer
Victor LaValle, Dietrich Smith
ISBN: 978-1-61398-732-2 | $19.99 US

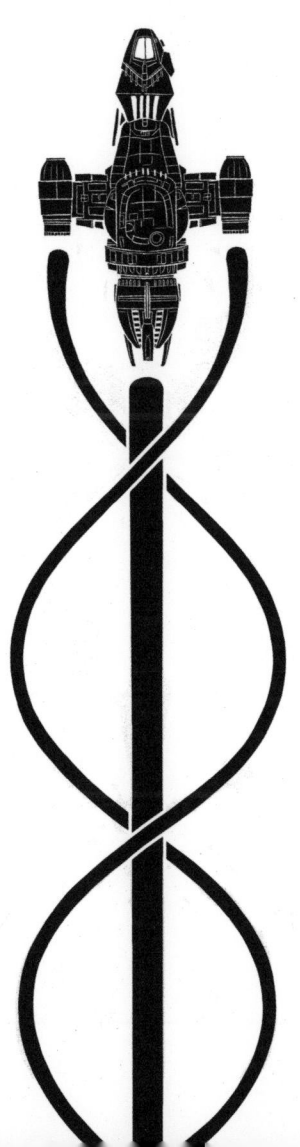